RUTH ELLIS
MY SISTER'S SECRET LIFE

RUTH ELLIS

MY SISTER'S SECRET LIFE

MURIEL JAKUBAIT
WITH MONICA WELLER

ROBINSON
London

DEDICATION

I dedicate this book to my sister Ruth Ellis,
whom I loved in life and love in death.

Constable & Robinson Ltd
3 The Lanchesters
162 Fulham Palace Road
London W6 9ER
www.constablerobinson.com

First published in the UK by Robinson,
an imprint of Constable & Robinson Ltd 2005

A copy of the British Library Cataloguing in
Publication Data is available from the British Library.

ISBN 1-84529-119-0

Printed and bound in the EU

1 3 5 7 9 10 8 6 4 2

CONTENTS

ACKNOWLEDGEMENTS

With the help of many people and archival resources, I have made discoveries about my sister Ruth. Each person or organization has helped me to see the whole picture. I would particularly like to thank Ernest Ranger for leading me by way of the *Leatherhead Advertiser* to John Leonard Skilton Steel to whom I am indebted. To Margaret Woodford for her personal memories about Ruth in Warsash; Maureen Gleeson whose evidence about my sister was ignored in 1955; Mr Casserly for his superb interview; Carey-Ann, daughter of the late Antony Beauchamp; Evelyn Galilee; Peter Nolan; Denis Roger; Mary Young of Hotel Bristol, Newquay; Arthur Waterhouse; Walter Carden; David Wooster; Tony Cox at Sherborne St John primary school; Jim Donovan; Bob Wallis; Vera Reynolds; Monica Suffolk; Deborah Kerr Viertel; Gordon Winter; 'Kim' Caborn Waterfield.

I could not have made progress without the following archive centres and archivists: The National Archives (TNA) formerly the Public Record Office (PRO); Margaret Harcourt Williams of the Royal College of Psychiatrists; Bethlem Royal Hospital Archives and Museum; Ian Mitchell of the Tatsfield History Project and his introduction to Elizabeth and Pat; Surrey History Centre; Old Michaelean Association; Leatherhead History Society; Westminster City Archives; British

Automobile Racing Club; Jean Linford of the Sherborne St John Historical Society; Centre for Kentish Studies; Centre for Buckinghamshire Studies; Croydon Local Studies Library; Aylesbury Local Studies; Lambeth Archives; Dorking Museum; *Illustrated London News*; St John's school; Harrow school; John Taylor at the British Museum; Joy Marshall of Taplow Parish Church Council; Martin Williams at Hurstpierpoint school; Camden Local Studies Library.

I would like to thank the British Film Institute; Getty Images Ltd; Companies House; The Family Record Centre, London; The Royal Court of Justice; House of Lords; Law Society; Terry Turner of The Camera Club, London; The Royal Photographic Society; Tom Samson of the British Institute of Professional Photographers and Croydon Airport Society; Carl Ward, Surrey and Kent Flying Club; National Museum of Photography, Film and Television; John Chillingworth; Bob Willoughby; BT Archives; General Dental Council; Governor of HMP Holloway; Imperial War Museum; John Ross, Crime Museum, New Scotland Yard; Tonbridge Registry Office; Mandarin Oriental Hyde Park Hotel, London; Hobbs at 37 Brompton Road, London; Central St Martin's School of Art; Smith and Wesson in USA; *Folkestone Herald*; Brookwood Crematorium; Randalls Park Crematorium; White Hart Hotel, Brasted; a special word of thanks to Diana Nutley; and others who must remain anonymous.

The following libraries have given tremendous service: The British Library; Newspaper Library, Colindale; Bookham; Ewell; Winchester; Portsmouth; Sevenoaks; Chelsea; Kensington; Folkestone. The following Record Offices: Hampshire, East Sussex and Kent. Mole Valley District Council; Chiltern District Council; Fareham Civic Office.

ACKNOWLEDGEMENTS

Thank you to Valerie Preston; Peter Finch; Jean Bowers; Dorothy Broome; Sheila Sandford; Alun Roberts; David Nicholls; Mr Hoath; Brian McConnell; Ron Callender; David Johnson; Roger Wildgoose; Moira Tangye; Patsie Blair; Roy Knight; Victor Styles; Julie Harris; Lord Rawlinson of Ewell; Michael Gibbons; Derek Ward; Sylvain Brachfeld; Patrick O'Callaghan.

My thanks go to those who encouraged me to tell my story, in particular to Robert Smith for his dedication, patience, good advice and guiding hand. And to my publishers, Constable and Robinson who made my story a reality.

I would like to thank my friend Ron Fowler for his kindness and for introducing Monica Weller to me – no words can ever express my gratitude for the work she has done.

To my children Christopher – who sadly passed away before this book was published – Joey, Pauline, Marlene and Martin, I say thank you from my heart. With your support and encouragement I have kept my sanity; and to Joseph, my husband, who has lived through the trauma.

My sincerest appreciation goes to everyone who has helped to remove the obstacles in my search for the truth.

M.J.
2005

ILLUSTRATIONS

Ruth aged 9 at Worting County Junior School, courtesy of Michael Gibbons

Berta and Arthur Neilson, from family collection

Ruth aged 24

White Hart Hotel, photograph by Monica Weller

Deborah Kerr and Tony Bartley, courtesy of White Hart Hotel, Brasted

George Ellis, courtesy of Popperfoto.com

1950's aerial view of School of Navigation, Warsash, courtesy of Roy Knight

Ruth in 1951 film *Lady Godiva Rides Again*, courtesy of Canal+ Image UK

Still of Ruth in *Lady Godiva Rides Again*, courtesy of Getty Images

Vickie Martin, courtesy of Vera Reynolds and Patricia Welham

Antony Beauchamp

Stephen Ward, courtesy of Mirrorpix.com

Desmond Cussen and Ruth, courtesy of Mirrorpix.com

'Dapdune' in Garlands Road, Leatherhead, photograph by Monica Weller

ix

Ruth in pub garden, *c.* 1953, from family collection

Dorothy Foxon with journalist Gordon Winter at Dorothy's Club, courtesy of Gordon Winter

Alex Engleman, courtesy of Ralph Engleman

What used to be the Little Club at 37 Brompton Road, Knightsbridge, photograph by Monica Weller

Ruth and David Blakely

Ruth and David at motor race meeting, from family collection

The gun that was retrieved after the shooting, photograph by Monica Weller

The Magdala in South Hill Park, Hampstead, photograph by Monica Weller

Hampstead Police Station and Magistrates Court, photograph by Monica Weller

Melford Stevenson, Ruth's defence counsel, courtesy of the Inner Temple Archives

Christmas Humphreys, prosecution counsel, courtesy of the Inner Temple Archives

David Blakely's headstone, photograph by Monica Weller

Passport photo of Ruth's son Andre, aged around 35, from family collection

Polaroid photograph taken by Andre of his bedsitter

Sale Place, Bayswater, where Andre lived and committed suicide, photograph by Monica Weller

The Paddock Club, courtesy of Patsie Blair

Muriel looking through documents, photograph by Monica Weller

Ruth's gravestone, from family collection

1

A Convincing Story

I couldn't say anything good about the film *Dance with a Stranger*. It supposedly portrayed my sister and the murder of David Blakely that she was hanged for in 1955. Miranda Richardson looked like a tart, nothing like Ruth. But they made people think that's what my sister was like – a tart, a criminal who was to blame for killing her lover David Blakely in a fit of passion. I cried all the way through. This was not the real Ruth Ellis. This was not the whole story. The producers had picked my brain, obscured the truth, put nothing of what I told them in and shoved a ten-pound note in my pocket for my train fare back.

I went home on that day in January 1985, after the film's private viewing in London. The house was empty. I walked through the tradesmen's entrance, the kitchen and dining room and sat down on the settee in the living room. I was alone. Suddenly while I was staring out of the window, I heard click-clack-click coming through the back door. I thought: 'That's Ruth's walk.' She always walked like that in her stilettos. It was a matter of seconds. I couldn't look up, just glanced to the side and recognized her dirndl skirt. They were fashionable in the fifties; hers was circular, black and had bands of coloured ribbon round the hem. If I'd only looked up. But I was afraid. I knew she was pushing me to do something about it – this miscarriage of justice. She was in me. She was obviously not at rest. Until her innocence was proven she probably wouldn't rest either.

I have lived for half a century with the story of how Ruth shot her lover. Here is a summary of that so-called convincing story, which I know now was based on lies and deceit:

On 10 April 1955, Ruth Ellis shot her twenty-five-year-old lover, David Blakely, at point-blank range outside The Magdala public house in Hampstead, north London. She was described as a twenty-eight-year-old peroxide blonde, divorced woman with two children, a nightclub hostess and part-time prostitute. Blakely was portrayed as a hard-up playboy whose passion was racing cars. Both were shown as jealous and emotionally unstable, Ruth's possessive attitude being blamed on insecurity because of her poor upbringing. People accepted the story as gospel. Her trial, two months after the shooting, lasted a day-and-a-half. The jury at the Old Bailey, on 21 June 1955 was out for twenty-three minutes, before returning a guilty verdict. A month later she was hanged in Holloway prison and buried in unconsecrated ground inside the prison wall.

During the Second World War, Ruth had fallen in love with a French Canadian soldier, Clare Andrea McCallum. She became pregnant, giving birth to his child Andre Clare McCallum in September 1944. Clare promised to marry her but at the end of the war he returned to Quebec to his wife and children.

She became a photographer's model and met vice-boss Maurie Conley who persuaded her to work as a hostess at his Mayfair club, the Court Club, where in 1950 she met George Ellis. He was forty-one, she was twenty-three. He was a dentist, an alcoholic and violent. They married in November 1950. In October 1951 she gave birth to a baby, Georgina, but Ruth and George parted before she was born.

David Blakely, a racing driver and ex-public school boy, came on the scene in 1953 at the Little Club in Knightsbridge, where Ruth had been promoted to manageress by Conley. Blakely and Ruth became lovers and he moved into her flat above the club. While Blakely was racing at Le Mans in 1954, Ruth began an affair with Desmond Cussen, a thirty-two-year-old wealthy businessman, an ex-bomber pilot and described as her sugar daddy. He wanted to marry Ruth but she refused him.

Blakely, like Ellis, drove Ruth to the edge of sanity. He beat her up, pleaded poverty, had affairs with other women, but she still wanted him. He convinced her he loved her. Because of money problems and Blakely's bad behaviour before Christmas 1954, Ruth lost her job and flat at the Little Club. He had smashed the place up because Ruth wouldn't give him money to finance his racing-car obsession. Ruth, now homeless, moved in with Cussen at Goodwood Court, a smart address in Marylebone.

Later she moved into a bedsitter in Egerton Gardens, Kensington, with Blakely, because Blakely was jealous of her staying with Cussen. But Cussen wouldn't let go. In March 1955 Ruth miscarried Blakely's child after being kicked in the stomach by him. She was emotionally disturbed, drinking heavily and taking tranquillizers. The situation was made worse by Blakely's friendship with Anthony and Carole Findlater who turned David against Ruth. Anthony worked as Blakely's mechanic on the Emperor racing car they were constructing together.

Just before the shooting, Ruth used Cussen as a chauffeur to stalk Blakely. On Good Friday morning Blakely promised Ruth he would spend Easter weekend with her but he didn't return home that evening. Cussen drove Ruth, who was in a frenzy, between London and Penn village in Buckinghamshire where Blakely had a flat at The Old Park, his mother and stepfather's prestigious place. Apparently Blakely had another woman in Penn. At 9 p.m. on Easter Day, she took a taxi to the Findlaters' house in Tanza Road, Hampstead, then went to The Magdala pub in South Hill Park armed with a .38 Smith and Wesson revolver. She murdered Blakely as he came out of the pub with his friend Clive Gunnell. One bullet hit Mrs Gladys Yule (a passer-by) in the thumb. At the police station afterwards Ruth reeled off her statement*. She said: 'I am guilty.'

At the trial on 20 June she appeared a cold-blooded murderess. Dressed in a smart suit, and freshly peroxided hair, she looked the part of a prostitute. Ruth did not help herself in the dock and swore she

---

* Ruth's full statement appears in the Appendix.

was given the gun by a client at the club, as security on a loan. She was found guilty on 21 June.

Despite thousands of petitions, the Home Secretary Gwilym Lloyd-George turned down her solicitor's request for a reprieve.

On 12 July, the day before the hanging, Ruth's original solicitors Victor Mishcon and Leon Simmons of Messrs Mishcon and Co. visited her in the condemned cell at Holloway prison. (Victor Mishcon is now Lord Mishcon QC, consultant to Mishcon de Reya.) Ruth had dismissed her solicitor Mr Bickford who had represented her since the shooting, because of his incompetence. She admitted to Mishcon and Simmons that Cussen gave her the gun and that he drove Ruth, by then drunk on Pernod, to the place where she shot Blakely. Ruth's statement was not published – the Home Office decided it would have been unfair to Desmond Cussen.

Who, after reading the summary, would believe that Ruth was actually involved in something entirely different? When I write the last word in this book I will say, I did it, I've shown that Ruth should not have died. I am writing this fifty years after Ruth was hanged – fifty years after she was murdered.

My sister was the last woman to be hanged in Britain. I've had her story with me all my life. To turn it into a book is something I must do for her, to prove to everyone what I always felt – that Ruth did not commit the crime she was hanged for. I want the truth, which was never published, or told. I want to make it clear she did not kill anyone. I knew her hanging was political but couldn't explain how. For fifty years the truth has been concealed. Justice wasn't given to Ruth in any shape or form. She was not the common peroxide blonde prostitute that she, conveniently for some, was portrayed as. We didn't come from a rough background. My father spoke properly like lots from good backgrounds. But to put the record straight and confine the rubbish that's been put out over the years to the dustbin, I needed more than feelings – I needed proof.

There's no quick route to the truth. What happened is complicated. By starting this story at the beginning of my life and taking it step by step, you'll see how everything that happened when Ruth came along slotted into a plan. How the shooting on Easter Sunday 1955, that affected so many lives, didn't happen out of the blue. Ruth fitted the bill for a dangerous game. Things I had no idea about. She was an ideal target. It's because of this horrible game played by wicked people that the truth about Blakely's shooting was concealed. If I hadn't found out it would have stayed that way for another fifty years.

Now I have enough evidence to show she was the victim of a big conspiracy, expertly concealed. Everything to do with her case was locked away for years – that alone was indicative. Even I can work out that the truth was too sensitive. That's why Ruth was hanged.

Six months into my investigations I found a link between my sister and Stephen Ward, the Secret Service agent involved with Christine Keeler and John Profumo, the Conservative Secretary of State for War in the early 1960s. Ruth's involvement with Ward has escaped public scrutiny for over fifty years. I asked myself: could Ruth, who was conveniently hanged for an open-and-shut case of cold-blooded murder, have connections with the Secret Service? On the face of it, I thought it was impossible. Then I discovered Desmond Cussen's name again, the man described as Ruth's sugar daddy. He had signed a business document in London in 1964 – a simple find. All the same I felt I had stumbled on something but had no idea quite how significant the discovery was. What I found *drove* me to find the truth.

I have searched endlessly through archives and electoral rolls for clues. I've looked through records in old-fashioned street directories. Local telephone directories from years ago filled in other gaps. I go into detail about devious people on voting lists. I've trailed gentry who should have been registered and weren't and people hiding all over the place. I call it my 'Party-Piece'. All I can say, nobody with whom Ruth was involved was who they appeared to be.

A diversion, that's all the shooting was. She was there to cause a sensation, to save the Establishment from embarrassment over the biggest spying scandal of the twentieth century – the defection of Burgess and Maclean. It was all wrapped up in a two-penny note, a phrase I used as a child, concealing what was really going on. Ruth had to be got rid of – she knew too much about important people. The murder case was open-and-shut. She had a gun hanging from her hand, pointing it towards Blakely's dead body. Therefore she was guilty. Nobody else was involved. All done and dusted in three months. At the time we thought they rushed the case because there was talk of abolishing hanging. We were wrong. Somebody at the top said pull the rope. An open-and-shut case was a perfect excuse for not investigating the case properly. No need for forensics on Ruth or her possessions. No need to consider if she was physically capable of firing a gun. Open-and-shut meant there was no need to check on the mischief-makers' backgrounds either. It was the 1950s. We were recovering from the Second World War and most things were in the hands of the gentry; they still ruled the roost – just. No questions were asked.

Ruth didn't help herself at the trial but nobody spoke up for her either. Her statement to the police was a mechanical story. Somebody had already decided what she was going to say. It was a brainwashing job. She lied all the way through the trial to protect someone. She kept her secrets and would not allow anyone to get blamed, only herself. I never could understand why she didn't fight for her children. I do now. She had no choice in the matter, irrespective of what she thought she had done.

It's no accident my sister carried the can. That murder was organized like a military exercise by experts. Ruth was hand-picked: she had the right background, needed the money and had two children and our family to support (her pay packet went on the table each week and my parents took every penny); and she had a family secret to keep. A gift she was. And she shielded those people who'd picked her. The ones who promised her she wouldn't die. She was loyal to them to the end. She'd been their eyes and ears, the innocent person trapped between madmen. And the death sentence didn't sway her.

They said the murder was open-and-shut, no one else was involved. That was not true. It was not the straightforward murder it was made to look like. Everybody had their hands in, telling stories in newspapers, spreading rumours, keeping the myth going. Not a word of truth came out. Top people were protected. Lies were covered up.

If it was an open-and-shut murder case, why was the evidence shut away in closed files at the Public Record Office for nearly fifty years and other files protected from public scrutiny for another thirty? A senior source at the PRO confirmed the rarity of such long-term non-disclosure. The usual closure period for any trial is thirty years, but this can be extended (even up to a hundred years) if the material is classified as 'sensitive', which can cover material of a sexual content or the protection of certain names.

The deception continued into the 1970s when intellectuals introduced stories of how Ruth was suffering from diminished responsibility. Some called it a crime of passion. No matter how well written those books were, nobody got near the truth. I can't think how many authors wrote about her but one thing is certain. For nearly fifty years there was no feeling for Ruth. Other writers tried to unravel her state of mind. How did these total strangers know what she was like? They didn't think it through. It had nothing to do with diminished responsibility. It wasn't a crime of passion either. But it was *made* to look that way. The clever thinking stuff played into the hands of the powers-that-be continuing the cover-up, developing the myth about the so-called peroxide blonde prostitute.

If the case had been investigated properly, the evidence could have been put together and Ruth would have been saved. You only have to read the transcript of the trial, released at the Public Record Office nearly fifty years after Ruth was hanged, to realize the inadequacies of the investigation and judicial process. The judge Justice Havers, Melford Stevenson, Ruth's defence counsel, and Christmas Humphreys for the prosecution, were all familiar with each other. At the end of the first day of the trial, without the jury present, they asked each other what they should do, transferring legal jargon backwards and forwards. Finally the judge decreed: 'It is my duty as a judge, as a matter of law, to direct the jury that the evidence in this case does not support a verdict of manslaughter on the ground of provocation.' Ruth had no chance of a prison sentence – she was bound to be sentenced to death if she was found guilty. Yet, at the eleventh hour Ruth could have been reprieved, her life could have been saved, but I know they just wanted to get rid of her.

Evelyn Galilee, the prison warder at Holloway, was with Ruth in the condemned cell that horrible morning before she stepped through the door to be hanged. She was the same age as Ruth. She told me recently how she prayed she wouldn't be there that day: 'When I looked at the roster, it was me. I've felt guilty. I am as much guilty as anyone who did that to her. I felt dirty. I have always said it. I walked with this guilt. I truly believe I was part of that. I never thought the girl should hang. Ruth has followed my life. I see her today as she was – beautiful, absolutely beautiful.'

To Evelyn I say: 'You're a wonderful woman. You told me the truth.' It must have been an effort for her saying that after all these years.

I have told you how things were hidden, how it was virtually impossible to get to the truth. There are many complicated links and connections in Ruth's story. That's why I explain in detail about particular characters that came into my sister's life, about complicated connections and false trails. Some people find it difficult remembering things that happened fifty years ago, but to me it's yesterday. Everything I've done in the last half-century was affected by Ruth's death. Ask anybody who has a connection with a crime like this and they will say the same. The thoughts are always with me. I think of Ruth every day of my life but the trauma has become more like a bad memory.

Young people say to me that their mums remember the case of Ruth Ellis and how they stood in the kitchen listening to the wireless for the nine o'clock pips of Big Ben. That's when they hanged Ruth. Nobody understands how my family endured that agony. How I coped with my sister, the only person I cared about, being hanged. I took everything as it came. I accepted it. I've lived under a trial all my life. Perhaps it's a karma I'm going through. To people who say put it in the past and forget it, I say, I will – when the truth is out.

With help from trusted sources all over Britain I've pieced together the truth. What I found was distressing. Step by step I'll explain the real story. Unravelling a complicated web of lies and deceit, I've found the truth at last. Nothing will bring Ruth back. What is done cannot be undone. But the support of the British people will go a long way to healing the pain.

Whatever happens I want to give Ruth a proper grave with a headstone with her name on: RUTH ELLIS. Everyone needs to be noticed.

This is my story. This is the truth. You may draw your own conclusion. I hope it will be similar to mine.

2

Our Early Years

I was born in Chorlton-upon-Medlock in what used to be the
county of Manchester on the eleventh of the eleventh 1920.
On my birth certificate the registrar wrote, Occupation of
father, Nelson Arthur Hornby, Musician (Bass Fiddle). They
got the spelling of my mother's maiden name wrong and put
her down as Bertha Elisa Hornby, formerly Grethals. It should
have been Cothals.

My mother had nine children, four died from scarlet fever,
measles and what-have-you and she had miscarriages. No
matter where we lived, my father walked around telling people
we weren't his children.

My oldest brother was Julian. He had the same surname as
Mother's – Cothals – and was older than me. Then there was
me, Irma Muriel Hornby. That's what I was called in those
days. Nobody pronounced it properly so Mother said I could
stick to Muriel. Then there was Granville Neilson. And Ruth
Neilson was born in 1926. Then came our brother Jacques
Neilson who died at eighteen months. Betty Neilson came
much later in 1937. We were all our father's children except
Julian. For some reason Father changed his surname to
Neilson after I was born.

We lived at 45 Nelson Street. Years later when I was on the
Kilroy-Silk television programme I discovered that Mrs

Downey, the woman whose little girl Lesley Ann was murdered by Myra Hindley, lived back-to-back with our old house.

I've no idea where my parents met and married but I know it was six months after the wedding that she had me. My father was ever after known as the black sheep of the family, I imagine because he'd married a Flemish woman who was also Jewish. In those days marrying foreigners was taboo. Mother was one of five sisters. Their names stick in my mind: Charmaine – Mother pronounced it gerry-mane – Rachel and Olga. Another sister died very young.

My earliest memory of childhood was when I was four years old. Father had returned from New York. During the 1920s he worked on ocean liners sailing between England and America, playing the cello in an orchestra. He brought back a huge teddy for me. I was walking along the canal (we lived near the Manchester Ship Canal) and I dropped it accidentally in the water.

Some people seem to think Ruth and I came from a deprived background – it's not true. Father was from a well-to-do family but our lifestyle deteriorated. He had one older brother, Uncle Douglas, then Granville who was my father's twin, and a snooty sister Marjorie who married Frederick Sennett. I remember hearing him talk about Auntie Lizzie who was headmistress of a girls' school but I never saw her. On her will after she died, it said her name was Jane E. Singleton. She left father £1755 17s 6d, a lot of money.

Auntie Marjorie caused a lot of trouble for Mother and looked down on her. I couldn't tell you what she looked like as we rarely saw her but she had two daughters, Sylvia and Joyce – another snooty pair.

I recall the day I walked up the stone path to Grandma's house. I was only little but I remember the horrible things quite clearly. Mammur said: 'I'm going to wait outside here,' and hid behind the bushes because she was scared to go to the house. ('Mammur' was broken English and Flemish all mixed up and means Mother.) I knocked on the door and asked Auntie Marjorie if I could see Grandma. She looked at me hard and said: 'Wait a minute, I'll see if Grandmother wants to see you.' She returned saying: 'Grandmother doesn't want to see you,' banging the door in my face. I don't know why she did that but Mother said the family despised her.

At sixteen Father had joined the army but his mother found out and went straight down and bought him out. They had enough money to do that sort of thing. She told them it was because he was under age. He also had awful eyesight and glaucoma. Mother often described how he felt his way round when he got up in the morning because he couldn't see. He was a well-educated man, it's just that he didn't use it in the right way. Father's father was Charles Hornby, a professor of music connected with Manchester Cathedral. Not long after I was born, he died aged forty-two, through 'overworking his brain' as Mother put it.

I know little about the Hornbys but I know even less of my mother's family. She was brought up in a convent in Bruges following the death of her mother. Even though my mother didn't know her own mother she was told how grand a lady she was. Mother's father was high up in a regiment in India. After their mother died the sisters were sent to a convent paid for by the army. Mother told us how as a little girl she'd been looking out of the window one day on to the square outside, when the Germans raided the Town Hall opposite. The nuns destroyed the birth certificates of the children as fast as they could, so the Germans couldn't get at them. Grandfather, as an

14

officer in the Belgian colonial army, would have been an enemy of the Germans, and his children likewise. She and her sisters escaped from the convent and got to England wearing only nightdresses and holding blankets round them.

So Mammur, as we called her, had a sad start in life. She was virtually alone. Her father, my grandfather Julius, followed separately from Belgium during the 1914–18 War after being chased out by the Germans – my brother Julian was named after him. I have never known Mother to have any peace. She never managed to escape from misery, poverty and work.

When they arrived in England, Mother and her three sisters were put into a Roman Catholic convent in Manchester until they were eighteen, when Mother went straight into service – she lost touch with her sisters and her life started to go wrong. The son of the family in the big house where she worked went from one servant girl to another raping them; he made my mother pregnant with Julian.

I was about five years old when we made the first of a succession of house moves. From Manchester we went to Rhyl on the north Wales coast. Granville my brother had something wrong with his legs and the doctor said he should paddle in the sea, it would do his legs good. I could take you to the big villa-type house where we lived. They said somebody famous once owned it. It had been turned into two flats, with an outside lavatory like everyone had in those days. Downstairs was a front room, sitting room and a big kitchen. We had four bedrooms and my mother rented the attic to a woman who crocheted milk jug covers with beads on.

I used to wander the streets in Rhyl till late at night, nobody would come looking for me. Then I started at Clwyd Street

School. I can't remember much, except I wasn't liked – probably because even as a child I was a loner. I've always stood back – a lesson I learned through the hardships. My younger sister Ruth got most attention from Mother. I had the feeling Mother didn't like me; not until Ruth died that is, then she clung to me. But I did my best for her.

Ruth was conceived in Manchester but born in Wales. I can't remember the day, but I can see the room she was born in, with just a sheet across a corner for a bit of privacy for Mother. Ruth never made a noise. She was definitely Mother's favourite but I didn't hold any grudge against her. It was just as Mother said in the tragic statement she hand-wrote in broken English at the beginning of July 1955 for Mr Bickford, Ruth's solicitor. He was trying to get a reprieve for Ruth from the Home Secretary a few days before she was hanged. I never knew she wrote it until I saw it at the Public Record Office. Mother wrote: 'Ruth grew up a sweet and lovely child. She never gave me any Trouble of any kind.'

When we were children, Mother had a big basinette pram. I remember one bank holiday being told to take Ruth and Jacques along the promenade. It was May Day, there was a parade and Mother warned: 'Don't let Ruth out of your sight.' I pushed the two of them in the pram, but Ruth was three years old and wanted to walk. For a split second I turned my back not thinking she'd run off. She was a skinny little child and fast with it. I can see the picture in my mind's eye of the town crier marching round the streets clanking his bell searching for her. Luckily a lady recognized Ruth and brought her home.

I had one friend who lived next door but I never saw her parents. They gave her a doll's pram one Christmas and bought a

16

tiny one for me. I preferred my brother's toy car. That Christmas morning while my parents were in bed we were outside half-dressed, riding down the street in the toy car like racing drivers.

Then we moved to a house near the railway line – I'll never forget that move. Going from Rhyl towards Colwyn Bay, there was a rope and plank bridge over the River Clwyd. It was called the Foryd Bridge and spanned the Marine Lake. It swayed when you went on it. Father had a three-wheeler car and we children squashed on to a 'dicky' seat in the back. Little cars like Father's had to be driven over the bridge slowly. The three-wheeler rocked from side to side and we nearly went into the sea below. The only things we lost were our beautiful hats.

Uncle Jack drove the steam trains. When he went past our house he'd pull the siren and go, Woo Ooh. He wasn't an uncle really, more a friend of the family. He and his wife were fond of my brother Jacques, and Mrs Jack as I called her could understand my mother's dis, dat and dems. Mother never dropped the way she said her words. She'd say to the kids who came to the door: 'You'd better go home to your mammurs now,' in her Flemish accent.

Father was happy in Wales. He'd left the ocean liners and was playing in cinema orchestras as first cellist, accompanying the silent movies and conducting the Welsh choir. He'd made friends with the Joneses; one of them used to play the piano in the church choir that Father conducted. My strongest memory is seeing him sitting writing his music. He would have a rehearsal and the fellas came to the house to practise in a downstairs room. That's why I like classical music now. It was after the Theatre Royal in Rhyl closed down that he went to Colwyn Bay theatre until that too went.

Father made more of a fuss of me than anyone else, probably because I was his first child and also because I didn't look like the Hornby family. I remember him taking me to the fairground on the back of his bicycle and catching my foot in the wheel. I never got to the fairground. We went another time but Father was ratty because I was scared stiff and cried on the helter-skelter that he forced me to go down. He was more interested in looking at the women.

Mother said Father was all right when his twin was alive. It all seemed to go wrong about the time his twin brother Granville was killed in Manchester. They were in their late twenties. Granville was riding his bicycle and stopped in the road between a steamroller and a bus. It sounds a bit of a joke but the steamroller rolled back, knocked him off his bike, ran over his legs and cut them off. Poor man. He had one child. Mother says Granville was the best twin and my father had relied on him for support. Father went queer after that.

I was still young, about six years old, when Father started his funny business, trying it on with me even at that age. He was in the parlour alone, where he did his cello practice. I'd just had a bath and all I had on was a thin nightdress. Mother told me to go and kiss him goodnight. I said: 'Goodnight Father.' He gave me a kiss. As he did he put his hand right between my legs. I was really young but remember exactly what he did. It's the things you shouldn't remember that I remember. As I walked away he put his bow between my legs. I told my mother but she hadn't been in the room and probably thought he was playing and I was joking. So she did nothing. I knew it was wrong. He'd pretended he was tickling me.

As I said, Father came of good stock and had a posh voice. The Hornbys were a well-to-do family. But something turned his brain. Whatever was he thinking when he started doing such horrible things to his girls? Why did the Hornbys blacklist their son and not want anything more to do with him? His family knew something about him. Perhaps his father was like it. I think that's why my grandmother begged my mother to get rid of him before they got married. She bribed Mother saying: 'I'll give you any amount of money if you leave him. Just get rid of him,' but didn't tell Mother why.

Looking back on those few years in Wales, they were otherwise fairly normal. I wasn't aware of any rows. My father earned £15 a week in the silent movie theatre, a lot of money in those days. That stands out – he always talked about how much he earned. But things were changing. As months went by he got upset with Mr Golden who'd been running the theatres around Rhyl. Mr Golden had given up and gone to America to try his luck making the new films. He'd promised my father he would send for him when he was ready, because he said he was a good cello player. He never did.

By the end of the 1920s the new Talkies arrived in Wales and Father was out of work. He heard that silent films were going strong in a place called Basingstoke. So we left Wales and moved to Hampshire.

3

A Hard Hampshire Life

I'm going back now to 1929 when I was nine. Father got himself into the orchestra at the Grand Theatre in Basingstoke where they still showed silent films. The job wasn't to last; there too the talkies arrived, and Father was out of work again, this time for ten years. We lived in a village called Bramley, where Mother had organized accommodation. In no time Father couldn't afford to pay the rent. We began wandering round the Hampshire villages – Baughurst, Brimpton and Tadley – shunted from place to place, running away from debts while Father looked for work. I can't remember any good days once we moved to Hampshire. The best thing was Ruth sitting on the back of my bicycle and going for rides along the lanes. I can see her today, about three years old and as light as a feather.

The locals in the Hampshire villages then were like my mother's in-laws, *they* didn't like foreigners either. The villagers stoned her as she cycled past, yelling 'Bloody foreigner'. The villagers still lived in an old-fashioned way with their church, Sunday school and whist drive routine. Mother went out to work every day in Baughurst as a cook for the Stokes family in a grand house called Inhurst. Three spinster sisters called Ellen lived there: Ellen Joe, Ellen Muriel and Ellen Sybil.

Julian and I went to school in Brimpton, close to Aldermaston where they had those anti-bomb marches in the 1960s. We hated it. Looking back, it's as though we were cut out to have terrible things inflicted on us. Father had shifted us miles out of the way to a remote cottage. I remember two things about the place. Freddie-never-sweat, so called because he wore three coats in the summer and never sweated. The second I'll never forget. It was the blackberry season. A girl knocked on the door, I was upstairs reading *The Red Letter* or *The Oracle* magazine – they contained sound advice and the girls and women loved them. It was the first time we could read love stories. The girl asked if Muriel could come blackberrying. I didn't know her but went off with her, dumb as I was. We were picking blackberries when suddenly this motorcyclist drove up. The girl ran off to him saying: 'I won't be long Muriel. I'm going for a ride.' They were gone a long time. Eventually they came back and she shouted: 'It's your turn now, Muriel, to have a ride. Off you go.' It sounded jolly so I climbed on behind him. We passed some woods but then he forced me off the motorbike. He threw me into the ditch. His hands went everywhere. I screamed. He was holding me by the throat and tried to strangle me. Then all this stuff went over me. I had no idea what dicks were for. It sounds ignorant for these days but in my life boys and girls never mixed. You must remember I was never spoken to about periods, sex or how to go about such things. I was lucky; a tractor came down the lane. It probably saved my life. The motorcyclist got on his bike quick, ready to drive off. 'Don't go off without me,' I shouted. He said he'd take me back to the common but he didn't, he dumped me miles from home. It was late at night when I got home. That was my first sexual experience apart

21

from the abuse I was getting from my father. Mother was at the gate: 'Where have you been? Where are the blackberries? You've been crying haven't you?' I said no. 'It looks as though you have to me.' She never troubled again. I went up to the bedroom to wash all the stuff off my legs. We didn't have the convenience of a bathroom with hot and cold water, just a companion set – a china bowl and a jug of water.

Our next stop was Monk Sherborne. Ruth, Granville and I went to school at Sherborne St John. We started together on 5 September 1932. It was a Victorian building and you had to eat your lunch outside even in the cold weather, that is if you had food. We didn't. We stood there watching everybody else eating. It's difficult to imagine what it's like unless you've been there. Ninety children attended the school. Ruth was in the infants when I was in class 4. We were always outsiders and never joined in. Other children stared, laughed and kept away from us. We wore ragged clothes – they called us raga-muffins.

I didn't smile and I never laughed. Not even at a joke. I hadn't the confidence to make friends, it was being knocked out of me every day at home. Each day I became more ex-hausted. The headmaster must have been concerned about Ruth and me – according to the school log-book, the school nurse was called out in January 1933 to look at both of us, and I was examined again by the school doctor, Doctor Tibby.

We lived in a cottage in Monk Sherborne and were poor like the Brewers next door. At least Mr Brewer worked, unlike my father who by now wasn't bothering even to look. We slept in the *cote* where shepherds would have slept. All the good stuff was sold off bit by bit – we sat on orange-boxes to eat our food and drank out of jam jars because we had nothing else. I know what it was like to have nothing.

I was still only a little girl, not twelve, when Father started seriously interfering with me. It was in this house he first tried to rape me but he couldn't get into me. When Mother was out he forced me to do things. I didn't realize what he was doing wasn't right. Mother must have known what he was up to but she kept her peace. When he started on Ruth she'd be the same. 'Why did you do that to me, Father?' I'd ask him. 'You're older than me and you know better.' He never answered.

He'd make me sleep with him in his bed when Mother worked nights in service. I'd lie facing the wall, rigid, and he'd put his thing through the top of my legs. He was attempting to rape me, but at that age I didn't know there was a word to describe what he was doing. I never murmured. I remember the horrible things and the mess he'd make over my back when he'd finished relieving himself. When he fell asleep I'd creep out of bed and wash myself. If I could have only washed his abuse away.

I hated what Father did. Sometimes he'd gag me to stop me screaming. I became a robot. I did what I was told, if I didn't I'd get a hiding. Some days I'd go to school with rings round my legs where he'd hit me with sticks. Whenever Mother wasn't there he'd start. Then even when she was there he did what he wanted. If only I'd had the mental make up to withstand his bullying. Sometimes when I escaped upstairs he'd threaten, yelling: 'That's where I'll hang you from if you don't do as you're told.'

Within a few years, as Ruth started growing up, it seemed strange that Father would proudly say: 'There's not a better-looking girl than either of you two in the village.' It didn't stop him beating us though.

My father was hard up. He hadn't got a job, he wasn't looking for one and there was no work anyway. He forced Julian to go begging for bread. I'd watch him knocking on people's doors just for a bit of stale bread. We were living a lowly, unfriendly life. We didn't know there was such a thing as a birthday. All I knew was that when I was fourteen I'd leave school. Every day mother would cycle to Captain and Mrs Kent's bungalow. She cooked and cleaned there and earned half-a-crown a week. I was allowed to visit the house once. Mrs Kent showed me her daughter's pretty dresses. I stood there in my one and only ragged dress.

Father had turned into a bully. If Ruth and I didn't get home from school early to get his tuppeny Woodbine he'd hit and kick us. Sometimes he'd pull me downstairs by my hair, threatening to kill me if he didn't have his cigarettes. On one occasion he took all the photos of Ruth and me, two lovely-looking girls, off the walls – one by one, glass and all, they went in the fire.

When he'd bashed the hell out of us, he'd show no remorse. He'd go out of the room whistling, pleased with himself because he'd upset my mother. When Mother cried, we all cried. Ruth learned not to, or to ask for anything from an early age. I'd choke back the tears when he walloped me but eventually learned not to cry. Ruth got out of the way as much as she could. In years to come she learned how to give him some of his own medicine, throwing anything at him that was in sight. Her jam sandwiches ended up on the wall after she'd missed his face because she couldn't see straight.

One night when my parents were fighting, Father left the house threatening to cut his throat. I lay awake crying under the bedclothes. I couldn't sleep that night, like most nights since – it had such a frightening effect on me. Needless to say Father didn't cut his throat, he slept on the common and came home at dawn.

Despite all this we were made to go to church every Sunday, to All Saints Church of England down the hill. It was not the 'Roman Catholic Sunday school' that Robert Hancock describes in *Ruth Ellis, The Last Woman to be Hanged*. We went to the morning service where one of my brothers would pump the organ for the organist Miss Raynbird.

There was no one to turn to or look up to. Except one summer, grandfather Julius came to visit us. He was a big kind man with one of those stiff moustaches. He was fond of Mother. He died not long after from his war wounds and it broke my mother's heart. I loved him even though I only met him a few times.

Granville and I left Sherborne St John school on 16 October 1934; Ruth left four days before us. She went on to Worting village school. I went to Fairfield senior in Basingstoke. I was there a matter of weeks but was so tired from rows at home, I'd have done anything to have a mattress to sleep on. At that time you'd be positioned in class according to your age and because I was approaching fourteen I sat at the back. The teachers didn't manage to bring the fear out of me. I couldn't conquer arithmetic, I was a bit dyslexic and more of an artist than anything.

I got bullied. The girls would either not talk to me or they'd call me names. There wasn't physical bullying except for the boy that thumped me on the nose every day on the way home from school.

Manor Farm Pond at Sherborne St John isn't quite the same today as it was then. It wasn't so watery then; it was muddy, and belonged to the nobs in The Vyne, a mansion on the other side of the lake. Major Charles Chute was the owner. There was no public footpath round the lake and it was definitely out of bounds. I remember my brother Jerry (Julian) was nearly shot by the gamekeeper for trespassing on their land when he was exploring the fields.

I was very close to Julian, he somehow safeguarded Ruth and me. I came home from school one night a bit late. It was getting dark but it didn't matter as long as I came in with Father's Woodbine. I asked where Jerry was. Mother said he was out. She let me walk miles on my own, past the chalk quarry behind the house and through the woods towards the village till midnight, trying to find him. I got scratched by thorns and horrible things ran through my mind. I cried because I couldn't find him. I was so tired I could hardly walk another step. I'd plodded all the way from our cottage to Manor Farm Pond and back trying to find him. When I finally got home all my parents said was: 'Where have you been?' I told them I'd been out looking for Jerry. Again I asked where he was. Mother said Jerry was in bed. He wasn't. She was lying. He'd gone.

I overheard my parents talking one day and discovered Father had thrown Jerry out. They hadn't said a thing or explained what had happened. I've never forgotten that awful day. None of us knew Jerry's whereabouts until years later when Mother received a letter from him. He'd joined a circus and was travelling round North America, where he cleaned out the animals and did the heavy work.

With Jerry gone it was left to me to get money. Mother sent me with a note to ask a local clergyman for half-a-crown. She did this to stop Father from hitting her. I was so shy and stood outside the gate for ages, waiting for the courage to go in. The vicar wouldn't give me a penny and said that my mother should go and see him. She didn't get a penny either. Occasionally he would come round with a quarter pound of tea for us.

We were on the move again, this time to a wooden chalet close to Park Prewitt mental hospital. I remember its French windows and the one bedroom we all shared. It would have been the year I was confirmed into the Church of England at Wootton St Lawrence church. I wore a white dress that Mother sewed for me by hand. I wore white gloves and a veil and carried a white Bible. Mother watched me walk down the road. There was a crowd of girls by the church with their parents but I was on my own. We took Holy Communion.

I remember Mother's words when I got home: 'Now you've been confirmed nobody can harm you.'

4

Abused by my Father

I found some 1930s photos of workers on Lord Ashcombe's estate in Dorking. It reminded me of my first job. The women were dressed in baggy dresses and Norah Batty stockings. I wore clothes like that when I went into service.

It was the beginning of 1935, I was fourteen and due to leave school. I'd spent a few months at Fairfield senior school, hadn't a certificate to my name and the headmistress was fussing about me leaving: 'This girl doesn't look ten, let alone fourteen'. Mother took my birth certificate in to prove it. She'd found me a job in Dorking on the Denbies Estate. Lord and Lady Ashcombe were an old couple, gentry through and through and their grand home was called the Cubitt Mansion. It had a hundred rooms. They had twenty-four indoor staff including maids, valets, chauffeurs, butlers and footmen. I was training to be a lady's maid because I was good at needlecraft – Mother had taught me crochet, embroidery and knitting. In the needle room I was trained to mend ladders, pulling thread from one silk stocking to mend another.

I was supposed to be there for nine months. It was a respite from Father's nonsense – it didn't last. He'd written to Lord Ashcombe, knowing he could get round anyone with his good handwriting and educated words, saying he needed me to look after the children while Mother worked. So again I became the unpaid servant, overworked with not enough to eat. A contrast to the life I'd escaped to at Denbies where I had a bath each day and good food to eat.

My parents had moved again, to a hamlet of two houses and a farm. As usual when Mother was out my father was at it. Nobody heard him bashing Granville and me around. Mother walked in once, asking what he was doing. 'She doesn't do as she's told so I gave her a good hiding.' Mother just said: 'You shouldn't do that.' She didn't know or didn't want to know what else he'd been doing.

Father found a job as bookkeeper at Park Prewitt mental hospital and we were given a hospital property in Dunsford Crescent. To begin with a couple stayed with us waiting for their own place to be built, so Father couldn't get up to his tricks but when they moved out he put iron bars on my bedroom window to stop me climbing out. I was a prisoner.

It was here that he'd get me to have sex with him any time he wanted. I feel sick thinking about it. He always tried to rape me in the kitchen when Mother was out working and Ruth was at her friend Pearl Wood's house. She used to get tea there and the two of them liked to practise singing in harmony. Ruth loved singing. As she got older she went to Pearl's to avoid Father's obscene behaviour.

He used to push me down on the edge of a wooden chair. My hands were tied behind my head with a scarf, my legs were pushed back and tied together so I couldn't escape. If I wriggled he'd kick me up the backside. He was like a dog on heat. But he couldn't get in because my private parts were sealed. He kept on until he did. He tried to kiss me on the lips.

I'd struggle and kick, but the more I struggled the more he held me down. In the end he got what he wanted. He raped me. The pain was agonizing. I remember moving around and seeing stuff that had come away – I'd lost my virginity.

Father raped me three times. I fought him each time. The more I moved, the more he threatened me with a razor blade at my neck. He'd remind me in his filthy language about the rope tied round the attic door: 'That's where you'll be hanging from.' And warned me he'd cut my tongue out: 'Then you won't be able to tell anybody anything.' He was a savage. He always abused me in the kitchen but eventually did it anywhere. One night he was beating my mother because he couldn't have sex with her. I screamed: 'Leave Mammur alone.' He yelled: 'Muriel's sleeping with me tonight.' I had no choice. I had no strength to fight him; I was left with an abscess in my ear and loose front teeth from his punches.

One day, Mother said I was going to have a baby. 'Where?' I said, looking around the room. 'Don't be stupid, it's there.' I hadn't noticed my stomach getting fatter. I'd had one period and he'd made me pregnant. I was about fifteen. Mother said nobody would want me the way I was. She and Father tried everything to get rid of it. They forced me into mustard baths, gave me Epsom Salts and douched me. They took it in turns rubbing my stomach until it was like raw steak. I went through agony.

An illegitimate baby was a terrible sin for a single woman. A child born through incest brought disgrace on the whole family. The girl next door, Mr Brewer's daughter, had four by her father, the dirty old dog, and was told not to have any more. Children born out of incest can be prone to weaknesses

30

that become noticeable as they get older. She'd push her babies around without batting an eyelid.

I went into an infirmary workhouse with a maternity unit where I gave birth to Robert William Neilson on 15 August 1936. I could have been put away permanently in the workhouse with other women who'd had illegitimate babies. Matron asked who the father was and reported it to the police. A policeman cross-examined me, repeating the questions: 'Who did it? Was it your brother? Was it your father?' I cried. Matron stared knowingly at Father when he came to take me home.

I remember giving birth to Robert as clear as anything. It was bloody hard-going over three days – no gas and air then. I worried about going home and not knowing what to do. My memories are of being imprisoned in an enormous secret. I had a pokey room upstairs and there I stayed, only pushing the pram out at night. Robert had to be kept a secret. Mother was petrified of any scandal. I tried to breastfeed Robert but it didn't work. All the while Father stood and stared. Ruth was too young to understand, all the same she was forbidden to talk about it to anyone. I realize now I was defensive when people asked questions about Robert's father and why they hadn't seen him around. I'd say anything, like he's in the army.

The Hutchinses were our neighbours and Mr Hutchins was a nurse at Park Prewitt. Ruth would take their little girl out for walks as a favour, and sometimes if she couldn't get to sleep at nights Ruth would cuddle her until she did. Mr Hutchins said something strange one evening when I was alone outside: 'One night, throw your mattress out the window, jump on to it and clear off.' I don't know what I would have done. I thought London was across the sea, I never knew it was just along the railway line. Can you be so dumb? Growing up, Robert had no one to call mummy. He was a little angel and clung to me like a shadow. As he got older he asked who his father was. We told him his father was in the Air Force and got killed. He accepted it. I couldn't say to him, your father is my father. He thought I was his sister, my mother was his grandma but he called her Mum. We all lived in the same place, even when I married Joe, and everyone called her Mum. I think he had an idea I was his mother. It was a muddled up affair.

In recent years my daughter Pauline said she guessed years ago that Robert was her brother but never knew her grandfather was Robert's father. She reminded me of an argument we had about Robert when she was pregnant. She asked why I couldn't kick him out. I was forced to say: 'You're talking about your brother.' Robert didn't even have a birth certificate. Mother said she'd registered him immediately but she can't have done.

Mother probably didn't want to keep quiet about Robert or Father – in her own mind she did it for the sake of the family. She probably knew Father could have gone to prison and her children would be taken away. All the same she didn't do anything to protect us against him, and turned a blind eye to his indecent acts.

Despite everything it still makes me mad the way she's been portrayed in books written about Ruth. Tony Van den Bergh and Laurence Marks gave the impression in *Ruth Ellis, A Case of Diminished Responsibility*? that she was a Roman Catholic maniac who spent her time knitting and praying. She hated the Church. She couldn't stand religion when she got out of the convent. She knitted and sewed, did embroidery and lace-making. But not how they describe it. She would do it in the evening if Father got night work. On the whole she was a good mother and worked long hours in service. All she did was slave to keep my father in cigarettes and never came in without a packet of fags, scared stiff she'd be beaten up.

I'll never forgive my father for doing those unthinkable things. We weren't told about periods or sex – we had to find out ourselves. Ruth was at junior school when she came running home one day, shouting: 'Muriel, I've got one of those political things.' She meant her period. I was frightened for her because of what had happened to me. I advised: 'For God's sake Ruth, don't have anything to do with boys until you get elderly.' She glibly replied: 'That's difficult because I sit next to two boys in class. What do you say to that one?' as if they only had to touch her to make her pregnant. She knew all the answers.

Ruth was subjected to Father's abuse when she got to eleven. I heard her scream the way I did. I knew what he was doing. She'd go into the new bathroom and wash herself when he'd finished, saying: 'Muriel, he's doing those dirty things to me. He's trying to put his thing in me.' She couldn't say the word either. But she knew what he was doing – she was more intelligent than I was.

I encouraged Ruth not to come straight home from school; it was safer to stay at Pearl Wood's until Mother came home. She kept out of his way as often as she could but he ranted and raved demanding to know where my skinny sister was. Most of the time I'd stand in front of her, trying to protect her, screaming for him to leave her alone. Nothing stopped him.

33

By the time Ruth was a young teenager she was determined he wouldn't ruin her life. But it didn't stop him trying. One occasion stands out. I was hanging out the washing and heard Ruth's screams coming from the house. He'd forced her, just like he did me. It was the same brutal treatment she'd have to endure later in life from her husband George Ellis and her lover David Blakely. I'm sure the way we were treated, the viciousness and abuse, affected our personalities. I still hear Ruth's words when she discovered that our father was Robert's father. She may have been six years younger, but acted ten years older than me: 'I'm not letting him do to me what he's done to you. You've got to promise one thing Muriel, never talk about Father's filthy behaviour to anyone.' I kept that promise – till now.

My youngest sister Betty was born in 1937. Mother was in her late thirties and ended up having a bodged hysterectomy in Reading Hospital. A few years later, the specialist at King's College Hospital in London, who treated the late Queen Mother, was appalled at how Mother had been fixed. In the meantime Father was accused of stealing money at Park Prewitt. He said a group of doctors were rolling drunk and had fiddled with the money box. Needless to say Father was blamed and lost his job and the house. We moved to another village. By now people suspected what he was doing to his daughters and were gossiping.

My brother Granville worked in a barber's shop till he was fifteen, then was marched down to join the army. That was brother number two gone. The next thing I remember was Mother leaving us for six months. She worked in the Red Lion in Basingstoke and left Father to it. I was in charge of Robert, Ruth, Betty who was just a baby and Father. It felt awful not having a mother but she couldn't stand it any longer – Father was still trying it on. She was afraid that I'd already got one child and what would I do with another. 'You'll end up killing her,' she'd scream at him. Apart from having Robert I had two miscarriages as a result of Father's abuse. He never stopped. It sounds silly that anyone could be so dumb but I didn't care any more. I let him get on with it. He had me where he wanted me.

The timbered cottage we lived in at Sherfield-on-Loddon is still there today. It may look like something off a chocolate box but in 1938 it was for the working class, not middle-class people like nowadays. Ruth went to the village school across the green, then on to Fairfield. By the time she was thirteen she looked more mature than I was at that age. She'd had a chance to grow up, was more advanced and managed to cope better with problems.

We'd go to dances together at the village hall. I remember my friend Kitty Bailey had just returned from London with more than she bargained on. Like all the girls who thought London was paved with gold, most brought babies back with them. So did Kitty. When mother wasn't around Ruth looked after Kitty's baby as well as Robert and Betty, while we went to the dances. But most of the time Ruth and I sneaked over there together. We did the veleta and quick-step. Ruth got all the dances with the fellas. She was a good dancer. I remember Mother made me a blue dress, a lacy affair with pleats set in from the shoulders. Another was green with a V-neck and leaves round the skirt. One of Ruth's dresses, bought in a second-hand shop, was altered to look brand new. Mother was good at making and altering clothes.

I can't remember the name of the bands that came down from London but they had five or six men playing clarinets and drums. What I see in my mind's eye is Father returning from work one day, discovering Ruth and I weren't home, and finding us at the dance. He marched into the village hall looking like Humphrey Bogart, yelling in his bolshie way: 'Out! Get out! Go home!'

Mother was back home at this stage. She and Father told me I had to go to work if I wanted to keep the baby. I got a job at Huntley & Palmers in Reading. First I had to be examined by the factory doctor. Just to pack biscuit tins! It shows how things have changed. He guessed I'd had a baby and could have refused to take me: 'Are you sure you're all right? I think you ought to go home and rest.' I said I was fine. I kept the job for two months.

Once when I was coming home past Bradley's printing shop where Father worked as a caretaker, he was waiting by the door: 'Are you coming in? We can get in the back seat of the car.' He wanted the usual, for me to satisfy him. I had no intention of doing it: 'No I can't. I've got to go home. I've got to give Mother some money. I don't feel well.' I said anything to avoid him. 'You know what you'll bloody get for that.' He meant a beating.

When I'd been at Huntley & Palmers a couple of months, Father made me pack in working there, just like the other two jobs I got in the paper mills and The Four Horseshoes pub. He wanted me at home when Mother was out at work even though I was supposed to be earning money for the family. His excuse was that Mother could earn more than I could. It was more like he was expecting all the things a wife does including having sex with him. I'll never forget how he cried on the steps of The Four Horseshoes, begging: 'I want my daughter back.'

I don't know what they must have thought. I walked out of the pub and didn't go back.

5

Wartime

It was wartime. We were living in Southampton Street in Reading. Father gave up the job at Bradley's virtually as soon as he started, to go up to London. He found a job advertised as a caretaker-cum-chauffeur at Porn and Dunwoody at Union Works in Southwark. He'd gone off on his own leaving Mother and me in Reading with Ruth, Betty and Robert.

Mr Porn was an influential man and bought a new Hillman car for Father to drive him round in. Not many had cars like that during the war. The firm had a flat above the factory that went with the job. That's where Father was living on his own.

Ruth knew where he was but it was her friend Edna Turvey who put her up to running away to London. It's difficult to describe Edna. Father told me to look at her because she walked like a queen. 'You'll never be like that,' he said. She was like any other woman except she always dressed in black. It was she who got Ruth into the fast life. Ruth was only fourteen, had just left school with no certificates. Edna was in her thirties when she met Ruth through my eldest brother Julian. He was back from America, had joined the Navy, was on leave and brought Edna home to where we were living in Reading. Anyway, Julian went back in the Navy leaving Edna with us. She didn't see him again.

Next thing, Ruth and Edna ran away to London, found Father and moved in with him. I can't explain why she ended up at Father's. She didn't run away from problems – she ran into them. As usual he was up to his tricks. Ruth was made to go to bed with him. Mother didn't trust him and she decided to join him, leaving me in lodgings in Reading with Robert. Needless to say as soon as Mother got to the flat she caught Father in bed with Edna. For once in her life she was furious, filled Edna's case with her clothes and chucked it out the window. That was the last Father saw of Edna Turvey.

After a few months of living in lodgings I went to London to join the family. I had a little room and looked after Robert in an attic room, with a balcony of some sort. I noticed a small hole in the floor and spied through it. In the room below I saw a young man. The next day I met him. He seemed pleased I'd been sneaking a look at him and said: 'I've been watching you peeping through the hole.' His name was Joe Jakubait. He was Porn and Dunwoody's first bound apprentice.

Joe had been going out with Ruth before I arrived. The first time I saw them together was when I was making my way into the air raid shelter. Four brick and concrete structures had been put up inside the factory so they could work during air raids. Joe had his arms round her. I think they'd been lovers but I wasn't like that with Joe once we started going together. He'd taken Ruth to Streatham Locarno, then took both of us to the pictures and it was my hand he held even though he was Ruth's boyfriend. When I talked to him about those days he couldn't remember much about what we looked like. 'Compared to Ruth, you were well formed,' he said. 'Ruth was more like a matchstick.' I don't know why he didn't stick with her; perhaps none of the awful things would have happened in her life, if I hadn't taken him away from her. But he fell for me and said it was love at first sight.

Ruth was turning into a lovely-looking girl with high cheek-bones and rosy cheeks. She was gorgeous. She'd hardly ever worn make-up but as soon as she left school she started wearing lipstick. We hadn't discovered the eyes in those days, no mascara, liner or anything. She didn't dye her hair either. She had thick, auburn hair – we both did. Joe describes her well when he first knew her: 'Ruth was young, thin and sort of skittish. Definitely not too clever with the eyesight and was supposed to wear glasses but never did. She was polite and friendly. When people used to sit and talk, she'd be up moving about. She couldn't settle. She was highly strung but there was nothing wrong with her and she was no trouble.' In those days you'd regularly find her in someone else's house in London. She was sociable and learning about the freedom of the city. She was a kind kid and still a bit clingy to Mother.

From the way books were written about her, I don't think people knew what she was really like. I want to put that straight. Ruth was referred to as a cheap peroxide blonde as if she was worthless and the only one who'd ever bleached her hair. Some sort of tarty blonde image was created from the word go to suit the fairy story. People were eager to read all about it. None of the authors stopped to think about the real Ruth Ellis. That made me angry. They wrote fabricated nonsense taken from press cuttings or passages of books published from time to time and regurgitated. Van den Bergh and Marks described her at age fifteen in their book *Ruth Ellis, A Case of Diminished Responsibility?*: 'Ruth had now shed all her puppy-fat. Her hair was growing darker, and she resorted to the peroxide bottle to remedy this. For the rest of her short life she was to be inordinately proud of her peroxide blonde hair.'

This wasn't Ruth at fifteen. Puppy fat? She was half-starved. What they had no idea about or didn't want to know was that Ruth didn't peroxide her hair till she was about twenty-four, four years before she died. The real fifteen-year-old Ruth worked across the road from our flat, at the OXO factory where I also worked at the time. We held the family together with our earnings. Imagine the smell when we had this terrific air raid not long after I started there. It blew up the factory and the smell was like a meaty stew. Then the Wright's Coal Tar soap factory on the corner and the firemen's hose factory next door went up – a right cocktail.

It was very different in those days. We'd go to work with curlers in our hair, done up in a turban made from a scarf, in case we got a chance to go to a dance. After some special training I started at Marconi's munitions factory where I did a bit of drilling and rewinding armatures. I was good at it because I had small fingers. Ruth worked there to start with but moved on to the Lyons Corner House restaurant near Trafalgar Square where she worked as a waitress. They wore black dresses and white aprons and caps to hold their hair in place and looked very smart. She didn't talk about it much though.

Father was now in his forties. Some time during the 1941 Blitz, when there was the terrible bombing of London, he'd been doing his fire-watching duty and was clouted on the head by a piece of falling timber. Ruth should have been downstairs in the factory shelter but she stayed outside with Father all night to watch the bombs dropping. She dragged him from the rubble and saved his life. After that he wasn't well enough to work as a chauffeur, got the sack, lost the flat and had to make his own way.

He found a caretaker's job in Herne Hill Road in a big garage right on the doorstep, a hundred yards from where we lived. But he collapsed one day on the floor of our lodgings. Joe carried him upstairs to bed. He said Father was as sick as a horse. He'd had a stroke. He couldn't talk. Mother had to go and find a doctor to see to him. That was difficult because we weren't registered with one. When she eventually found one we had to pay him and that was a problem because we had no money.

At that time the evacuations were going on. They took Father from Camberwell in south London where we were living to the new hospital in Poplar Road, Leatherhead, in Surrey. At the time I couldn't understand why they sent him that distance but learned it was excellent for specialists; food by all accounts was good for wartime and the nurses were pretty, so the men who'd been in the same ward as Father reported. I have to say I didn't care where Father went. I was glad to get rid of him.

While he was away Mr Bright, the works foreman at Porn and Dunwoody, was paying attention to Mother. He helped her out with money because she had to look after Robert and Betty while Ruth and I went to work. Father didn't come home for a year. He was unable to speak or walk. But Mother went once a week to the hospital. She never told us anything about how he was. I never asked. By then I'd started going with Joe. I was my own person and no longer a prisoner.

I was working on munitions and had just turned twenty when Father came home from hospital. He thought he'd carry on with me as before. I put up with none of his nonsense and ignored him. I don't know what it was but something gave me the strength. It didn't stop him trying though. I'd be making

42

myself up in the mirror over the hearth and he'd be watching me, trying to start all over again. He knocked me across the leg one morning with a hairbrush when I refused him and I had to lie at work about the egg lump there. He'd come down early in the morning when I was getting ready to go out and sit in a chair crying because I wouldn't let him touch me. He was sex mad. I understand how not carrying on his career as a musician must have made him feel bitter. But I'm not making excuses for him any more.

That same year Ruth became ill. We'd been bombed out and moved so many times, and had to live in any building that still had windows. It was 16 March 1942. Our address was 19 Farmers Road in Camberwell. During the night Ruth kept crying. I rubbed her hand to make it better. I'd been awake all night and was worried because I was on munitions first thing next morning. I went through to Mother: 'You'd better come and see Ruth because her hand's hurting.' Mother just said keep rubbing it, it'll be all right, there's nothing wrong with it. I did as I was told and went off to work. When Mother went in to her in the morning she told me how she'd carried Ruth into the sitting room, put her on a mattress on the window seat and went searching for a doctor. Ruth was rushed to St Giles Hospital in Camberwell in an ambulance with acute rheumatic fever.

According to the hospital report I've seen in the Public Record Office, Ruth must have been very ill for longer than anyone thought; she'd had three weeks of pain, swelling and redness of the left knee. Followed by pains in the ribs, left wrist and the back of her left thumb and ring finger. She had an X-ray on 4 April and they diagnosed acute infective arthritis of a joint on her left hand: 'Destroying the bone on each side of one of the first inter phalangeal joints and periostitis of the first phalanx.' On 3 May 1942, two months after she'd been admitted to hospital, she was discharged. Ruth's arthritis and crooked fingers stayed with her for the rest of her life. The pain never stopped.

At the bottom of another report in the Public Record Office there's a p.s. from W. Mackenzie the Medical Registrar: 'I should be interested to know from the medical point of view, the present condition of her joints.' The report, prepared for Ruth's solicitor, Mr Bickford, was dated 27 May 1955 – six weeks after Ruth allegedly shot her lover David Blakely with a heavy .38 Smith and Wesson revolver. Nothing was made of this at Ruth's trial.

Robert was christened, in 1942, as a Catholic because my mother wanted him to be. He would have been about six years old because Betty was christened at the same time and I can see to this day what happened. She ran in and out of the church pews and down the aisle. She'd be four-ish and was shouting: 'I don't want no bloody bath. I don't want to be bloody christened.' I had to run and grab her and remember that I couldn't stop laughing. It was one of the funniest things in my life. The priest said it was the devil coming out. He would say that. Robert looked on quietly, probably thinking silly sods.

Mother would do anything to avoid bringing more shame on the family. When Robert had to go into hospital that same year, she told a pack of lies about him because she was petrified we would be social outcasts. She called him her son when she filled out the papers. I can't remember what was wrong and Mother wasn't a woman to come and tell me what it was about. She just said: 'Don't worry.' End of conversation. It didn't stop her reminding me that nobody would want me because of what had happened. Robert was six years old and abnormally small, probably a genetic defect. The hospital told Mother that the blood test they'd taken proved she wasn't Robert's mother. She went completely mad and told them they were wrong.

Mother hadn't told me anything about what had happened there – she'd always go off and do things on her own. It was much later when she was rowing with Father that it all came out in the open. I think that's when she finally faced the truth about who Robert's father really was – her own husband. I don't think she knew for certain before that or just wouldn't accept it despite covering up for him in hospital. It must have been awful for her but she never said a thing. Like me she was a very forgiving person.

While this trouble was going on with Father, Ruth and Robert, I was courting Joe. We saw each other two dozen times in the early forties. Joe was in a reserved occupation. That meant he wasn't called up but travelled a lot, working on ships all over the country. His mother died in 1939 and he couldn't get on with his father because he wanted everything his own way. So when he wasn't travelling he stayed at our house. I suggested we should live together because I couldn't stand my old man around me. I didn't tell him anything that was going on though. He didn't suspect either because during those war years Joe was always working. As he said he wasn't putting his mind to anything other than work.

We had a three-storey Victorian house in Bengeworth Road, Brixton, which our whole family rented together. It was a reasonable sort of place – unfurnished and owned by an elderly Italian woman who owned most of the property round there. Joe got on with Mother except she smoked a lot and always scrounged money for cigarettes. That annoyed him. He remembers her constantly complaining in her strong accent there wasn't enough money. He thought differently about my father: 'My first impression of the family was that they seemed all right. Then I noticed Arthur sort of wanted to control Muriel. He wanted to tell her to do things his way.' Joe thought it odd that Ruth and I didn't bring friends round but soon realized it was because Father would have got in a tantrum about it. 'Most families would have had an open door for friends and a house full of kids, but not Arthur. You go back to the early days. That wasn't homely, that was purgatory. The family was never together. You're going back to Charlie Dickens' time. All the way along the line there was a strange atmosphere. Going back to the beginning when he came as a caretaker-chauffeur to Porn and Dunwoody, I can't remember it as a family. I never could.'

Once Ruth was on the mend from rheumatic fever, she started going down to what the Yanks called dives, where she and her girlfriend would meet Canadian servicemen. Dives were like air aid shelters. Sometimes she'd sneak out to meet her boyfriends without father noticing, then she'd tap on our bedroom window and climb back in so the old sod didn't know she'd been out. She was just mischievous and having a bit of fun like any normal teenager would.

I've never told anybody about this before because people may think I was two-timing Joe who was away doing his secret work with ships. Ruth said: 'Come on Muriel, I'm going to the nightclub tonight. Do you want to come?' She was years older than me in her thinking despite being six years younger. I was a bit scared but said I'd go.

The dive was like a dark underground cellar where everyone was fondling each other. The Yanks didn't care what they did or who they did it in front of. There were seats round the edge of the room. You couldn't dance even if you wanted to, it was too crowded. I felt uncomfortable and told Ruth if we sat there much longer I'd go home although I had no idea how I'd get in because she was the skinny one and would have to climb in through the window to let me in.

Just as we were about to go a soldier in khaki uniform came over. I noticed he'd been sitting opposite, looking as though he was sick of the place. He was taller than Ruth. She was 5'2", he'd be about 5'6". He had all the usual things the Yanks had, like rings, a watch and good clothes. He came over to our table and it was funny, he tried to get off with me. I said there was no point looking at me – I was going out with someone and I'd only come to keep my sister company. I introduced him to Ruth. He said: 'She's nice.' He was French Canadian. His name was Clare Andrea McCallum. That's how they met and how their love affair started.

We walked round town and had a bag of chips with salt and vinegar wrapped in newspaper. He walked us to the station, insisted on taking us on the tube, then walked us from Camberwell Green station to Herne Hill. He asked Ruth if he could see her again. She said yes. I left them outside after she'd climbed through the window to let me in. She hadn't been there long before Father opened the door yelling: 'Hey you, come in.' She thought Clare was smashing. I was pleased to think she'd met someone. This was her first serious relationship. Ruth adored the man.

They'd go to shows and cinemas – in those days, mainly cinemas. As things got more involved he lived with us when he was on leave. We were in the Bengeworth Road house and each of us had a flat. Ruth was in the top one with Clare, I lived under her, my parents were on the ground floor. They encouraged him to stay with us because we were short of food and each time he came back he'd bring a haversack full of rations like tinned food and cigarettes for my parents. That's all my father cared about – fags.

When he went away Ruth was very good and never went out anywhere. She'd spring clean her flat – I've never seen a girl work like she did. She even had the inside lace curtains off the windows once a week to wash them. Fanatical about cleanliness she was. She spoke to me about him but when they were together they were very private. Each time he came home they'd stay in the top floor room with the door locked like a loving couple. They never went out. She was so much in love with him.

I knew my sister well but there was never any talk of contraception between her and me. She wouldn't have discussed it with Mother either. Nobody talked about it then, it was taboo. Ruth and Clare had been going together for a year but we were all surprised when she became pregnant. She was still such a little girl of sixteen. Not that I should talk, I was only sixteen when I had Father's child.

Anyway, Ruth was in for a rough time. My parents turned against her. As soon as she started to show at about five months pregnant, that was it. King's College Hospital that Ruth was under sent all the girls away who were having illegitimate babies. She was sent to a nursing home in Gilsland in Cumberland well away from gossiping neighbours. I wasn't there when Ruth told Mother the news. But Mother told me she wouldn't have anything to do with it. She didn't want to know about any more babies or anything to do with Ruth. I said somebody would have to help her but that was it as far as Mother was concerned. No more babies in the house. Father, as usual in these circumstances, had a filthy mouth about it.

Clare was in France when his son Andre Clare McCallum was born on 15 September 1944. Ruth wrote afterwards asking if Joe and I would meet her under the clock at Waterloo station. I sent her a shawl for the baby to come home in. Baby Andre was done up in a ball and didn't wake up. He was gorgeous. 'Doesn't she look pathetic,' I said to Joe. I cried a lot for her. She was alone in the world. Clare had told Ruth he'd marry her after the war, but for now it was tragic to see her alone with the baby.

Joe and I by now had the top flat in the house. There was a separate small room with a little bed that I made up for Ruth and a tiny cot for Andre. He was a quiet baby and she was a decent mother. Eventually Mother was crawling to her, wanting to see the baby. So Ruth went back to live in my parents' flat, the last thing she should have done. The only thing my father said on the subject was that Ruth could give them money for looking after the baby if she went out to work.

The horrible bit for Ruth was still to come. In 1945 at the end of the war she found out from Clare's commanding officer that he was married with three children in Canada. Normally she covered up her emotions, she'd had years of practice, but then Ruth went haywire. If anyone had ever loved anyone, she really loved Clare. She was heartbroken.

Clare was sent home to Quebec in Canada, leaving Ruth alone with his one-year-old baby – the worst thing that any man could have done to her. She really took it to heart. Just before he left England Clare sent Ruth a dozen roses from the ship. I don't know what must have been going on in his mind. Perhaps he thought it would make everything better. Ruth never saw him again.

6

Ruth's Marriage to George Ellis

Joe and I were married on 5 February 1944 at Brixton Town Hall. After signing our marriage lines, we had a hot cross bun and a cup of tea in the ABC restaurant opposite. We got married on the spur of the moment. Ruth didn't come. I'd imagine she was feeling pretty sick – she'd be two months pregnant with Andre then. We'd wanted to marry before 1944 but Joe's father wouldn't give his permission. As soon as Joe was twenty-one we went down to the Register Office.

Porn and Dunwoody, where Joe served his time, did marine diesel and electrical engineering. Porn's were ship repairers for the war effort and Joe was doing secret war work. He said the owner Marcel Porn, a Rumanian, was a powerful man and could have been the Lord Mayor of London. But he didn't make it.

After our wedding we went to the pictures. Joe has a memory of seeing *Casablanca* starring Ingrid Bergman and Humphrey Bogart. We were watching the film and a flash came up on the screen for Joe to report home. That's how they'd get hold of you. Outside the house was a dispatch rider with instructions for Joe to go to Croydon Airport. He was flown to Cornwall to look at a ship. He told me recently it was a special ship for D-Day: 'They were called Q ships by Naval Intelligence and were fishing trawlers converted to carry commandos that blended with the rest of the fleet.' Our married life started with Joe being away for thirteen weeks, and my not knowing when he'd come back.

We were still with my parents. Joe remembers what it was like living with them:

> In my younger days it was hard being brought up as a cockney in the East End. You don't take no nonsense from people. Seeing Muriel being controlled by Arthur didn't go down well. He probably knew he'd get a wallop from me if he tried anything on. We'd moved from Bengeworth Road to Padfield Road. He came home one day, shouting. That's when I got stroppy and put him in his place. I threw him in a chair and he got stroppy with me. I threatened him once with my fists.

Resilience was Ruth's special quality. She bounced back no matter what was thrown at her, or how much she'd gone to pieces. She became as good as she could be at managing her life. After she'd heard Clare McCallum was married with children she changed. The shock was almost more than she could stand especially as she had a toddler with no father to support him. She loved Clare. Apart from Joe, he was her first love.

Ruth started working again at Lyons Corner House and wouldn't get home before five in the evening. By 1946 she'd got a job as a photographer in the Streatham Locarno taking snaps every night of hundreds of dancers who'd then buy copies. She'd do anything to earn money: modelling; taking photographs; you name it, she did it. She was desperate. It was more than her life's worth to go home without a few pounds in her pocket. That's all my parents waited for – money for cigarettes.

Ruth looked after Andre in the mornings and I'd take over for the rest of the day, but soon she was working full-time. Andre was growing into a lovely boy. Mother was packing parcels in a factory and doing cooking as well to make ends meet. I ended up looking after Andre, Robert and Betty, and Christopher who was Joe's and my first baby, born at home on 5 March 1945. Joey followed in 1946, Pauline in 48, Marlene in 49. Martin was born in 1953, two years before his Auntie Ruth was hanged.

The children were in bed when Joe went out in the morning and tucked up when he came back late from the coastline. It was hard work looking after four noisy children, so the housework was left till they were in bed. The situation was dire. Joe was under apprenticeship, we were living off a pittance. It was hard for people like us.

Shortly after we were married Joe and my parents decided they didn't want Robert living with us. When Christopher arrived, Robert was sent away. Joe reckoned I'd enough to do with his children. Their decision was justified when Robert borrowed a bike, without asking permission, to come home on. They sent a policeman round, and the council paid for him to be sent to Darrenth Park, a special boarding school in Kent for backward people. I was upset because he was only a little fellow and hadn't harmed a soul. There was something wrong with him. Experts say incest can cause problems and there's a good chance of producing children with disabilities. As he grew up he appeared a bit slow, although he turned out all right in the end. Occasionally I'd see Robert at weekends, if I could get someone to look after the children.

It was plain Joe wasn't keen on him. He says Robert is a blank in his mind: 'I don't think about it. He lived with us, I couldn't care less where he come from. He was a sod at times, and got on my nerves. But you tolerated him. I wasn't putting my mind to anything other than work. After the war you had to earn a living because you had children to bring up – the hardest thing in the world.' Joe helped me in many ways though. I respected him; he was a good father. But I married him to get away from my father. Even though I had sex with Joe, after everything I'd been through, I hated it. Despite that, I grew to love him and managed to conceive five children.

We had all been living at Padfield Road but were on the move again, this time to Joe's parents' house in New Eltham, built by Davis Estates who stated they could build a semi-detached in three weeks. Joe bought it for £575. My parents moved into a flat in Herne Hill. I'd broken free from Father's abuse at last.

Ruth was still with us. I remember walking down the street with her. Every man whistled. We just walked on and ignored them, although she'd never have seen who'd whistled – she was so short-sighted, like my father and Andre. All the same she was too vain to wear her standard issue spectacles and wouldn't dream of stepping outside until her make-up was perfect.

We'd occasionally go to Granville Arcade in Brixton and buy clothes from a Jewish fellow. Ruth bought a blouse or two. She'd fall back on my clothes when I got fed up with them. Later, once established in nightclub life and earning money, she bought her own gear. I'll always remember my black coat with a crinkly skirt. When I'd finished with it Ruth wore it. She was a size eight with a tiny waist, you'd have got two of her in it. Ruth was a perfectionist in her clothing.

We'd walk the children together when she was around. Ruth pushed the posh white pram with a lace top and canopy that Clare brought back from France. Nobody else had one like it. I'd push a utility, wartime pram, more like a tub on wheels, that could carry six children.

I'd got away from Father but Joe and I hadn't got away from problems. I can't imagine what normal life was like. My sister Betty would arrive at our place because Father was beating her up. Ruth stayed for long periods, then moved out, then moved back in, depending on what work she got. Joe was never aware of her problems, I had to deal with them. He'd gloss over anything and wouldn't want to know. I was responsible for the household, his job was to find money to live on. We were still living in austerity. Our life was nothing other than working and survival. Joe had it engrained in him by his father that you don't work to live. You serve an apprenticeship. You become a tradesman. You live for work.

Fifty years on, I'm piecing together what really happened to Ruth in the late forties, early fifties. People say she broke away from the family home early on. That's the type of misleading information authors made up, giving the impression she didn't care about Andre. She came home every night to my parents' place or mine. What they didn't know was that Father would be hurling abuse at her, calling her an old bag or slut, no matter how hard she worked.

I'm often asked what jobs she did before going into nightclub life. I've discovered that Ruth had a walk-on part in a film and got to know actresses like Diana Dors. She mentioned she was very friendly with her.

Although she wasn't exactly secretive, if anything was confidential to Ruth you wouldn't be told about it. She'd think twice before telling you anything. There came a time, she was coming up for twenty and well into club life, when, except for the odd phone call, Ruth stopped communicating with us. As Joe said: 'She vanished off the scene. Left our sort in 48 or 49. Went off with the funny people.' She'd got a flat in Tooting Bec. Somebody else must have been paying the rent because she couldn't have afforded it. She was still in touch with Mother though, who she paid to look after Andre. My parents took nearly every penny she earned. Whatever Ruth gave them, it was never enough. They'd think nothing of phoning her at work for money if she hadn't been round.

She kept the family going. Mother certainly wouldn't have looked after the children for nothing because she could have earned money in service. That woman slaved into old age. When she got cooking jobs at private parties and at Longlands Laundry, I shared looking after Andre. I'd got three children of my own by then, Betty spent a lot of time with us, and Joe and I weren't well off, but Mother still tried to get money. She'd send me threatening letters, no doubt Father was egging her on:

Dear Muriel,

Could you send us some money because we're very hard up. If you don't we'll write to Joe and tell him about Robert and what happened to you.'

Mother

I can't believe she did it out of choice. If I'd known what I know now I would have returned the letters saying 'Try it Mother, it won't do you any good.' Even so when Joe gave me

55

the odd ten pounds (a fortune then when you could buy a lot with a pound) I gave her half.

The first I knew about Ruth marrying George Ellis was shortly after 8 November 1950. I'd called at my parents' place on impulse, a three-storey house in Herne Hill divided into flats during the war. As I went in that evening, I knew I wasn't welcome. There was an atmosphere. I knew nothing about what was going on. The dining room table, usually against the window, was in the centre of the room and laid for two people with white tablecloth, serviettes and place settings with the correct number of knives and forks. Mother knew about those things – she'd been cooking for rich people over the years. It looked like there was going to be a celebration and one of her professional dinners, because two sets of wine glasses were set out. They didn't know I was coming. Mother said as I arrived that there'd been a telegram from Ruth saying she was coming round to see them with someone. That's why the place looked spick and span.

Ruth hadn't mentioned George to anyone. My knowledge of her relationship with him at that time was as simple as this: they got married; they came round; they went off to Southampton; Ruth came back a few months later without George and she'd had her curly auburn hair cut short in the Italian bob and dyed black.

From the minute they sat down they didn't look like a loving couple. Mother whispered to me that it was George her husband. I'll describe the scene. It was as if she'd brought him round to prove she had a husband. She didn't introduce him or act excited. He looked elderly compared to Ruth. I said how-do-you-do and covered up how shocked I was. He didn't look at me. I couldn't understand why there wasn't any talking. It was like a play where everyone had forgotten their lines.

I felt it wasn't for me to speak, that he should have said something. But he didn't. When he spoke the once, I noticed he had a gruff voice which I couldn't understand. That was it in the way of communication. His shifty manner was like Desmond Cussen's, who Ruth would meet two years later. Both in the same league – both getting on a bit, both snaky characters. George had a pasty complexion, a fair-coloured moustache, lightish hair balding on top – a Brylcreem boy. He was around 5'8". His face was gaunt, not particularly pleasing. I remember the scar down one cheek but didn't scrutinize him in case Ruth thought I was staring. What possessed her to go for this ferret-looking old man? I could only think this was a marriage of convenience, not a marriage for love. Clare McCallum was meant for Ruth. He was her type.

Mother was plainly cross that I'd turned up but invited me to sit at the dinner table. Ruth didn't look best pleased, she wasn't herself and sat there staring. George was silent. What was going on? I felt I was intruding on a private arrangement. Mother had made a chicken broth for starters: soup was her speciality. It was only me who broke the silence. I wish I hadn't: 'This soup is lovely.' Nobody spoke. It sickened me seeing Mother putting herself out, just because George was a dentist. Father didn't sit down to eat, he'd been told not to. There was no sign of Betty. She was not allowed downstairs to see Ruth which was odd. My parents treated Bet terribly. I didn't see Andre either – it was eight o'clock and he'd been put to bed.

I stayed for the soup and watched a bit of telly – the early type with a magnifying glass around it; I was frightened of the ugly thing. I stayed an hour but then decided to beat a hasty retreat. I wasn't welcome, I told Mother I didn't want anything else, and went. I said cheerio to Ruth who didn't answer. It was as if she'd changed her character. For some reason they weren't going to say a word in front of me. I felt uneasy. I'd brought my daughter Marlene to see my parents for the first time but they didn't make any fuss of her, so I picked her up and left.

George had entered Ruth's life while she was hostessing in the London nightclubs. I felt she'd joined a secret world. I didn't know everything about her life. I wasn't part of it. I had four children under five to keep me occupied. But I knew the minute Ruth walked into the flat with George Ellis she wasn't herself. I've mentioned how she coped with problems but that evening she was different; she was morose. And they didn't want me there.

She'd gone into hostessing because the money was good. She had to take plenty of it home to my parents or there'd be hell to pay. One of the cruel things I remember Father doing was hitting Mother and Ruth with a copper stick (used for laundry work) when the money wasn't there. Ruth had to make ends meet. If she couldn't earn enough waitressing or modelling she could earn good money in the clubs selling drinks to willing, rich men at exorbitant prices. She was good. As everyone knew, the hostesses were there to keep the men happy. To Ruth it wasn't only about money. Club life gave her something she loved and longed for – glamour, cars, mixing with the wealthy and upper class. Above all it made her feel a 'somebody'.

Ruth was a refined-looking girl, she'd draw a refined type of man. She spoke well enough without needing elocution lessons. Even if she had a high-pitched voice it was still good.

We did after all come from a good family. There was no reason for people to look down their noses at her.

Apparently she met George in 1950 at the Court Club, later called Carroll's Club, in Duke Street when she was working for Maurie Conley. It's obvious why he picked her for the job. She had startling looks. He must have had his oats and realized she could attract high-class men like royalty, politicians and people with money. She was in the right spot for listening to the prominent, hearing about their private and business lives and about their wives who didn't understand them. They knew she would keep quiet and for that she was well paid. Clubland was where the people who were in the know would go.

But I have made an important discovery: it would appear Ruth knew of George Ellis at least two years before she officially met him at the Court Club. Arthur Waterhouse was the chef at the White Hart Hotel in Brasted, the next village along from Westerham on the Surrey–Kent border, from just after the war until 1950. He said that the pub was known as the 'unofficial HQ of Battle of Britain pilots'. All the top-ranking RAF personnel went there. Mr Waterhouse recalled:

> Mr and Mrs Preston owned the pub. They had a daughter Valerie. Ruth Ellis came in occasionally towards the end of the 1940s with her boyfriend and her best friend Deborah Kerr, the actress, and her husband Tony Bartley. He was a Battle of Britain pilot and decorated. They were great friends. Ruth was a very charming lady. I thought she was a nice looking girl with lovely auburn hair. I knew her ever so well. George Ellis came to the White Hart at the same time. I sobered him up a number of times. He'd come in

totally drunk, he was often under the influence. I used to give him cups of black coffee in the kitchen when he staggered in.

Imagine my astonishment, fifty years later, on learning that my sister was associated with *the* famous actress Deborah Kerr and mixing with the RAF elite. Somehow she'd achieved a sophisticated makeover which allowed her to associate with these people. This is a side of Ruth previous biographers failed to uncover. But who was Ruth's boyfriend? Mr Waterhouse could not describe him except to say that he was smart and had straight hair – fifty years is a long time to remember details. At every opportunity over the next few months, photos of Ruth, Miss Kerr and Tony Bartley were shown to people connected with the White Hart Hotel just after the war. But nobody recognized Ruth in the photo.

I dread to think how Ruth ended up marrying George Ellis. Previous so-called biographers thought they knew. But I'm only interested in fact not hearsay. To those writers I say they should have looked for the facts. Take Van Den Bergh, for instance: he didn't listen to anything I said. When he wrote, 'George Ellis waited with ever growing impatience for the blonde hostess to come tapping down the street,' he didn't get that right. Ruth had auburn hair then.

George Ellis was an unknown quantity. This is obvious in all accounts of his and Ruth's relationship. There's nothing much about him. He is fluffed over as though he was a nonentity. He's come, gone and forgotten about in a few paragraphs. Basically they say he was a dentist; he'd married Vera, lived for some time in her home town of Warrington before moving south to Sanderstead in Surrey; they had two sons; they got divorced; he was a drunkard, married Ruth and was always ready to hit her. I couldn't believe there wasn't more to him than that.

I agree that Ruth went to Warsash, Hampshire, with George. Mind you, the first I knew about that was when she came back under her own steam. I knew nothing of what went on with her then. There was a gap – where she was, what she was doing. So the Warsash episode was a good starting point to pick through first-hand evidence, not the regurgitated nonsense that's created the big lie about Ruth.

Ruth and George's daughter Georgina Ellis wrote: 'He [George] was offered employment together with a house at Oak Bank, Warsash Road, Warsash on Southampton Water.' Warsash fifty years ago was a village in the sticks with a handful of houses, where everyone knew everyone. I found out that in Warsash, by the water's edge on Southampton Water, is the College of Maritime Studies, formerly the School of Navigation in the fifties, and before that it was called 'HMS Tormentor' where they trained navigation officers for the merchant navy.

Why exactly did George and Ruth go to Warsash? In the books about Ruth, the story is told that George couldn't hold a job down as a dentist, was virtually on the scrap heap and had no money. They say he was briefly employed in Hampstead in north London in 1950, and in and out of Warlingham Park Hospital in Surrey between 1950 and 1951, drying out from his alcohol problem. While George was in hospital he wrote to a dentist who ran a group of practices around Southampton asking for a job. Then the books go into overdrive about Ruth's jealous behaviour towards George in Warsash and the beatings he gave her while in his drunken stupors. But I've discovered there was more to Ruth's story in Warsash than anyone imagined.

George Johnston Ellis was a mystery man. He was born on 2 October 1909 in Chorlton-upon-Medlock – quite a coincidence as it's where I was born. I was curious and wanted to find out for myself who George really was.

George entered the Manchester University School of Dentistry in 1929, graduated in 1933 and registered his address in West Didsbury, Manchester, with the General Dental Council. It appears from Georgina Ellis's book that George worked in Warrington and lived there with his wife Vera. She wrote: 'They had lived together in her home town, Warrington, where they moved in the upper circles of professional society.' Conflicting evidence shows he was registered on the electoral roll at Woodlands on Sanderstead Hill in Surrey, where in 1936 he shared the house with Emily Spear, a year later with Maria Pedley. According to the GDC, in 1935 his registered address was Elmswood, seven doors along from Woodlands, and he was there with Ada Mary Spear. George married his first wife Vera Hume in her home town in Surrey, on 24 September 1938. Not in Warrington, as Georgina Ellis suggested in her book, but in Sanderstead at the parish church. They lived at Woodlands in 1938 and 1939 and again after the war until 1948. In 1949 he lived there alone. It's odd, Ruth and George stayed only one night with my parents after their wedding but from the end of December 1950 he registered his address with the General Dental Council as 7 Herne Hill Road, London, my parents' address. There must have been something in it for Father. Money was his god. The GDC says: 'Dentists must give an address for inclusion in the register, somewhere for mail to reach them. Some dentists may not want to be traced at their practice.' From 1951 until he committed suicide in 1958, his registered address was 16 Soho Square, London, prostitute land, despite the fact he was supposed to be working in Warrington. His dental practice phone number was still in the Croydon telephone directory in 1953.

Fifty years on and it seems possible he was trying to confuse somebody. George could have been anywhere doing anything. Why else give those strange forwarding addresses at which he didn't appear to be living?

Trying to find first-hand information from fifty years ago is difficult. I was pleased to discover Dorothy Broome, one of George Ellis's private patients from the early 1940s until he disappeared from Sanderstead in 1950. What she said threw new light on his character, particularly his disappearing acts. She was nineteen when she started consulting Ellis in 1942. She'd been working as a personnel manager in Purley:

> Mr Ellis had done some excellent dental work for the general manager. He'd originally been seeing someone in London who I think was Mr Ellis's dentist. I think he did the ballet dancers and the stars and that sort of thing and that's how the general manager heard of him. He was referred back to Mr Ellis in Sanderstead. I was very keen for someone to do cosmetic dentistry if ever I needed it and George Ellis was the man. I was impressed he'd done this posh stuff. He did bridge work which was top class in those days. It was a classy practice and I saw him privately and regularly during the wartime, every six months. Were dentists a reserved occupation?
>
> I used to go to George Ellis's on Sanderstead Hill. It was a big detached house with a nice garden. He wasn't an attractive man. Not the sort of person a

nineteen-year-old would fancy. He was round-shouldered and pot bellied. He was fairish with combed-back hair. Actually he was a little morose, a quiet sort of man, not outgoing. He never chatted. There was never a nurse when I was there although he had a receptionist. He never smelt of drink. He was quite often not there when you turned up for an appointment. I went two or three times and in the end I phoned before I arrived to check he was there and hadn't gone off somewhere else. He hadn't always been like it. Early on he was very reliable. It was around 1950 when he was less reliable and disappeared.

Coincidentally, when I was working in Purley one of the girls there had been a receptionist at the dentist's. I said I went there. She said: 'Oh do you?' She'd worked at the dentist's quite a while when she came for the job at the aeronautical instruments factory. She was twenty-eight and called up to do war work at the office. I remember her telling me about an incident at the dentist's. George Ellis had a sun lamp. He said: 'Why don't you go under the lamp?' He insisted but she wasn't that bothered. In the end she stripped off and got ready to read a magazine while she sunned herself. George Ellis walked in. He feigned surprise, evidently making out he didn't realize she was there!

At the time I assumed he was married. I seem to remember seeing this young pregnant lady waft in and out. She was older than myself. Funnily enough I was talking about Ruth Ellis to a hairdresser recently who said she went to a private school in Croydon in

the 1920s with Vera who later became Mrs Ellis.
George Ellis never told me he was leaving the practice. It was odd. He just wasn't there any more. When
I phoned for an appointment I got the new man. The
last time I went up there was 1953.

I have discovered Ruth and George's marriage lines – I've never
seen it before – 'married on 8th November 1950 by Licence'.
Mother told me they ran away for a shotgun wedding in Gretna
Green and were tiddly when they got there. Why did she tell me
that, I wonder, when they'd actually got married at Tonbridge
Register Office in Kent: 'Ruth Neilson, 24 years, spinster and
George Johnston Ellis, 41 years, divorced husband of Vera Ellis,
formerly Hume.' His father, James Edward Ellis, was a wholesale
fish merchant. They gave the King's Arms Hotel, an elegant
coaching inn in the market town of Westerham, as their address.
It wasn't so much shotgun after all.

It was the biggest mistake Ruth ever made. Whatever
writers said about her marrying him for security or status, I say
it is *not* true. Living like she was, earning the money, why did
she want security? Surely she knew he was a drunk. As for
wanting a father for Andre, as Georgina Ellis stated in her
book, George didn't even know Ruth had a little boy. Georgina
misleadingly wrote: 'Ruth was forever packing her bags, with
or without Andy in tow and returning to Brixton for a few
days.' Andre was not with Ruth. She left him with my parents.
During the time she was in Warsash she made no contact with
Mother, except for one trip home to Mother's for a few days,
which I found out about recently at the Public Record Office.

I looked on the map and found the places on the Surrey-
Kent border where the wedding part of the story happened.

Sanderstead, south of Croydon in Surrey, to Westerham on the Kent border was a straight run south on George's motorbike, about six miles. In between was Warlingham Park Hospital. Tonbridge is a bit further south from Westerham. Two other places are significant, as I shall come to later: Tatsfield, a village of a thousand people in 1950, was three minutes south-east of Warlingham. It became famous because between December 1950 and May 1951 double agent Donald Maclean resided in a house there called Beacon Shaw. Our Secret Service agents in Russia lost their lives because of Maclean and his spying friends Guy Burgess and Kim Philby. Chartwell, Winston Churchill's place in the country, is a mile down the road from Westerham.

Between the end of December 1950 and May 1951 Ruth and George disappeared to Warsash. At some point for the first time in her life Ruth changed her auburn hair colour. George apparently booked in to Warlingham Park Hospital as an in-patient straight after seeing my parents until the end of December. It was a big Victorian-type institution, and had the first alcohol unit in a mental hospital in the United Kingdom. It was convenient for him as it was revolutionary in its time: patients came and went, like in a hotel. Looking at it now, his disappearing acts to the hospital between the winter of 1950 and spring of 1951 must have been more than drying-out sessions.

Nobody in Warsash could be sure when Ruth and George arrived or when they left. So I was lucky to find Mrs Margaret Woodford in the village who could talk about the time they were there:

When I think about Ruth Ellis in relation to Warsash,
I used to cycle every day and saw her around the

village most days at lunch time. She'd often walk down Newtown Road close to the School of Navigation as it was called. She'd be in her short fur coat, it was before the fake ones came in. I remember it because I compared it to my New Look green coat from C & A. All her clothes looked short because she was only so high. She wore high stiletto heels which weren't suitable for the village. It was a really rough road. Everyone looked at her because of the way she was dressed.

She was very tiny, very attractive for the era. I do remember she looked very fashionable – a glamour girl. At a time when nobody else had very much after the war she seemed out of place in Warsash. One of the first things that struck me was her hair was very curly. I thought it was permed but apparently it wasn't. It was shoulder length and bordering on blonde. I can remember seeing her coming out in an open-top sports car one Friday afternoon when I was on my bike. I know it was a Friday because I was cycling home early, taking time off in lieu of working the previous Saturday. In those days you only had one car pass an hour, they're weren't many cars then. This one was certainly no old crock. I had to put my foot on the pavement because he reversed out so fast, showing off. The driver was dark haired, a man in his thirties. I have this vision of them reversing out, speeding off in the direction of Fareham and seeing her fair hair flying in the breeze.

Next I saw her in the dentist's at Oak Bank, a house in Warsash Road. She could have been the receptionist but I'm not certain. She just appeared in the hallway when I was waiting. It's a faint memory now but I believe she wore a white coat. She was definitely the only lady working there. There wouldn't have been the work for anyone else. She wore a lot of make-up and I seem to remember red nails.

It seems most people knew her as the nurse and apart from her glamorous appearance she didn't mean a thing to anybody until, as one local man said: 'This storm broke with the tragedy in London.'

Mrs Woodford also recalls another glamorous young woman from London appearing with Ruth in Warsash in that short space of time, a fact never discovered by commentators:

It was well known around the village that Colonel Bradshaw, retired, had quite a reputation for his young lady friends. One of them, another smart girl who'd come down from London, was very friendly with Ruth Ellis. Colonel Bradshaw was a big 'Colonely' sort of man with a moustache, in his fifties, had gout and wore a navy blazer and grey flannels. He was a yacht broker [and] had his office in Shore Road in Warsash – Monty Bradshaw's Yacht Brokerage.

One thing's certain. There's no evidence of the 'physical fights of the marriage' between Ruth and George that Robert Hancock described in *Ruth Ellis, the Last Woman to be Hanged*. Mrs Woodford recalls there was never gossip about Ruth having fights or black eyes and cut lips. Nor was Hancock correct in saying Ruth 'abandoned the heavy make-up she normally wore' or that Ruth's only companion was 'Mrs Bourne the daily who came in to clean'. Margaret Woodford knew for a fact that Ruth and George mixed with a couple they knew from London.

She continued her recollections:

> I remember someone telling me that Ruth was caught going on the premises of the School of Navigation. There was a big hoo-ha there but it was hushed up. The director ruled with a rod of iron and told her never to go on the premises again. What I would say is that she was definitely a diversion. She was the talk of the village with her glamorous appearance. If anything else had been going on it wouldn't have been noticed. People were homing in on her. When you think what the village was like she appeared to be blatantly parading around by the college as if she was doing it for a reason – as though she wanted to be noticed. I would imagine Ruth was put in a corner somehow. But I can't describe how. That's the impression she gave. It's funny how Ruth and George were there for just a few months then were gone.

Despite it being a quiet village, Warsash had its share of prominent people including Prince Philip and his uncle, Lord Mountbatten's. Prince Philip used to go sailing at the same time that Ruth was in Warsash. He'd leave the Bentley that he and the Queen were given by the RAF as a wedding present in the car park at the School of Navigation. One reliable source described how the director, in the same way he'd ordered Ruth out of the premises, shouted out to get that 'bloody Bentley out of his billet'. The Household Brigade Yacht Club had its HQ in the School of Navigation premises. They had to walk through there to get to their yacht club. Then they'd go down off the pier and the launch would take them across to Cowes to go sailing.

I believe Ruth and George's visit to Warsash was not the innocuous sojourn spun by commentators – it was part of something much bigger. No previous writer has touched on Ethel Gee and her boyfriend Harry Houghton's connection with Warsash. They were the two British members of the Portland spy ring, finally broken up in 1961, who passed secret weapons information to Russia, the ring being organized by Gordon Lonsdale and Peter and Helen Kroger. It's a peculiar coincidence that Ethel Gee lived in Locks Villas opposite the dentist's at Oak Bank in Warsash and was employed in 1950 at the Underwater Weapons Establishment at Portland in Dorset. I discovered from the electoral register that Harry Houghton also lived in Warsash, a mile away, and also worked at the Underwater Weapons Establishment. Strangely, at the time of their arrest, the Hampshire and national newspapers did not disclose Gee's and Houghton's association with Warsash. Eventually, following their release from prison in 1970, after serving nine out of a fifteen year sentence, the *Southern Daily Record* wrote of Warsash people 'who prefer to remain nameless and are talking behind their hands about Ethel Gee and Harry Houghton.'

Something doesn't add up about George Ellis in Warsash. Why doesn't anybody remember the dentist with the deep scar down his cheek that he apparently acquired in a scuffle outside a London club in 1950? Past patients were shown his photograph but nobody recognized him. A master of disguise, perhaps.

On the other hand everyone knew who Ruth was. To see her in this sleepy part of the country was out of this world. But why was my sister parading by the School of Navigation in such a noticeable fashion? She was a diversion. Ruth was providing a cover.

I have stacks of papers from the Public Record Office concerning my family. This one, like all the documents I saw for the first time in 2002, was painful to me. It was handwritten by Mother, two weeks before Ruth was hanged. Mr Bickford, Ruth's solicitor sent it to the Home Secretary in July 1955 trying to get a reprieve for Ruth. He said it was a 'convincing but somewhat illiterate statement'. I'd say it was written from the heart even if she didn't know the truth. There were so many spelling mistakes, she was a nervous wreck. It didn't do any good – it didn't stop Ruth from hanging. I'm quoting it here because it says more about Ruth and George's relationship:

'She met George Ellis a Dentist. They were married but he was a alcoholic drinker and turned out to be a cruel man. They went to live in Warsash near Southampton. It was a lonely house, my daughter sitting by herself night after night, her husband coming home in a taxi because he was unable to stand he was so drunk. On one of these occasions he told my Daughter to go in the kitchen. Once she was there he locked the door. He pulled her hair and banged her head against the Wall six or seven times. After that seen she started bleeding from the nose. Losing pints of blood. She suffered from terrible head-ages for a long time. On another occasion he ill-treaded her by knocking her on the floor and kicking her. She was black and blue all over. She ran into the garden and stayed behind a bush all night. She was terrified of him and she ran away from him the next day. She stayed home with me for 3 days. Her husband asked her to return to him, he would phone her two or three times a day. She went back to him. But within a forthnight she was back home again. This time for good. Both her eyes were swollen. She had a bald patch on the left side of her head. Her legs were bruised. She was a very sick girl. I put her to bed and kept her there for several days. I refused to let her return to this Brute of a man. She told me she was pregnant. I feared for this unborn child.' *HO291/237*

Ruth's so-called marriage, a set-up I'd say, can't have lasted more than five months. Mother said she was half-dead on the doorstep and was depressed enough to want to kill herself. I don't know how Mother coped because Ruth was her favourite. It upset me to think that someone could do that to her. Not that it was the first time – she'd had enough good hidings at home without going and asking for it.

Just as when Ruth got married, the first I knew of her going to Warsash was when she returned. Knowing what I know now, the episode of her marriage to George is even more confusing. It makes me think the so-called matrimonial problems were to create a diversion. Ruth, as George's wife, was an instrument of some sort. It doesn't make it any easier to explain. Nobody was aware of her being knocked about in this small village in 1950, a place where you'd think the smallest bit of gossip would be around in no time. As Mother's statement said, Ruth was beaten black and blue. According to Mother all she had on was a white dental overall, nothing else. George had locked her in an upstairs room, she escaped through a window. A lorry driver stopped and brought her all the way home. He told Mother how he'd picked her up covered in bruises and a big lump of hair had been pulled out of her scalp. That's what I was told. My mother said Ruth did this, Ruth did that and the driver was so good and over the years I believed exactly what she told me about how it happened.

She must have been at Mother's for some time because by the time she arrived at my place in late spring 1951, the bruising was better, but the bald patch on her head was still visible. It had been bleeding and there were bits of hair stuck in it. Ruth came to us for safety because George was trying to get her. Mother wasn't having any of it. He banged on her front door. Mother shouted from the window: 'She's gone. We don't know where she is. Clear off.' After what appeared to be another boozing binge he'd come crawling. Only this time, looking at the time sequence, he must have just come out of Warlingham Park Hospital.

I kept her well out of his way while this was going on. It meant Ruth couldn't go out. Her mind was absolutely at war. I remember this next episode clearly: what she was doing was strange, she was all of a dither, getting het up and in no fit state for anything yet she was dashing backwards and forwards telephoning somebody the whole time. Because I wasn't on the phone, she had to go to the public phone box up Domonic Drive. Up and down like a jack-in-the-box she was, really upset as if she was scared of something and looking round all

73

the time. It was a mystery. She didn't tell me anything about Warsash, she was as secretive as ever.

Ruth was a good four months pregnant and must have been getting money from somewhere. Somebody was supporting her. It certainly wasn't George Ellis. She lived with us for a while. Then she went again.

7

The Stephen Ward Connection

I was under the impression Ruth became a club hostess in the late 1940s because she had been swept off her feet by Maurie Conley, the London club owner. He'd seen her waitressing and offered her a job at one of his clubs. Ruth told me he was in love with her. But there was more to her arrival into the Mayfair club scene than I realized. The intrigue deepens as new characters appear and as the true story starts to unfold.

Most people will know the names John Profumo and Christine Keeler and the scandal involving them in 1963. It didn't mean much to me. But I knew it was a scandal about prostitutes, spies and a government minister. In the same way that Ruth Ellis was a household name in the fifties, Christine Keeler was the name of scandal in the sixties. One of the major players in the affair was Stephen Ward. He stood trial in 1963 for keeping a brothel, living off prostitutes' earnings and offences to do with abortions, under the Sexual Offences Act of 1956.

Ruth never spoke about her modelling at the Camera Club – like most things it was done in secret. The first we knew was when Father came to our place in Padfield Road, sometime about 1947, carrying a bundle of black and white photographs to show Joe and me. The dirty old sod was gloating over them. He'd raked through Ruth's cupboards when she was out. If she'd known she would have been furious. I instructed Father to put them back where he'd found them.

The photos looked as though they'd been taken in a studio with special backgrounds. She looked like a film star. I'd never seen such lovely photographs of Ruth. They weren't pornographic. Ruth's hair was auburn and done in a chignon. In some she stood full frontal leaning against a chair, her legs turned in to cover up the bit down below. She'd shaved herself, leaving a narrow strip of pubic hair. Ruth never had a lot up the top, just enough. In some she wore lace panties and matching bra. She knew how to pose. The photographer skilfully covered up the crooked left hand she was left with after rheumatic fever. I didn't care for those of her naked on a stool. Joe says he wasn't interested. I never saw the photos again.

I don't blame Ruth for wanting a better life. The war was over but there was a shortage of money and food rationing, and she was trying to make a living.

Most girls doing this type of work, acting, hostessing or modelling, used other names, something easy to remember. Ruth's best friend and flatmate Valerie Mewes became Vickie Martin. Patricia Creaton became Vickie Page when she was acting, dancing and modelling in London. Ruth wouldn't have been known as Ruth Neilson. Terry Turner, the longest serving member of the Camera Club in London, said the impression a 1990s television documentary gave of Ruth at the Camera Club was wrong:

> The Camera Club used models and I am sure Ruth wasn't on our books. She must have met somebody who brought her along and probably posed privately for them. As she wasn't one of our models there

wouldn't have been thirty or so photographers taking pictures of her like they showed on the television. It would probably have been one photographer who hired the studio for a private session with her.

Terry remembered seeing Ruth in The Magdala tavern in Hampstead when she was a blonde and said she was striking, but didn't see her at the Camera Club. But would he have recognized her with long auburn hair when she modelled there? She would have looked different to the image most people have of her between 1953 and her death in 1955.

The Camera Club was in Manchester Square. It was *the* centre of photographic activity in the country, nothing like the seedy establishment portrayed in Van Den Bergh and Marks' book *Ruth Ellis, A Case of Diminished Responsibility?* Their offensive words, 'The fact that most of the photographers had no films in their cameras was neither here nor there,' drove me to find out what the place was actually like in the 1950s. Terry Turner said:

It had top photographers amongst its membership. The thing about the Camera Club in the 1950s was that you had to be somebody important to belong. They wouldn't admit riff-raff and you had to show you could take pictures. You had to be proposed, seconded and go before the committee. It was up-market, for people with money. Past presidents included Lord Paul who was the official photographer for Kodak. It was a gentlemen's club with big RAF connections, more like a club with photography as a sideline. Lord Snowdon, then Antony Armstrong-

Jones used to come here. He used Camera Club
models for all his stuff.

According to Terry, Diana Dors started at the Camera Club in
1946 and modelled there till 1951. In her autobiography *Dors
By Diana* she says she got an evening job there for 'the princely
sum of one guinea an hour . . . the extra money from posing
nude came in most handy.' Ruth hadn't told us anything about
her friendship with Diana Dors, except that she was a friend.
As usual she kept the details quiet. She and Ruth were to meet
up in the spring of 1951 during the filming of *Lady Godiva
Rides Again*.

What happened to Ruth after she left Warsash came like a
bolt out of the blue to me. It says this about Ruth – she knew
how to keep quiet. The mystery about her began slotting into
place after investigating Diana Dors's recollections in her
autobiography. I don't like what I've learned but it explained
much about Ruth's life that I never knew, and puts things into
perspective:

> . . . I commenced filming [*Lady Godiva rides Again*,
> 1951] on location at Folkestone, where I met a
> beautiful young girl named Jane Hart who was
> playing a small role . . . the day we were due to return
> to London she offered me a lift with her boyfriend,
> who was coming to fetch her . . . when the boyfriend
> arrived at our hotel I did not take to him at all: he
> looked devious and was something of a show-off . . .
> he found fame as a slick society doctor among the jet
> set, being regarded as some sort of Prince Charming
> with women. My earlier opinion of him was

confirmed in 1963, however, when Dr Stephen Ward died from an overdose of drugs after it had been revealed that he was behind the Christine Keeler affair that led to the Prime Minister's resignation and the eventual defeat of the Conservative government.

Lady Godiva Rides Again starred Dennis Price, and Kay Kendall who was a friend of Stephen Ward's. People may find my next discovery hard to believe. I had a hunch: could Ruth have been one of the starlets in the film, a comedy about beauty contests? The British Film Institute (BFI) found three stills. One showed a line-up of twenty beauty queens. Amongst them I saw Ruth alongside Diana Dors and starlets Joan Collins and Jane Hart (also friends of Stephen Ward). I was stunned. It was one of Ruth's best-kept secrets. She looked different. Her hair was short and dyed black. She'd put on weight. But it was Ruth. I knew she wanted to make a name for herself. But I couldn't believe my sister moved in the same circles as Stephen Ward.

Ruth probably mentioned to Mother she was doing walk-on parts but Mother didn't tell me. Joe wasn't surprised: 'Knowing what she got up to, to earn money, she'd be up there.'

I have read about Stephen Ward. He was known for spotting glamour girls to make them into something. I can't see Ruth liking being dominated by him. That's what he did with girls. She would have had a very much, I don't trust you as far as I can throw you type attitude. But if there was money, Ruth would have thought differently. He probably promised she would earn a fortune once he changed her looks and personality. Joe reckoned you could easily transform Ruth because she knew nothing to start with: 'It would have been like taking a kid out of school and altering her.' Knowing how Ward worked on his girls you can see how Ruth became different. I can see it now. This was the time she changed so much – her confidence, her sophistication, her hair, although it was another year before she peroxided it. To think I knew nothing about it, other than seeing she was different. What happened behind the scenes was a blank to me.

When did this happen? *Lady Godiva Rides Again* was released in November 1951. The *Folkestone Gazette* reported that the beauty contest scenes were filmed on 4 and 5 May 1951. Everything fitted together – the timing was right. Ruth had long curly hair in Warsash – it was black in a bob when she returned to London – and the stills photograph shows she had put on weight: she was four months pregnant with Georgina.

Ruth must have known Ward before she went to Warsash. Her part in the film must have been planned in advance. She can't have met him while she was staying secretly with me on her return to London. Ruth clearly knew Ward before she married George Ellis in November 1950. She probably met him at the Court Club, where she suddenly started dating George. I suspect Ward introduced her to him and was involved with their quick marriage. Just like his connection with Ruth's best friend Vickie Martin and her love affair with the Maharaja of Cooch Behar later on. Stephen Ward arranged things. Everyone knew that. I think Ruth was set up to marry George Ellis, and she went through with it for money and with a naive willingness to act as a partner in some plot.

Some say Ward was evil. I'd say he didn't do most girls any favours by transforming them because they weren't used to the circle they moved into. He corrupted them. They couldn't cope with their new lives. He wouldn't care. He obviously had something else in mind – use them and lose them. Damon Wise wrote in *Come By Sunday*: 'Ward had a singular talent for finding young ladies and shaping them for society. His notable success was Vickie Martin . . . but Ward was not running a call-girl racket, he was merely trying, somewhat high-mindedly, to play Pygmalion.' That was the impression Ward wanted to give, about the underdog being given a chance to improve themselves. What sort of man goes out of his way to find girls who want to be made something of?

Stephen Ward was in his late thirties when Ruth knew him. He was a clergyman's son, qualified in America as an osteopath and joined the army in 1941. After the war he began practising his osteopathy amongst the wealthy set. People like Winston Churchill, his daughter Sarah, Harold Macmillan and Douglas Fairbanks Junior were amongst his patients. Ward's consulting room in Devonshire Street was paid for by Lord Bill Astor, his friend from Cliveden near Maidenhead, who was also a patient. Ward was an accomplished artist and sketched famous people. Prince Philip and Princess Margaret sat for him. In 1949 Ward married a twenty-two-year-old beauty queen, Patricia Barnes. But the marriage was over by the end of 1950 because of his 'instability'.

When the name Stephen Ward cropped up I remember how I'd weighed him up when the scandal was splashed across the papers in the sixties. He may have got girls to say, 'The rain in Spain stays mainly on the plain,' but to me he was a pimp. He brought them on as so-called society girls, educated them, told them how to pose and say thank you but he also used them as high-class prostitutes for powerful men – and he wasn't doing it for nothing.

Ward may think he prepared Ruth for getting on with influential people at the nightclubs but she was left high and dry when it came to normal life. It makes me livid when writers described her as a common West End tart. She wasn't. But it was the image ordinary people could relate to. And it sold books. Nobody knew what Ruth went through to get away from an abusive father, then the same kind of husband, before she became the manageress of an exclusive London club. It didn't happen overnight. She learned about make-up, hairstyle, clothes and how to talk to well-off people. For somebody in the 1950s, without education, that change was enormous. But she wasn't prepared for the next three years and what was thrown at her.

We were led to believe Ward was doing his stuff in the 1960s. Now I know he was getting into practice fifteen years before – just after the war and in the early 1950s. The time we called the Cold War when Russia, America and Great Britain were at loggerheads about communism. Joe talked about infiltration by communist agitators. I didn't understand other than feeling frightened reading about communist countries in the *News of the World*.

I picked up titbits about Ward from *An Affair of State, the Profumo Case and the Framing of Stephen Ward* by Phillip Knightley and Caroline Kennedy:

> The end of the trial and Ward's dramatic suicide swept the Profumo scandal off the British scene. It was as if one moment the newspapers had been full of only that and the next moment there was nothing . . .

Another, more senior MI5 officer involved in the operation said it was a pity that Ward's true role had not been revealed at the time of his trial. 'I think that everyone involved did feel sorry about Ward and the final outcome,' he said. 'Nowhere in the Denning Report does it say that Ward was acting under our instructions. That is very unfortunate.' The officer said Ward would have been encouraged to see himself as a patriot working for his country. MI5 had no idea that the operation would end in the manner it did . . . But could not MI5 have found some way to have confirmed that Ward was working for the service? 'Yes . . . Ward might have been alive today if that had happened . . . we were very cut up when we learned he was dead.'

Ward's activities clearly went much deeper than the pimping of which he was accused in his trial and in the Denning Report, both of which failed to refer to his spying for MI5. His skill was finding uneducated girls from a poor background with a good face shape, moulding and manipulating them into girls that could go into society. I believe he took the ones who were most gullible, desperate for money, and could keep a secret, then used them for something more dangerous: as prostitutes to draw out secrets from influential men during the Cold War. He probably had a dip in the till although I heard he preferred watching sex to taking part. I'd say the girls didn't want to be prostitutes – they wanted to go with men with money, to make money for themselves. Ward set them up in flats, which is how I imagine Ruth came by her flat in Tooting Bec. For Ward though, the sex side of the business was a shady cover for his Secret Service activities, he was spying for the British and quite possibly at this stage he had become a double agent.

At the end of 1951 it was all happening. Ruth gave birth to Georgina on 2 October. On the 25th of the month the Conservatives beat Labour in the General Election. My family had always voted Conservative. *Lady Godiva Rides Again* was screened, although Ruth's part remained a secret for fifty years! My parents moved from Herne Hill. As usual they were in debt with the rent and Ruth let them live at her place in Tooting Bec. This was when Ruth's friend Vickie Martin moved out of the flat she shared with Ruth and met Stephen Ward. She couldn't have stayed in the same place as my parents – Mother was there looking after Ruth's children, Andre and Georgina.

Mother said Ruth nearly died giving birth to Georgina. When I went to see her in Dulwich Hospital she was sitting up in bed and told me to look at the baby. We didn't say much. She had come up in the world and was different and acting out of character. She was in hospital for two weeks until she got her energy back. Within three months, when she could take the pace again, she was back at Carroll's (previously the Court Club). With two children she had to work. My parents were living in her flat and expecting money.

I'm not sure when Ruth met Vickie Martin. The first and last I knew of her was at the beginning of January 1955 after she died. Mother broke the news: 'Ruth isn't very well and it's because she's just lost her friend Vickie.' Ruth mentioned that they worked together as hostesses in London clubs. That's all we were told, apart from Ruth asking Mother and me if we'd read about Vickie's death in a car crash in the papers, which we hadn't.

I began piecing together the friendship between Ruth and Vickie.

Old Etonian 'Dandy Kim' Caborn-Waterfield is described in *Honeytrap* by Anthony Summers and Stephen Dorril as a 'better class of criminal'. He has insider knowledge of the social scene in the early 1950s. He remembers the time when he knew Ruth and Vickie when they worked together as hostesses at the Court Club in Duke Street, Mayfair. He mentioned a regular visitor to the club – Stephen Ward. For his own reasons Kim would not give permission for his words to be recorded but I can summarize:

> Over a period of two years I went to the Court Club half-a-dozen to a dozen times. I originally met Ruth when I went there with Diana Dors and a butch girl in the early fifties. Ruth was very kind. I can't imagine that she and Vickie would ever have broken up – they were best friends. I recall Stephen Ward being there. I only remember him in a dark suit, a quizzical look with his eyebrows and his stand – a shade camp. He loved pretty girls around him. He lived round the corner to the club in Cavendish Square.

Vickie Martin was born Valerie Mewes. She was from Egham in Surrey and was a penniless nobody till she met Stephen Ward. Then she became a somebody. Knightley and Kennedy wrote in *An Affair of State* that she met Stephen Ward in a doorway and he liked her bone structure. Ruth is mentioned briefly: Valerie told him how she had quarrelled with her boyfriend and was about to lose her accommodation. She had been sharing with Ruth Ellis . . . Ellis had just found a job as the manageress of the Little Club in Knightsbridge.

Ward spent time on Vickie and turned her into a star. She became a model and posed for society photographer Antony Beauchamp and got her one and only film part in the 1952 film *It Started in Paradise* playing the part of a model. She also fell in love with the Maharaja of Cooch Behar, a wealthy playboy educated at Harrow school and Cambridge University, and another friend of Prince Philip. The Maharaja asked her to marry him. But he realized he would lose his prince's income if they got married. Next thing, she is killed in a car crash in Maidenhead, a mile or so from Cliveden where Stephen Ward's friend Lord Astor entertained just about everyone who was anyone – Winston Churchill, the Rothschilds and in the sixties Christine Keeler and Profumo.

The papers reported that on 9 January 1955, the date of Vickie Martin's accident, a journalist called Terence Robertson and Vickie were returning from a restaurant near Henley-on-Thames at about half-past-three in the morning. Mr Robertson sustained a broken leg and lost his memory. The driver of the other car died.

Newspaper reports varied in their details of who was driving the car in which Vickie was travelling. The 10 January 1955 editions of *The Times* and the *News Chronicle* stated that Vickie Martin was driving and Mr A. Robertson was the passenger. But according to the *Maidenhead Advertiser*, 'The police have established that Miss Valerie Mewes, 23-year-old model better known as Vickie Martin was not driving the car in which she was killed,' and Mr Terence Robertson, a journalist of Lowndes Street, Westminster was the driver.

Mr Robertson's name didn't appear on the voting list at that address at any time; his home at 30 Smith Terrace was a quarter-of-a-mile away. Terence Anthony Robertson had served in the war, wrote fact-based spying books and was forty years old at the time of the crash. I believe he committed suicide in America in the 1970s.

The inquest on Vickie's death opened on 11 January but was adjourned until 2 March 1955. The result was not made public. Vickie's aunt, Vera Reynolds, was aware of some puzzling aspects surrounding her niece's death, that have never been explained:

> Vickie was very close to her grandmother Alice Reynolds who was my mother-in-law. Alice told me Vickie was with this writer the night she was killed, returning from a big do at Cliveden, Lord Astor's place. It's not what they wanted to put in the papers at the time. Vickie told her sister Doreen that she was going up there. They used to have those big weekends at Cliveden with Stephen Ward – Vickie went there frequently with him. They had some pretty influential people there and Vickie was in the circle. This guy [Terence Robertson] wasn't a friend. A friend of Doreen's who was there told Alice he was punch drunk and kept shouting, 'I want to take you home' to Vickie. It's not true what the newspapers wrote about Vickie having thirteen car crashes; to put the record straight she never drove a car because she was frightened of having an accident. Nor did she have a driving licence – the Driver and Vehicle Licensing Agency checked their records and confirmed this. If she came to see her grandmother, either Bhayai [Maharaja of Cooch Behar] or Stephen Ward would drive. Otherwise she came down from London with a

friend who ran a club; I met her once at Alice's house in Chandos Road, in Staines. I remember Vickie saying, 'she looks after me, auntie'. The woman was blonde and middle-aged. Vickie wasn't the only one she had under her wings – she looked after other girls apparently. I think she was called a Madam.

Something big was going on when Ruth was working in the clubs. Knowing her she probably didn't have a clue what it was all about. Joe reckoned: 'She didn't know her arse from her elbow and was easily manipulated if there's money involved. It goes back to the family, the way they were conditioned.' Reading about MI5 and MI6 and comparing what was going on in Ruth's life with her husband George Ellis and Stephen Ward at this time, it didn't take me long to realize there were dates, people and places that matched and were connected. Everything in Ruth's last five years seems to overlap everything else. No wonder the truth about her didn't come out.

With the help of John Steel from Leatherhead, who comes into the story again later on, I discovered that the photographer Antony Beauchamp, a close friend of Stephen Ward, was an official war artist in Burma – he photographed the Wingate expedition in 1943. The only portrait photograph I have of Ruth used to be in an old velvet frame which fell apart because journalists over the years handled it roughly. I believe it was taken by Antony Beauchamp. The black and white photograph was tinted like a watercolour painting. Her green eyes are exactly the right colour. On the back it was dated 1951. She was twenty-four and at her best. I've studied the photograph and worked out it can only have been taken immediately before she went to Warsash, about the time of her marriage to George Ellis. I keep it on the mantelpiece. Ruth looks like she was going through a transformation. Her make-up was beautiful. Her hair was long, still her natural auburn colour, and done up in a chignon at the back – different to how people remember her in 1955. She looks sophisticated, very royal, every bit the young lady she was. You can see her exceptionally long neck. Father used to say: 'All the better for hanging with.'

Tinting photos was Beauchamp's trademark. He wrote in his autobiography that the *Sketch* described his portraits in the 1950s as 'studies in fumed oak'. That describes Ruth's portrait well. After the war he became a society photographer, some called him a glamour photographer. He photographed beautiful, rich and glamorous women like Marilyn Monroe before she became famous, Greta Garbo and Mae West. And political people like his father-in-law, Winston Churchill, Anthony Eden and Duncan Sandys. In 1949, Sarah Churchill, Winston Churchill's daughter and a talented actress, was unmarried. Beauchamp wrote in his autobiography: 'She would have been a prize catch to any man of means aspiring to a political career. It was clear to him [Churchill] that I had no such cravings.' On 17 October 1949 he secretly married Sarah in America. Ben Lyon and Bebe Daniels let them use their house in America at Sea Island, Georgia for the honeymoon. Ben Lyon was casting director for Twentieth Century Fox and the person who originally signed up Marilyn Monroe.

Despite his top-class connections, I could not find any photographic organizations with information about Beauchamp. Nor could the *Tatler* magazine find evidence of Beauchamp's sketch-cum-photograph series that he boasts about in his autobiography.

By 1950 Beauchamp was moving in the right circles. As Winston Churchill's son-in-law, he became brother-in-law to Duncan Sandys, Anthony Eden and Christopher Soames, and to their wives, Diana, Clarissa and Mary. He photographed them all. The upper-class women with money adored him. Anyone going up in the world wanted their photograph taken by Beauchamp. I have it on good authority that all the gorgeous girls would model for him with no clothes on. If I'm to learn the truth about Ruth's short life I have to question everything. I've never forgotten that Ruth in the prison told Mother that she hoped the truth would eventually come out after her death. I had to start digging. I started reading around what was happening in the fifties particularly about spying – something I never understood. Having learned about Stephen Ward I asked myself, was Ruth's death connected with the secret services? Would I ever find out? I would have to look where I've never looked before.

I return briefly to George Ellis. There's no doubt he too had another side. As far as I know George Ellis wasn't on the scene when Ruth was back at Carroll's. Not that she'd go back to the drunken brute anyway, she'd completely broken off the arrangement with him before Georgina was born. By the end of 1951 he had taken a job as a school dentist in Warrington in Lancashire, not exactly the Chief Dental Officer he's described as in various books, and Ruth was fighting for a divorce. However, it didn't stop him from pestering her once she became manageress at the Little Club in Brompton Road in 1953 – he was thrown out more than once.

I've looked at recently opened papers at the Public Record Office that mention George Ellis. Even I, without an education, can see there was funny business going on. My father gave a statement to the police on 17 April 1955: 'Ellis treated her cruelly and assaulted her on numerous occasions. In the end she had to apply for police protection and was advised by the police to leave him and apply for a separation which was granted.' This section of the report has 'Slashed' written next to it. Why wasn't this used in the trial to show what Ruth had endured? None of this background detail came out.

In one document prepared for the trial, Brief to Counsel to Appear on Behalf of the Accused, eleven documents are listed in Folder B. All documents relating to Ruth and George's matrimonial affairs, numbers 8–11, are missing. If George Ellis was a nonentity in the case, why has this information been concealed from public view until 2032?

Not a scrap of evidence about their marriage, nor the way Ruth was treated by George Ellis was used in her trial. Ruth was described purely as a divorced woman. Why? Because their marriage was a marriage of convenience. There was more to it than anyone imagined. There was a web of secrecy. That's the way it was going to stay.

I'll never forget reading a little piece in the *News of the World* after Ruth died written by George Ellis's sister. She said: 'I blame my brother for what happened to Ruth.' It was just a strip of news pushed into a story. She knew how cruel he was, she'd heard. On the other hand it may not have been the cruelty she was hinting at. It could have been something else.

8

Enter Desmond Cussen

Ruth's lover Desmond Cussen came on the scene in 1952 after George Ellis had made his exit up north to Warrington. Like Ellis and various other characters Ruth was caught up with, very little is actually known about Cussen. Yet there was so much more to him than we realized. My intuition told me that Cussen, who played a big part in Ruth's life, was responsible with others for making the shooting of her lover David Blakely in July 1955 look like a crime of passion. She lied at her trial to protect Cussen and signed her own death certificate: 'I took the gun from my bag and I shot him . . . This gun was given to me about three years ago in a club by a man whose name I do not remember.'

Ruth met Desmond Edward Cussen at Carroll's Club in Duke Street in 1952. He has been described in books as a docile father figure, quiet, unassuming, greased-back brown hair, a round boyish face and a pencil-thin moustache. He was a director of the family wholesale and retail tobacconists business, Cussen and Co. All my mother told me about him at the time was that Ruth was going out with a rich man.

Finding anything about Cussen's early life was not easy. But I made a big discovery. Three hundred yards from where Father lay in Leatherhead Hospital during the war was the house called Dapdune in Garlands Road where Desmond

Cussen lived. In the 1940s it was a select road with few houses. General Ironside lived in one house. The not-so-well off neighbours in Copthorne Road thought he was a Colonel Blimp-type person – they never saw the owner who lived behind a high brick wall next door to Dapdune. Ironside was one of Churchill's generals in the Second World War and Commander- in-Chief Home Forces (in charge of the Home Guard).

Mr John Leonard Steel, a retired Leatherhead gentleman who has helped me with several pieces of research, was an ARP warden based in Garlands Road during the war. In 1941 the Home Guard's HQ was in General Ironside's house. Their job was to guard bombed places and watch out for parachutists. What Mr Steel said about the young chap he paired up with proved to be important in my search for the truth:

> Two rooms in the house next to Dapdune were com-
> mandeered by the government for the Home Guard.
> At night there would be two guards in the front and
> twelve in the back room. I can remember a colonel
> somebody, not in uniform, coming to introduce
> himself to the men and thanking us for what we were
> doing to help the war effort. I know now it was
> General Ironside, I saw him on television.
>
> I teamed up with a young man from a well-to-do
> family, who lived next door in Dapdune. It had a high
> fence round it. I think he was an only child. He would
> have been about eighteen ears old and his father was
> a city gent type. The young man and I worked to-
> gether at night-time. We met up two or three times a
> week from mid summer 1940 till about April 1941.

We'd be together in the front room. There was a desk
and a typewriter and a bed for one of us to sleep in
while the other stayed awake. We talked about girls
and the war – normal things young men talked about.
He had straight sandy hair, was about 5'9", of muscular build and handsome.

One night we were on duty at the telephone
exchange in Leatherhead. Outside was a letterbox. I
remember this occasion well. A lady appeared in the
dark. My partner said: 'Home Guard. Hands up.
You're a spy.' His bayonet was nearly in her stomach.
I told him to be careful and steady on. The lady said
in a pathetic voice: 'I'm not a spy. I'm Mrs Smith,
come to post a letter.'

Important documents were found in Germany
after the war. It seems capturing Leatherhead was
part of Germany's invasion plans. It was an important junction on the road to London and was to be
taken by the 9th Panzer Division. We had to be on
the lookout for flashing lights signalling to German
aircraft. We'd seen some lights coming from the
Ridgeway as we left the depot on Hawks Hill. We
marched out in the blackout and got the spooky
feeling that somebody would stick something in our
backs. We approached the house in the Ridgeway. I
said to my partner: 'We'll get this sod. You go this
way, I'll go that and meet in the middle and grab
him.' It turned out to be a bonfire. Everyone was
warned, there were strict instructions that bonfires
should be doused before dark, but this house owner
hadn't taken any notice. We got him out of bed to

teach him a lesson and put it out. A report went in to our platoon commander but we never knew if anything was done about the incident.

My partner was a good shot. We'd practise on St John's school rifle shooting range opposite our HQ, using 303 rifles. You try picking up a 303, you'll see they're heavy. He was good with it. He had more strength than me. I envied him. As you fire the gun it comes back and hits you but he had a thicker body than me and could take it. He was a crack shot. Other times we'd be taken in a lorry to Bisley for shooting practice.

One thing that struck me about him – coming from a well-to-do home, why wasn't he at college? People from wealthy families automatically went to college. I couldn't understand why he was around in those days. He was a cut above the rest of us, well spoken and well educated. I failed my eye test at an air crew examination later in April 41 but at the beginning of July I went for training in Skegness and became an RAF radio mechanic. I never saw the young man again.

Mr Steel couldn't at first remember the young man's name. It was sixty years ago. Then out of the blue it came to him: 'I remember now. His name was Cussen.'

Fourteen years later at my sister's trial at the Old Bailey, Desmond Cussen, Mr Steel's Home Guard partner, was referred to by Christmas Humphreys, prosecuting counsel, as Ruth's alternative lover. Desmond Cussen was registered at Dapdune, opposite St John's school with his father William David Cussen and mother Mary Cussen in 1947, 1949 and 1950, his father having owned Dapdune since 1921. It would appear that Desmond, born in December 1922, was an only child.

Robert Hancock, in *Ruth Ellis, the Last Woman to be Hanged*, wrote of Cussen: 'He was not particularly outstanding in anything he did.' Georgina Ellis described him as: 'A drip. Failure to impress academically or socially. Of wisdom had he none.' She said he joined the RAF aged seventeen, underwent training mainly in South Africa to be a bomber pilot, flew Lancasters and was demobbed in 1946. But the facts are that when Cussen was seventeen he was in the Home Guard working alongside John Steel. He was not then in the RAF. In the Air Force List the entry for D.E. Cussen 197248 states he joined the RAF as a Pilot Officer in General Duties Branch on 10 April 1945 and left on 10 October 1945. He was in the RAF for six months.

Come 1947 Cussen described himself on company documents as a motor car dealer and director of T.J. Carey and Co. Ltd. He took over the tobacconist business, Cussen and Co. that his father acquired in 1946, with shops in Hammersmith, Stepney, Barnet, Peckham and Finsbury Park, and premises at Lower Marsh and Falcon Road in London and another in Aberystwyth. The property in Lower Marsh, a scruffy bomb-damaged market area near Waterloo station, was opposite Steve's Café where in January 1961 the spy Ethel Gee, of the Portland spy ring, handed a package containing Admiralty secrets to the Russian spy Gordon Lonsdale.

Cussen was a director of Longley and Co., named, according to his accountant whom we traced but cannot name, after Longley Road in Harrow where he supposedly lived. The accountant mentioned, in passing, that Cussen told him in the early 1960s that Ruth had been a friend of Stephen Ward. More proof of their connection.

I might never have known Ruth was caught up in something to do with espionage if I hadn't stumbled across Cussen's signature on a business transaction in 1964. To think the truth about my sister surfaced because of a paid-up loan on her lover's properties in Lower Marsh and Falcon Road. By signing that document Cussen slipped up. For me it opened a new line of investigation. Hidden amongst microfiched hand written documents at Companies House was a 'Memorandum of Complete Satisfaction' dated 29 May 1964. On it Cussen gave his address as Flat 543 Atlantic Hotel, Queens Gardens, London W2, where he'd lived for two years. That hotel was frequented by Christine Keeler, Mandy Rice-Davies and Stephen Ward in the early sixties when Cussen lived there. Before that he lived at Lanterns Hotel in Craven Road for about two years. I was horrified. I thought he was in Australia. Even worse I discovered he never left his flat in Devonshire Street after Ruth was hanged – he was there till 1957.

The police wanted to question him the night before Ruth passed away but couldn't find him. Ruth was due to be hanged on 13 July. She had dismissed her solicitor Mr Bickford on the evening of 11 July. By the time she'd confessed to her original solicitors, Mishcon and Simmons, on the morning of the 12th that Cussen supplied the gun used to kill Blakely, Cussen had disappeared. The police maintained they looked for him but couldn't find him. PRO documents revealed they arrived at his flat on the 12th at 9.30 p.m. waited twenty minutes, made a phone call and left. A porter at the flats saw him leave at 9.15 a.m. on the 12th with suitcases – twelve hours earlier!

How did Cussen know to leave when he did? Did he know Bickford had been dismissed and fear that Ruth would tell the truth? He had some sort of immunity. I suspect that he may have been a member of M15 and was watching Stephen Ward who, at that time, according to Anthony Summers and Stephen Dorril's book *Honeytrap*, was suspected of being a double agent. Somewhere hidden in books written about the Cold War, Cussen's true identity is waiting to be found.

What would the papers have said if they knew he had not been interviewed by the police? In 1955 there was a grounds-well of opinion that Ruth should not be hanged. There are thousands of letters in the Public Record Office, begging to reprieve her. They nearly broke me apart when I read them. Those at the top weren't going to listen. Despite the fact that 90 per cent of women sentenced to death after 1900 were reprieved, Ruth was to be an exception. What if the people of this country had been told that Ruth Ellis simply knew too much about Burgess and Maclean, the biggest spying scandal to hit Britain. Imagine the damage it would have done to the new Conservative government that only just scraped in at the May General Election for another term, following Churchill's resignation – there would have been a public outcry.

I'm in no doubt this is what my sister's story was about – spying. The real Ruth Ellis story was not about a crime of passion, the Establishment just made it look that way. The shooting of David Blakely was a diversion. It obscured the truth about the country in the grips of a spying scandal. If only Ruth could have told the truth at her trial in June. Instead she was hanged to protect that bunch she mixed with, taking her secret to the unconsecrated grave at Holloway prison.

It was a fact there was a Cold War between Britain, the Soviet Union and America after the war. We know now spying was going on but then people in Britain didn't know anything about it. Not till the late 1950s or early 1960s did we start to hear murmurings. It wasn't till Sir Anthony Blunt, Surveyor of the Queen's Pictures and a double agent who passed secrets to the Soviets during the war, had his knighthood taken away in 1979, that information started coming out. Everything had been under cloaks – my phrase that's half-way between under wraps and cloak-and-dagger. We were patriotic after the war effort, thinking Great Britain was great. Only when the books about spying came out in recent years did you realize what had actually gone on. The public is aware now that Stephen Ward was involved in spying in 1963, although at the time they thought he was just a pimp as the Denning Report portrayed him. Now it seems Ward was possibly operating in the early 1950s.

When Burgess and Maclean defected to Russia in 1951 we didn't think about it. The war was still on our minds, we still had its after effects. Demolition boys were still cleaning up. In June 1951 the papers only touched on Burgess and Maclean's disappearance – they were just described as men missing from the Foreign Office and not portrayed as traitors. It didn't mean much to us. Joe was trying to get on in life, to earn enough money to feed the family. It wasn't till later we discovered what damage the traitors had done.

The Government White Paper about the 1951 defection was anonymously written by Graham Mitchell, head of D Branch, MI5's counter-espionage section, and published on 23 September 1955. When I read it in Nigel West's *Mole Hunt* I could see that the government had kept the crisis under wraps for four years, probably deciding how and what to tell the press and the British people – it's called 'spin' now. Here are some excerpts:

> Report concerning the Disappearance of Two Former Foreign Office Officials,
>
> 23rd September 1955
>
> On the evening of Friday, 25th May 1951, Mr Donald Duart Maclean, a Counsellor in the senior branch of the Foreign Service and at that time Head of the American Department in the Foreign Office, and Mr Guy Francis de Moncy Burgess, a Second Secretary in the junior branch of the Foreign Service, left the United Kingdom from Southampton on the boat for St Malo. The circumstances of their departure from England, for which they had not sought sanction, were such as to make it obvious that they had deliberately fled the country. Both officers were suspended from duty on 1st June 1951 . . .
>
> 2. Maclean was the son of a former Cabinet Minister, Sir Donald Maclean. He was born in 1913 and was educated at Gresham's School, Holt and Trinity College, Cambridge . . .
>
> 3. In May 1950 while serving at His Majesty's Embassy, Cairo, Maclean was guilty of serious misconduct and suffered a form of breakdown which was attributed to overwork and excessive drinking . . . After recuperation and leave at home he was passed medically fit, and in October 1950 was appointed to be Head of the American Department . . .

5. Burgess was born in 1911 and was educated at the Royal Naval College, Dartmouth, at Eton and at Trinity College, Cambridge . . . In August 1950 he was transferred to Washington as a Second Secretary.

6. Early in 1950 the security authorites informed the Foreign Office that in late 1949 while on holiday abroad Burgess had been guilty of indiscreet talk about secret matters of which he had official knowledge. For this he was severely reprimanded.

7. In Washington, however, his work and behaviour gave rise to complaint . . . The Ambassador requested that Burgess be removed from Washington and this was approved. He was recalled to London in early May 1951 . . . It was at this point that he disappeared.

8. Investigations into Burgess's past have since shown that he, like Maclean went through a period of communist leanings while at Cambridge . . .

10. In January 1949 the security authorities received a report that certain Foreign Office information had leaked to the Soviet authorities some years earlier . . . Highly secret but widespread and protracted enquiries were begun by the security authorities and the field of suspicion had been narrowed by mid-April 1951 to two or three persons. By the beginning of May Maclean had come to be regarded as the principal suspect . . .

11. It is now clear that in spite of the precautions taken by the authorities Maclean must have become

aware, at some time before his disappearance, that he was under investigation . . . he may have been warned.

13. As a result of these and other inquiries it was established that Maclean and Burgess together left Tatsfield by car for Southampton at midnight, caught the SS *Falaise* for St Malo and disembarked at that port at 11.45 the following morning.

18. Lady Maclean received a further letter from her son on 15th August 1951. There is no doubt that it was in his own handwriting. It had been posted at Herne Hill on 11th August.

23. In view of the suspicions held against Maclean and of the conspiratorial manner of his flight, it was assumed, though it could not be proved, that his destination and that of his companion must have been the Soviet Union . . . one or other of the two men became aware that their activities were under investigation. This was reported by them to the Soviet Intelligence Service who then organized their escape and removal to the Soviet Union.

24. Two points call for comment: . . . how Maclean and Burgess remained in the Foreign Office for so long and second, why they were able to get away.

26. The watch on Maclean was made difficult by the need to ensure that he did not become aware that he was under observation. This watch was primarily aimed at collecting, if possible, further information

and not preventing an escape. It was inadvisable to increase this risk by extending the surveillance to his home in an isolated part of the country and he was therefore watched in London only.....In the event he was alerted and fled the country together with Burgess.

Oddly enough, I know Point 13 was incorrect. Frank Watson, who owned the garage in Tatsfield, regularly picked up Maclean from Woldingham station on his way home from London. Frank's sister said her brother took Maclean in his own Humber Super Snipe to Woldingham station the night he defected and was told to drive the car back and 'garage it for a few days'.

The West End clubs where Ruth worked were meeting places for secret agents – risky places for people with brains and money. They weren't just the dens for gangsters they were portrayed as in books about Ruth. That was a smokescreen. It's where the police, royalty, politicians, intellectuals and journalists went, and high-ranking homosexuals gathered in secret behind closed doors. Homosexuality was then illegal. Club owner Maurie Conley was painted as the biggest gangster in London. But according to historian David Johnson he wasn't as black as he was painted. He wrote to me in 1993: 'One description of Morris Conley for instance, puts in everything except the horns and the tail, and is unrecognizable to a friend of mine who actually knew (and liked) the man.' To me, Stephen Ward and his Secret Service colleagues that Ruth mixed with, were the most dangerous. It was the easiest thing in the world after the war for Ward to pick up uneducated girls like Ruth, knowing they needed money, do them up, make them street-wise and get them into clubs. They were easy prey. Ward in his role as osteopath had many upper-crust clients. Top men were poncing on him because he was promoting the girls. Done up, the girls attracted influential people. It wasn't so much a call-girl service, more a listening service and pillow talk. They'd free up their tongues messing around with sex. I doubt the girls knew they were actually spying – they'd have been brainwashed first. Even in this big time men's game of spying, they still had to use women and sex to gather intelligence. Sex was the ultimate.

Ruth was mixing with high-risk characters who seemed to have a darker side: Stephen Ward, the smooth society doctor, was acting as a vice peddler; Desmond Cussen appeared to be a boring businessman; and George Ellis, the alcoholic dentist whose frequent spells of 'drying out' may have covered up something more sinister.

In Chapter 6 I showed how convenient it was for George Ellis to get to Warlingham Park Hospital from Sanderstead. Was being classed as an alcoholic George's cover? Add to this the truism that marriages of secret agents aren't necessarily love affairs but convenient cover operations. No wife – at least at that time – would give evidence against her husband in court. George's first marriage to Vera in 1938 ended in divorce in November 1949. She'd allegedly had enough of his brutality. Come 1950, without a wife, George no longer had a cover. If George hadn't married Ruth nobody would have noticed he was a drunken bully. With Ruth around, she made sure that everyone knew she'd been beaten up by the alcoholic dentist. Thanks to Ruth his disappearances into Warlingham Park were convincing.

Was Warlingham Park Hospital, or somewhere close by, a safe house where Ellis and Maclean met up? Dates between 1950 and 1951, when Ellis was displaying mad, drunken behaviour, coincide with events surrounding Burgess and Maclean, both of whom had apparently been suffering from drunkenness, been reprimanded for bad conduct and recalled to London from abroad. Burgess had behaved badly in Tangier in 1950. In the spring of 1951 following three motoring offences in America involving a homosexual with a police record, he was instantly dismissed from the country. In May 1950, Maclean was called back from Cairo to dry out from excessive drinking and recover from a breakdown. According to the experts Maclean's cover was about to be blown. He returned to London. Seven months later, at the end of December 1950 he moved into a house in Tatsfield, a stone's throw from Warlingham.

Maclean's drunken behaviour, like George Ellis's, is complicated. If he was being dried out as the 1955 White Paper implied, and pronounced fit to return to work at the Foreign Office in November 1950, it's strange that he regularly visited the pub in Tatsfield from December 1950 till May 1951. Elizabeth, a Tatsfield resident, moved to the village in the summer of 1950. She said: 'Donald Maclean used to come back on the 706 Green Line at that time. I used to see him walking down to The Ship. My husband saw him on several occasions – he'd always be sitting on his own.' Geoffrey Hoare, Maclean's friend and author of *The Missing Macleans* said Donald didn't socialize at this time because of his drink problem. That wasn't true. Elizabeth confirmed:

These two couples in Tatsfield, Jack and Fran Crowther from Manor House and Malyn Knight and his wife from Neville House, called on Donald and Melinda Maclean and asked them for dinner. In those days you called on people if they were in similar circumstances. By coincidence I was introduced to Malyn Knight during the war when the local doctor in Bracknell in Berkshire had a party. I got the impression he had affairs with everyone he met. He was stationed in one of the big houses nearby that was commandeered by the army. It's funny, when we came to Tatsfield he said I've met you somewhere before, but I didn't recognize him. When I heard his name I remembered because it was an unusual name. I think the Knights moved soon after the Macleans left.

Cyril Connolly wrote in *The Missing Diplomats* that Maclean had champagne and oysters for his birthday lunch, the day he disappeared in 1951. Was drink really his problem? Drunkenness, it seems, is a good cover when you need an excuse to disappear. It suited their purpose to appear drunk, people expected that conduct from them. They weren't acting out of character. In *The Missing Diplomats* Connolly wrote:

> Donald's drinking followed an established routine. The charming and amiable self was gradually left behind and the hand which patted his friend on the back became a flail. A change would come into his voice like the roll of drums for the cabaret. It took the form of an outburst of indignation. . .

Desmond Cussen's cover was his string of tobacconist shops

and being involved in motor racing. Not that he was a racing driver, but it gave him something to talk about in the clubs. It was a good cover. To Ruth on the other hand, being in motor racing meant glamour. And Cussen knew it and exploited it.

Public Record Office files show, and later chapters reveal, that David Blakely, the man Ruth was convicted of murdering was bisexual. Ruth's need for money and Blakely's thirst for male sex would have provided suitable ingredients for intelligence gathering in London's clubland about spying and the activities of high-ranking homosexuals. Burgess and Maclean, both homosexuals, were in the frame. Ruth and Blakely's paymasters, like Cussen's, may have been the British Secret Service. As minor players, with the sensitive information they'd gathered, Blakely and Ruth would become expendable – but not before Ruth had passed Blakely's secrets to Cussen.

Was this behind the shooting of David Blakely?

9

Problems in the Family

It was 1952. I was sweeping up in the flat, I didn't have the luxury of a Hoover. I couldn't hear anything going on whilst I was working but when I'd finished there was blood-curdling screaming coming from the garden. My daughter Pauline was in flames. I threw a bowl of water over her; it was the only thing I could do. 'Aunt Peggy' from over the road wrapped her in a sheet and we got her to Sidcup Hospital.

Pauline was four years old and we were living in Domonic Drive in Eltham. We had a gas cooker with long legs with a plate-warming space at the top where I kept the matches so the children couldn't get them. I had to stand on tiptoes to reach. Pauline that day had other ideas: 'I set myself on fire in the summer of 1952. I got a chair and climbed up. I loved the taste of sulphur and used to lick the side of the matchbox.' I'd always thought she'd had an accident with the electric fire and burned the hairs on her legs. Twenty years later she told me she'd lied because she thought she'd get told off: 'I went down the bottom of the garden with Marlene and Jonathan, from next door. I wondered what would happen if I put a match on my leg. I had a flammable seersucker dress on; it caught the dress and went up quick. It wasn't an electric fire like I'd said as a child. It was one match.' After Joe had seen her in hospital he gave me a hell of a telling off. At the same time he said I'd done the right thing flinging water over her. They reckoned it was sixty-five per cent of the body got burned – all down one side of her and each leg. We didn't know if she'd survive.

In Sidcup Hospital they cut squares off Pauline's skin and stuck them on places that bled, then bandaged her up. Doctor Clark looked after her. Then she was shipped off to East Grinstead, a far better hospital with a plastics unit, established by the Sir Archibald McIndoe, the plastic surgeon famous for his treatment of wartime burns victims. Archie MacIndoe had performed several pioneering operations using a cheese-grating technique for this type of burn. Instead of cutting the skin with a knife they grated it. Then wrapped it in gauze to be stored in a skin bank. When holes appeared on the wounds they'd stick more skin on. Pauline remembers Dr MacIndoe drawing on her body with biro to show where he was going to release the tightness of the skin. He was very kind and very clever.

The doctors said it was most important I should be there with Pauline. Mother came to look after the other children while I went in every day, then Ruth took over for two weeks while I went to and fro. She was very edgy though – up and down. I expect she wanted to get back to work.

Not long before Christmas 1952 we had to give up our house. Joe had run into debt with the payments. We left there to live with my parents who were looking after Georgina and Andre in Ruth's flat in Franciscan Road, Tooting. My parents were waiting to find their own place. The flat was opposite the grounds of Newlands House which used to be a private mental home but was turned into a secret prisoner-of-war interrogation centre. I do not know why Robert Hancock stated in *Ruth Ellis, the Last Woman to be Hanged* that Ruth lived in my parents' flat at 11 Lucien Road (which was a turning off

Franciscan Road). It was not true. The flat was in a big Edwardian house. They had plenty of beds. Ruth was supposed to be living there but wasn't around much and said we could move in. It would have been this time that Ruth's friend Vickie Martin had to move out of the flat. I'd tramped everywhere to find a place but they wouldn't take children into flats. There were two massive rooms, one for Joe (he occasionally stayed the night) the four children and me. The girls slept at one end of a single bed, the boys down the other. In the second bedroom were two folding beds, one for Ruth when she was there, the other for Mother and Father. Ten people in one flat wasn't as hellish at it sounds. Some families lived like this in the fifties and councils treated you like muck if you wanted accommodation. For months Joe slept under the railway arches in his workshop near Rotherhithe Tunnel in the East End of London. He rented two arches where he slept and repaired ships. It was rough. If he needed a bath he'd go to the public baths in Commercial Road.

Andre was going to school in Tooting Bec. My two boys went there as well. I don't even know where the school was; they just went off one morning with Andre and joined. Nothing like today when you check out schools first to see how they're doing in league tables.

Only three things stand out in my mind about Ruth while we stayed at her Tooting Bec flat, probably because we weren't there long, also because Ruth wasn't around much. I remember Ruth playing cards. It's just a scene that flashes into my mind. I can 'see' her as she lay on the sofa looking glamorous, sorting and shuffling cards. She learned how to play in the clubs but wasn't a gambler. She and my parents were playing whist till late at night and I can 'see' them watching her. That night she stayed in the flat. Funny how you remember little things like this. Then there's the big Christmas tree she dragged through the streets that year, and piles of presents she'd bought for everyone.

It must have been around that time that she'd had an abortion or miscarriage. She was in the bathroom trying to wash and was doubled up in pain. I remember she was bleeding and I had to see to her. Somehow she got dressed to go out but was very quiet. I asked if she would be all right going off on her own but she went out without answering. Now I know she took herself to hospital. According to Public Record Office documents she had a fallopian tube pregnancy in December 1952 which required an operation at Middlesex Hospital.

In another PRO document it said her solicitor had difficulty piecing together her medical history. I thought it was because Ruth never went to a GP. Then I discovered she didn't want her medical history revealed at the trial for some reason: 'A supplementary proof dealing with the Accused's past history is attached. Unless material, she does not want too much detail – particularly relating to previous pregnancies referred to below – to come out.' *HO291/237*

She never went to the doctor, not even to show the bruises after she'd taken a beating from David Blakely. Instead she'd come home – the worst place – knowing how many beatings she'd had from Father. Between 1953 and 1955 she was a pitiful sight on so many occasions, especially as there was nothing of her to knock about. I remember the time I bathed her because Mother wouldn't. She told me to look at Ruth's body. My God, the bruises were black and green. Sometimes her eyes were black and her body so stiff she could hardly move that she had to stay at home. When I think of poor Ruth,

I wonder what she did to deserve this. She'd casually say: 'Look at these marks on my body. I can't go out until they're gone.'

The abortions were something else. Don't forget they were forbidden by law and not legalized till 1967. I knew when Ruth had got rid of something. Whether Mother fetched them off, I'm not certain but she knew all the tricks of the trade – look what I went through. It's possible Ruth used the services of the gynaecologist first, perhaps the tall man with black-rimmed spectacles to whom I was later introduced to at the Little Club, but whose name I didn't learn. Mother would do the dirty work afterwards. Once Ruth dashed home in a taxi because of the bleeding. I'm surprised she got around like she did. But Mother helped out by giving her a Parrish's pick-me-up tonic.

It was the beginning of 1953; Pauline had come out of hospital after eight months. I gave her salt baths twice a day because she'd been covered in scabs. Her skin was tight and tender. If she fell over she was frightened and screamed like hell: 'Oh my burns!' But she was a fighter. Within days of Pauline coming home my mother got nasty. She said suddenly that she wanted us out even though it was Ruth's idea we stayed there. We'd given them food and rent and I cooked the evening meal for everyone, but she just told us to go. Mother created all the time because I gave Pauline special food, when all I was doing was keeping up with the hospital's recommendations. And another thing – my brother Julian turned up out of the blue and decided he didn't like my children as much as Ruth's.

I was five months pregnant with my fifth child, Martin. I put all the children's things and mine into a suitcase and walked out. I heard the door being bolted behind me. What sort of mother would do such a rotten thing? I was pregnant, had four children including Pauline suffering from burns. We walked to the police station. I was desperate. My children were tired and I asked the police where I could get into a rest home. He told me to go back home. I said I couldn't, my mother had locked me out. I walked to the half-way house at 367 Fulham Road; it's where we stayed for approximately two months. Those are the days I try to forget. We slept in a dormitory-type ward with beds either side. There were people whose children had TB. Joe wasn't with me because the refuge was for women. All the time I was writing to the council begging them to get me out of there.

We eventually moved into a four-bedroom council maisonette in Cotmandene Crescent in St Paul's Cray. It was above a green-grocer, then a bank took over and opened up. The Richardsons, the notorious London gangsters, lived in that area. He was a window cleaner but that was a sideshow to cover up what he was really doing. I knew the wife and only knew the name Richardson because Joe said to me: 'He's a bloody gangster.'

Martin was born on 21 September 1953. Pauline remembers how she and Marlene hung around outside Joe's and my bedroom waiting for him to arrive. There was a box outside the door, which they thought he came in, a bit like a gift. Pauline still has memories of the first few days at St Paul's Cray and of Joey and Christopher pushing her like the clappers in a pushchair around the balcony. It was on that balcony, exactly two years later, with our baby Martin in a big pram, that I was willing myself to die – I couldn't live with Ruth's death. My feelings will never be any different.

I hadn't seen Ruth for two or three months. She was up in the West End club and not coming home at night and I'd been in the Fulham Road hostel with the children. Then one day I had a surprise. I was cutting the hedge outside our maisonette in St Paul's Cray and could see someone who looked like Ruth carrying baby Georgina but I couldn't be sure it was her. She'd always had a big stride and walked fast like my mother but now she was walking like a model, swinging as she walked and really confident. I thought, who's this striking blonde coming up the road? She got nearer and I could see it was Ruth. She'd been totally transformed. She was thinner than I'd ever known her to be but it was the hairstyle and hair colouring that made the difference. I remember to this day my words: 'Oh Ruth you've gone blonde and I like it.' She'd had her original auburn colour stripped and changed to platinum blonde. It was immaculately styled. She'd been back to Carroll's but was soon to be promoted to manageress of the Little Club in Brompton Road. I remember sweet rationing ended about that time and she'd brought loads of sweets for the children. She talked more confidently about things I'd never heard of and probably never would. She asked if she could stay. I gave her a big mattress to sleep on. Why she wanted to stay with me I'm not sure. She spent most of the time carrying Georgina up to the phone box. There is a lot about Ruth I didn't know.

From the time she started bleaching her hair her character changed. It was like two different people. Being blonde does that. It made her confident and more carefree. She looked beautiful. She didn't look like a cheap painted doll which was how the papers described her – they made that up. She looked like that other victim, Marilyn Monroe.

I've worked out that this was the time in 1953 that my sister became the Ruth Ellis whom two years later everybody would know, her photograph would be on every newspaper in the country.

10

The Little Club

I had a head and shoulders pencil sketch of Ruth drawn on beige paper. RUTH ELLIS was written in capitals at the bottom. Over the years the picture fell apart and I threw it out. I'll never forget the name of the artist – it was signed Alex with a curl underneath. It was short for Alexander Engleman. He was the commissionaire-cum-doorman and also sketched people at the Little Club at 37 Brompton Road. When Ruth became manageress in 1953 she employed him. He was fifty-seven. Maurie Conley would often take on older men on the door.

In the statement the police took from him on 6 July, seven days before Ruth was executed, he described himself as an 'artist-receptionist'. He didn't mention his main job which was checking members as they came in and keeping the riff-raff out. You had to sign in, in a hardback book. It was very strict – if someone didn't have the right name they didn't get in. It was a high-class, members-only club to begin with, different to other London drinking clubs. Engleman would have guarded the membership book with his life.

Ruth's favourite song in the 1950s was 'Dance with a Stranger'. That's why the 1985 film had that title. Ruth and the Little Club weren't anything like they were portrayed in it. The film made it look more like a saloon bar in Texas. It wasn't like that, except when Blakely was smashing the place up in December 1954, during bouts of drunken, aggressive behaviour. The film made Ruth look like an old tom with a silly high-pitched voice. Her voice wasn't like that. It's typical of how they all missed the point, how the myth about my sister was invented.

In reality the Little Club's membership list read like a *Who's Who* of top people – I saw a few myself. Anyone with money including politicians, royals, scientists, solicitors, barristers, doctors, photographers, racing drivers, magistrates and journalists; CIA, FBI and visiting policemen from abroad; MI5 and MI6 agents working for England, all covering each other; homosexuals; bent coppers; and Blakely, Cussen and Ward. And rich gangsters in and out of prison according to an ex-manager of the club. They all passed through the doors of the Little Club. It was a safe place; most had something to hide. But nobody told tales on anybody. Ruth was in the middle of it. She knew everyone – all the wealthy people and all their secrets. It would have turned any girl's head to work there. The people who congregated at the Little Club were the ones who influenced the government without actually having to go to parliament.

If, as the authorities kept saying, Blakely's shooting was an open-and-shut case of cold-blooded murder, why was the Little Club membership book seized?

The answer is easy; the Establishment needed to hide something about the members. Just like they covered up what happened in 1951 with Burgess and Maclean. In 1955 some important people were being protected, including Cussen and Ward. So where *is* the Little Club membership book? There's no evidence of it in Public Record Office files. If it was destroyed, who destroyed it and on whose authority? Who decides what evidence is destroyed and what is kept?

It is strange that the club is only mentioned casually in passing in the trial. Christmas Humphreys, prosecuting counsel, says right at the beginning: 'Mrs Ellis was a hostess at the Little Club in Knightsbridge. She lived in a flat over it.' That was the only mention – and she was manageress not a hostess. Conveniently Ruth had left the club before the shooting. That's no coincidence, somebody made certain she left to divert attention away from the club and its members.

When she started at the Little Club in 1953, Ruth was earning good money. She'd got a flat that came with the job and shopped at Harrods for her clothes. She always looked glamorous. Each time I went to her flat, three times in all, she'd been washing her beautiful lace panties and bras – black, white, pink, a multitude of colours. They'd be drying round the electric fire. She wore a particular perfume that a man friend gave her: Christian Dior, expensive even then. I gave Georgina a bottle that had been empty for years; it still retained its smell.

I told Ruth that I'd like her life, she seemed to have fun. Her reply was always: 'Muriel, I'll tell you what. Don't ever think about doing club work. I wouldn't want you to do it. You wouldn't like it. It takes ten years off your life.'

In her case it took the rest of her life.

I was nervous going to her flat but Ruth insisted that the prostitutes upstairs would never know I'd been. Why she said that I don't know. Andre was having his sandwiches that day when this noise started above us. I didn't know what was going on. Ruth banged a broom on the ceiling shouting: 'Shut up you dirty buggers.' I knew then it was the prostitutes upstairs.

Everything in Ruth's bedroom was white – including the eiderdown decorated with tassels and bobbles and the sheets. She was a spotlessly clean girl. Which is why I couldn't understand a witness statement that said she was untidy at her flat in Egerton Gardens, Kensington, where she lived for two months prior to the shooting. Mind you at that time she was out of her mind, brainwashed, filled up with Pernod and acting like a demented robot.

I'd stay two hours and have a cup of tea with her when the club was closed. She'd always give me a bone china cup and saucer and sardine sandwiches. There was no sign of drinks around the flat. She had a bed settee in the sitting room that Mother slept on – she stayed to look after the children till she and Father went into service in Ferncroft Avenue, Hampstead.

One Sunday afternoon I was there. Auntie Vick, Joe's sister, had the children because Joe wasn't around. He was dodging about, 'ducking and diving' everywhere as he said, trying to feed the family. He worked for F. E. Walkers at the Tower of London. They had three pleasure boats. (Ruth always asked about him: 'How's the old man, the miserable old so-and-so,' she'd say. Then she'd remind me about my promise not to say anything about Father raping us because she was making a life for herself.) Ruth had slatted Venetian blinds that she complained had to be washed regularly. There was a lot of tooting outside. I glanced through the slats. She immediately whispered, pointing to the window: 'Put that down quick Muriel. If he knows I'm in he'll come in and wreck the place.' She was talking about Blakely. He and his friends were crammed in a racing car – the car Ruth's money went on. He was banging on his hooter to come in.

Peter Nolan, who managed the club soon after Ruth died, when it became known as Dorothy's Club, said there's a lot of mystery attached to the place. I'll tell you what I can because it was quite a place. The doorway's still there but in the 1950s there was a jewellery and umbrella shop downstairs, the club was on the first floor, Ruth's flat next and two flats on the fourth and fifth floors. When we went in, to me it was mainly mature, refined-looking men in there. You could tell by their faces how refined they were and by the way they spoke. It was a place for men to ease their frustrations, between three o'clock in the afternoon and eleven o'clock at night. It was for the more mature type, not the youngsters who had rock 'n' roll clubs to go to. I felt comfortable but it got noisy with swanky people's la-de-da voices. That's all that were allowed in, so-called gentlemen and ladies. There were lots of flighty ones – rich men are worse than the poor.

On my first visit, there was an upright piano in a little alcove; a girl called Maria or Maureen used to play classical music. She was older than Ruth and was either French or German. I remember Ruth saying she used to transmit secret messages during the war via the piano wherever she played. Then suddenly Maria disappeared, Ruth never saw her again. She was very vague about it.

I sat at the bar on a high stool with long chrome legs. There were eighteen or so people in there including the hostesses. Ruth was the lady of the place. I can see her standing there in a black dress, with a dotted bow at the neck and a pleat that opened up like a concertina. She wasn't over made up, just right. She didn't do bar work unless they were busy. It was the hostesses' job to sell as many drinks as possible. The more they sold the more money she'd make. As manageress she had to talk to people, encouraging them to spend at the bar.

I was impressed with her. She never appeared excited at seeing up-market people. She enjoyed the thrill of working there and wanted to be one of them. I'd never seen her so well dressed – she looked refined and lovely. Only that day I thought she'd aged a lot. She was more like a woman of thirty-eight than twenty-seven. She was blonde and it suited her. The trouble is men had the wrong opinion of blondes, they thought they were ready to fall into bed at the drop of a hat.

Ruth made the customers feel welcome. Far from being the dumb blonde she's been portrayed as, she chatted to guests about politics, motor racing, horse racing and dancing. I think she had been tutored about politics knowing she'd have to talk to educated people. She'd learned a lot in a short space of time from her friends Dorothy Foxon and 'Irish' Molly, and while she was being transformed.

Dorothy took over running the Little Club, with Peter Nolan as manager, renaming it Dorothy's Club, immediately after the suicide of the interim manageress after Ruth's sacking, Linda Justice, another of Ruth's friends. She was twenty-eight and was manageress for only a few months.

Dorothy was a white South African war widow in her late thirties. Peter Nolan said she attracted the young boys. He described her as short, homely-looking with a round face, highlights in her dark hair and 'heavily veiled,' in other words she wore lots of make-up. She wasn't interested in cigarettes and drinks. Cards were her thing – she was a seasoned poker player and played illegal 'chemmy' games (*chemin de fer*) in posh homes. She told Peter (and it became common knowledge) that she'd met her husband Keith Foxon in South Africa during the war, that he was from Dorking in Surrey and was killed in action in the Fleet Air Arm. And she stayed with her late husband's family in Dorking after the war when she arrived in this country, before moving to London.

Foxon was an uncommon name. I found only two on the voters' list in Dorking – William and Mildred Foxon. Their address was Bembridge in Pilgrims Way, coincidentally a stone's throw from Lord Ashcombe's home where I trained as a lady's maid. When Monica Suffolk, a neighbour of the Foxons, recalled her memories of Bembridge and Mr Foxon and his South African girlfriend I realized I did not know the whole truth about Ruth's friend Dorothy. Mrs Suffolk lived in Pilgrims Way during the war then, following her marriage, moved to Sorrento opposite the Foxons' house in 1945. She is probably the only person now with first-hand knowledge of the Foxons at Bembridge. She had a story to tell:

The Foxons, I don't remember anything at all about the parents, but we knew their son who lived at Bembridge. We were in the same social circle. We were told in confidence that he, I can't remember his name, was shot down in the RAF in Germany and miraculously got back to England through all the escape routes – but they wouldn't discuss it.

It would have been between 1946 and 1948 that we socialized with him. I recall one occasion, I was about twenty-two, we went as a foursome – he and his South African girlfriend, my husband and myself – to the Mirabelle nightclub in Berkeley Square in London. There were two bands, Joe Loss and Edmundo Ros, the Latin American band. She, the South African girlfriend, was something to do with nightclubs and was close to somebody influential in the nightclub world. I can't think of his name. She had big connections. In those days it was top of the list to go to the Mirabelle and we stayed overnight in the Hyde Park Hotel. We had to buy whisky at an extraordinary price. I should imagine her life was in London and she'd met him [Mr Foxon] at one of the Forces clubs in London. He had a boyish face and she seemed to be older than him. She was quite dark, vivacious and extrovert. And there was money there. He was a bit enamoured of her. She was the leader of the young man. She reckoned she could get us a brand new car from South Africa, I don't know what she was but we paid her the money, about £400 and never saw the car. Mr Foxon left in 1952, we moved out in 1961 and lost touch with him.

So much for Dorothy's husband being killed in the war. What was Dorothy's motive for telling Peter Nolan a false story? I didn't understand. Or were these just people of the same name mixing in the same circles at the same time? If so, what a coincidence. Mrs Suffolk did not remember Mr Foxon's first name or that of his South African girlfriend. There is no record of Keith Foxon on the electoral roll at any time; between 1945 and 1952 the only voters at Bembridge were William and Mildred Foxon.

I thought Ruth knew Dorothy from the original Blue Angel nightclub at 14 Berkeley Street, infamous in its time, and where Dorothy was manageress. But I discovered their friendship went back further. Ruth and Vickie Martin had actually

122

known Dorothy since their days at the Court Club, where Stephen Ward was a regular visitor. Peter told me that Dorothy was a hostess there. He said: 'That's where she came into the picture with Ruth along with 'Irish' Molly. Most girls would have moved from club to club as and when they needed work.'

Back to Ruth at the Little Club. She went from person to person saying 'How do you do' and shaking hands, never giving them a kiss. She wasn't that way inclined and she didn't talk about sex. She was sociable and pleasant – in other words a good manageress.

She never spoke about the clients. She was extremely confidential; she had to be. She ran the club well. That's why Maurie Conley gave her the job. The posh people could go there, almost like a den, and not be recognized. And it was a place where they wouldn't get found out. To begin with the Little Club was very up-market; that is until the girls upstairs spoiled it and turned it into a place of prostitution. But they still did get rich and influential men continually running up and down the stairs with them – some were more discreet than others.

When customers bought Ruth drinks she'd leave them on the counter and drink a glass of water from underneath. She only had the odd drink. Her job was getting everyone else to drink. She apparently liked Pernod and made more commission on it than G and T.

People often ask who I saw at the Little Club. Here is a list of members who would have been known to Ruth. Compiled from thorough research and first-hand information, it is just a glimpse of a few members while she was manageress there.

Little Club Members 1953/1954:

King Hussein of Jordan, who became king in 1952, ex-Harrow school and Sandhurst, racing car driver and well known to David Blakely

King Farouk of Egypt, who was forced into exile by President Nasser in 1954

King Feisal of Iraq, ex-Harrow school, cousin of King Hussein of Jordan, assassinated in 1958.

(The double agent Kim Philby was connected with King Farouk, King Hussein and King Feisal. Kim Philby's father, Harry St John Philby had been associated with Middle Eastern politics since 1920, Kim had Arab half-brothers from his Arab stepmother Rozy.)

The dashing American film star, Douglas Fairbanks Junior.

The socialite Duchess of Argyll.

Donald Campbell, who achieved the world land speed record in the racing car 'Bluebird'.

Ben Lyon and his wife Bebe Daniels, American stars of film and radio, particularly popular in *Life with the Lyons* on BBC Radio.

Richard Lyon, actor son of Ben Lyon and Bebe Daniels.

Character actor Ronnie Fraser.

Film stars Victor Mature, Stanley Baxter and Burt Lancaster.

Rugged looking actor/singer Paul Carpenter.

Peter Rachman, the London landlord who exploited slum tenants.

Raymond Nash (the partner of Peter Rachman).

Paul Adam, middle-aged band leader at Les Ambassadeurs in Park Lane.

Lady Docker, known for her ostentatious style of living. Her husband Sir Bernard owned gold-plated Rolls Royces. Her son Lance Cunningham was also a member.

Danny Kaye, the Hollywood star of Russian parentage.

Billy Butlin, the holiday camp entrepreneur.

The Marquis of Milford Haven, the Duke of Edinburgh's cousin, and best man at his marriage to the present Queen Elizabeth.

The Maharaja of Cooch Behar, educated at Harrow and Trinity, Cambridge, playboy and lover of Vickie Martin.

Lord Montagu of Beaulieu, involved in homosexual scandals in the 1950s; owner of the most successful car museum.

Michael Pitt Rivers, involved in the 1950s scandal with Lord Montagu of Beaulieu.

Journalist Peter Wildeblood, also involved in 1950s scandal with Lord Montagu. He was called as a witness on the 1954–1957 Departmental Committee on Homosexual Offences and Prostitution.

Gordon Winter, journalist, played illegal 'chemmy' card games with his great friend Dorothy Foxon.

Diana Dors, larger-than-life blonde British film star.

Dennis Hamilton, married to Diana Dors, played illegal 'chemmy' games with Dorothy Foxon.

'Dandy' Kim Caborn-Waterfield, a better class of criminal.

John Caborn-Waterfield, 'Dandy' Kim's brother.

Sir Mortimer Wheeler, TV archaeologist and Keeper of the London Museum.

Tony Van den Bergh, journalist and co-author of *Ruth Ellis, a Case of Diminshed Responsibility?*

Antony Armstrong-Jones, photographer, became Lord Snowdon when he married Princess Margaret.

Stephen Ward, osteopath, pimp and secret agent.

Antony Beauchamp, photographer, friend of 'Baron' Nahum and Stephen Ward and a member of the notorious Thursday Club (a post-war group of hard-drinking men from top London society, including the Duke of Edinburgh, the Marquis of Milford Haven and Stephen Ward). His wife Sarah Churchill was the daughter of Prime Minister Winston Churchill.

'Baron' Nahum, friend of Antony Beauchamp, Stephen Ward, Prince Philip and a member of the Thursday Club.

Patsie Morgan, fashion model.

Stirling Moss, the brilliant driver, who won sixteen

Grand Prix races but never won the Formula 1 World Championship.

Peter Collins, the quiet racing driver who won three Grand Prix races and crashed to his death in 1958.

Mike Hawthorn, the flamboyant, blond racing driver, who won three Grand Prix races.

Clive Clairmont, racing driver and good friend of Ruth.

David Blakely.

Desmond Cussen.

Carole and Anthony Findlater.

Jackie Lockhart, who was a friend of Ruth.

I went to the Little Club one evening to collect Easter eggs from Ruth. The clients were coming in. Two distinguished-looking men came over to me. They didn't introduce themselves but one said that he 'takes those bits away from you women'. He was a gynaecologist. I said: 'Oh really.' He thought I didn't know what he was talking about. He was tall with tinted, black tortoiseshell pebble-glasses; he almost looked in disguise. I said to the other one, a grey-haired, well-dressed man in his sixties: 'What do you do?' He replied: 'I'm an archaeologist.' He wasn't kidding. It doesn't matter what their job is, they all have the same urge. He said he'd take me to dinner to some nice hotel and 'if I played my cards right I'd come home in a taxi.' I said no. He kept touching my legs. Rich people don't care what they do in front of anybody. He thought I was one of them sitting there, I mean the prostitutes. He'd taken a fancy to me. Ruth told me afterwards he was famous, he was Mortimer Wheeler. They hadn't been speaking to me for long when I felt Ruth was rushing me out of the club. Originally, I thought she didn't want me chatted up by her clients. Looking at it now, it's more likely she didn't want me recognizing anyone and talking.

Ruth didn't introduce me to Cussen and Blakely; she just pointed them out. Cussen looked like a snake, an old-fashioned spiv with dark Brylcreemed hair and a thin moustache that didn't look natural. Something about him was immediately obvious to me. In the same way nothing added up about her marriage to George Ellis, which was a set-up, I knew as I looked at Cussen sitting alone at a table, that Ruth was involved in something shady, but I didn't know what. That was the first and last time I saw him until the day after the shooting when he brought Andre and my parents to Haverstock Court, though he told a different story at the trial.

The way Cussen came on the scene in 1952 was peculiar. He'd met Ruth at Carroll's Club, run at that time by a horrible man called Ronnie so I've heard. Cussen introduced her to Blakely there, then allowed Blakely to steal her – an odd thing to do. What never came out and was new to me is that Blakely was bisexual. I read a letter at the Public Record Office from Mr Bickford to the Under Secretary of State at the Home Office, dated 9 July 1955. It confirmed what everybody in the motor racing world knew, including Cussen. Bickford refers in the letter to a conversation he had with Ruth where she spoke of the homosexual practices Blakely was addicted to at school. So why did Cussen introduce Ruth to him? It was clearly part of the plot. Between them they'd make a suitable combination for intelligence gathering within their social circle; both attracted to men for different reasons. That is why Cussen wanted the relationship between the pair to flourish.

Ruth fell in love with motor racing. Blakely was a racing driver and to her that meant glamour. And Cussen knew that. He knew Ruth wanted glamour more than anything, and to be away from the poverty at home. From the time she met Blakely she never mentioned anyone else.

My first impression of Blakely at the Little Club was that he looked like a panda with big black staring eyes and a thin, pale face. He wouldn't look at me; he was too busy showing off like a schoolboy. He leaned against the bar wearing his smart suit and schoolboy tie that was the style in the fifties, laughing with the girls and watching Ruth at the same time. He was a bit taller than she was. She was five feet two, the same as me.

Mother met Blakely regularly when she stayed in Ruth's flat to look after Andre and Georgina. He didn't live there full-time, he slept with Ruth two or three times a week, then took bouquets of flowers to make it up with her after he'd beaten her up. Although he lived in Culross Street, off Park Lane, and was kept by his wealthy stepfather Humphrey Cook, he pretended to be very hard up. Ruth gave him up twice but he wouldn't leave her alone. I wished Mother had told me what was going on but she wouldn't. She was like all the women in our family – if someone says don't say anything you don't.

Another extract from Mother's 1955 statement for Mr Bickford, exactly as she wrote it, describes Ruth at this time:

She became manageress of the Little Club. she took a great interest in the bussenis and made this club pay. She was very happy for about a year. Of course David blakely paid her visits all the Time. Not of and on as it was said in the Court but all the time I was living in the flat. and I wasn't blind to the fact, I did not care for Blackly. (reason) this man lived on my daughter's hurnings. He would sneak in the club every night just about when all the costumers left and sneak out again at 9 in the morning. She paid his drinking Bills and paid for his sigs and paid for several other items. He would get drunk time and again if she talked to the men in the club. This was her business of being pelight. He would knock her about terrible. One night when the people had all gone I could hear voices down below. It was coming from the bar. He was saying something to her but could not hear clearly what it was about. A few minutes later I heard a voice altought someone was being shooked. I ran downstairs. He had my daughter by the tooth. She had marks on both sides of her neck. Several of her friends asked her how she got them. On another accation the left side of her face was swollen, she had a black eye. Her left leg was in bandiges. She attended Middlesex hospital for these injuries. He reminded me of the second George Ellis. Yes David Blackley was a brute . . .'

Blakely used amyl nitrate for sex. Public Record Office files reveal that it was found in Blakely's pocket after he was shot. It's a prescription heart stimulant kept in ampoules and broken under the nose during sex. This wasn't mentioned at the trial, probably because Mr Lewis Charles Nickolls, director of the Metropolitan Police Laboratory didn't have time to explain. It sickens me to read how Christmas Humphreys called him at the trial: 'My Lord, I will now call Mr Nickolls because I know he is anxious to get away.' It was my sister's life on the line. He merely said amyl nitrate was used 'in cases of heart disease to cause dilation of the veins and also in the relief of asthma'. Nobody questioned at the trial if Blakely suffered from these problems. Blakely's own GP hadn't prescribed them.

Blakely gave me the shivers. I looked at him and thought he looked like a mother's boy. He acted childishly when he was speaking to Mike Hawthorn the racing driver. Hawthorn was smart and I remember his blond hair and ruddy complexion. He was good-looking and a proper racing driver, although my driving instructor who taught Hawthorn to drive said he might have been good on the track but hadn't a clue about driving on the road. He took me out on drives to where Hawthorn wrapped himself round a tree on the Guildford by-pass in 1959 and killed himself.

I remember Stirling Moss came in but apparently he doesn't remember going to the Little Club. He was smart, wearing evening dress and looked as though he was going out for dinner, and was standing with Patsie Morgan, his girlfriend at the time. She was much taller than Moss. I noticed this tall, sophisticated figure in her twenties, who had all the men hanging round her. Ruth whispered: 'That's Patsie Morgan the model and that's Mike Hawthorn and Stirling Moss.'

11

The Ruth Ellis Network

The following words written by Ruth's solicitor for her defence counsel may not sound intriguing, but to me, reading them along with papers at the Public Record Office that have been in closed files for half a century, they are important: 'Apparently the Findlaters got to know Blakely when Blakely was in the Army. They were a foursome consisting of Mr and Mrs Findlater and Blakely and his sister.' *HO291/237 A.3 (9)*

I point this out because it's an example of how the public has been misled. According to previously published information Blakely first met Anthony Findlater in 1951 when Blakely replied to Findlater's advertisement regarding an Alfa Romeo. Maybe Blakely did look at the car that year, but the fact is he and Findlater met up in 1949, when Blakely was in the army, a detail not mentioned at the trial.

These are the final 'cast' in Ruth's story: David Blakely, Ruth's lover, was a public schoolboy down on his uppers, aspiring to be a racing driver; Anthony Findlater, also a public schoolboy, tinkered around as a car mechanic and was unable to get a permanent job; Carole Findlater, Anthony's wife, was a journalist of Russian origin and jealous of Ruth; Desmond Cussen, Ruth's 'alternative' lover, a tobacconist businessman, about whom very little was known; Clive Gunnell, a friend of

David Blakely's and Anthony Findlater's, who described himself as a Mayfair car salesman.

I will not repeat misleading descriptions that camouflaged the true identities of these people over the years. It's clear from the transcript of the trial and police investigation, that nobody was interested in people's backgrounds. In an open-and-shut case of cold-blooded murder, which is what it was made to look like, where a prostitute has murdered one of her lovers in a fit of passion; it didn't matter about anybody else. But it did matter. Those individuals should have been thoroughly investigated.

Christmas Humphreys, the prosecuting counsel at the trial, defended his opinion twenty-seven years later when he said to Andre, Ruth's son: 'As a barrister for fifty years I was just putting the facts of the actual murder. I knew nothing of the background and I didn't care.' Andre secretly taped their conversation at the Buddhist Society in London, just weeks before committing suicide. How blinkered Humphreys was. For it was *exactly* what was going on in the background that led to the shooting of Blakely on Easter Sunday 1955 outside The Magdala in Hampstead, and to my sister's death by hanging two months later.

The truth about the crime is hidden in the backgrounds of the bunch of people Ruth mixed with – characters more complicated than you'd gather from their simple statements made in court – who I believe conspired against Ruth. A common factor drew them together. What was that factor? The puzzle started unravelling when I learned that Stephen Ward, now known for his spying activities, was involved with Ruth – a fact previously unknown to the public. Cussen's mysterious behaviour also pointed to undercover operations.

To me, the Public Record Office was quiet and scary. Even scarier when I walked with files about Ruth under my arm, then opened them to find thousands of letters begging that Ruth shouldn't die. Most were handwritten. Some were religious, praying for Ruth. Most were addressed to the Home Secretary, Gwilym Lloyd-George, some to the Queen. A handful received standard replies from the Home Secretary, saying there was no reason to give a reprieve. Sometimes his secretary left him notes saying: 'Do you think this letter warrants the usual reply?' I could have rammed the letters down the politicians' throats.

I saw some documents to do with the case, not everything though. What seemed to be missing is itself partly suggestive. Snippets added to the jigsaw – concealed in screeds of technical words. Bits about a homosexual relationship between Blakely and Anthony Findlater. A long memorandum from journalist Peter Grisewood to Lord Mancroft mentions a conversation he (Grisewood) had with Mr Bickford following Ruth's death. Mr Bickford 'hinted at homosexual relationships' between Blakely and Mr Findlater, saying he (Bickford) had evidence of this but had felt it unwise to call it. What was going on?

There were other findings. At the PRO you can read in the transcript, released forty years after Ruth's death, what the witnesses said at the trial on 20 June 1955. More interesting is what witnesses said at the magistrate's court on 28 April 1955. It becomes clear that the prosecution witnesses were influenced. Certain points made at the magistrate's court were modified by the time the witnesses gave evidence at the Old Bailey, giving statements a different meaning and so guaranteeing it would be an open-and-shut case. In Christmas

Ruth *(centre)* aged 9 at Worting County Junior School, Hampshire

My parents, Berta and Arthur Neilson

Ruth aged 24 with auburn hair

White Hart Hotel in Brasted, Kent, today

Ruth's friends Deborah Kerr and Tony Bartley

George Ellis

1950's aerial view of School of Navigation, Warsash
with Household Brigade Yacht Club in foreground

Ruth (*4th on left*) in 1951 film 'Lady Godiva Rides Again' Diana Dors and Joan Collins (*8th and 5th on right*), Jane Hart (*far left*)

Ruth in 'Lady Godiva Rides Again'

Ruth's best friend Vickie Martin

Antony Beauchamp

Stephen Ward in his sports car

Humphreys' set of magistrate's court documents (Crim1/2582) words were crossed through.

This one caught my eye. Clive Gunnell was with Blakely at The Magdala during the shooting. Gunnell said: 'I saw Blakely lying on the pavement and the accused firing a gun. She was pointing the gun at his back.' The transcript was altered to read: 'And the accused was firing a gun into his back.' This from Police Constable Alan Thompson who was drinking in The Magdala at the time of the shooting: 'She was holding the revolver loosely (*crossed out*) pointing it downwards at a slant' (*crossed out*) becomes 'She was holding the revolver in her right hand pointing it downwards.' She is no longer holding it loosely at an angle – it's pointing straight down. Those witnesses either had bad memories or were persuaded to change their statements sometime between the magistrate's court hearing and the Old Bailey trial.

Furthermore, you can only find those alterations by comparing the transcript at the PRO with the magistrate's court documents, which weren't at the PRO but should have been. The file was opened from Long Closure and removed. The PRO could not say where it was. A friend mentioned an essay about Ruth called 'No Angels'. Its author Annette Balinger stated the file Crim1/2582, which she'd used for reference in 1996, was at the Royal Court of Justice. Six years later it was still there. That's not in the public domain. After being given the run around, Monica Weller was permitted to view it at the Royal Court of Justice in April 2002. The file was still listed as FRUSTRATED (not available) at the Public Record Office in June 2003. It was eventually made available at the Public Record Office on 12 January 2004.

What else was omitted about witnesses at the trial? Who were they and how were they really involved at the time of

Blakely's murder? And why, according to one document, did Ruth's learned defence counsel Mr Melford Stevenson decide on Monday morning, the day of the trial, to 'Subject the witnesses of the prosecution to a minimum of cross-examination'? Who was being protected? Seeing these documents it's obvious that Ruth was short-changed by our justice system.

To find out how these people came together meant going back in time. What did they have in common? What is the connection between Findlater a car mechanic, Gunnell a car salesman and Blakely a racing driver? And between businessman Desmond Cussen, dentist George Ellis and journalist Carole Findlater? And there's society photographer Antony Beauchamp. And Stephen Ward, osteopath, artist and pimp. And Ruth. What drew them together?

David Blakely was born on 17 June 1929. He went to Shrewsbury school, paid for by his stepfather Humphrey Wyndham Cook, about whom little is known, and was called up for National Service in 1949. He was in the Highland Light Infantry. Van den Bergh and Marks wrote: 'His army career was a facsimile of his school record. He did nothing outstanding but managed to remain out of trouble.' But they didn't mention that he was not in the army for the usual two years. He was in and out in 1949. The Army List states: 'Blakely D.M.D 'R' December 1949.' The Index says R 'denotes release to unemployment or from embodied service under the terms of the Royal Warrant dated 18.6.45 or Army order 1945.' The Army Personnel Centre explained that every soldier will discharge under certain paragraphs. R means he's been released from regular army service for a reason as undramatic as flat feet: 'It seemed he had an ultra brief military career. Things maybe didn't go well for him. If it had been a gross breach of discipline it would have been court-martial.' But he wasn't court-martialled. And it can't have been his health that gave him an 'R'. Dr R.G. MacGregor, Blakely's own GP, is on file as saying Blakely's health was good.

Like David Blakely, Anthony Seaton Findlater went to public school – Hurstpierpoint. He was born on 29 April 1921, making him thirty-four at the time of Ruth's trial, and eight years older than Blakely. Ruth obviously felt Findlater was involved with the shooting. I've read Mr Bickford's Plea for a Reprieve, sent to the Home Secretary shortly before she was hanged. He said Ruth entered the witness box 'disheartened and somewhat bewildered' because Findlater had not been seriously cross-examined. Bickford quotes her: 'I don't mind hanging – but why should they [Findlaters] get away with it.'

From the transcript of the trial, we learn the following about Findlater's background. Prosecuting counsel Christmas Humphreys, examines him:

Q. Anthony Seaton Findlater. Is that your name?
A. Yes.
Q. And you live at 29 Tanza Road, N.W.3?
A. Yes.
Q. You are a motor engineer?
A. Yes.
Q. And you live there with your wife and little girl?
A. Yes.
Q. How long had you known Blakely the man who died?
A. About 5 years.

Melford Stevenson, defence counsel, cross-examined:

Q. You for some time received £10 a week, did you
    not, from Blakely for your services in connection
    with a racing motor car which he was building?
A. Yes, that is right.
Q. Was that at that time your sole source of income?
A. Yes, it was.

The document 'Brief to Counsel to Appear on Behalf of the
Accused' indicated that Blakely paid Findlater £10 a week. Blakely
became short of money so Findlater found a job with a man
named Simmons where he worked with Clive Gunnell, another
prosecution witness. Before that Findlater had not been earning
his living – it was left more or less to Carole Findlater, who
according to Robert Hancock was woman's editor at the *Daily
Mail* in 1955, though I have been unable to substantiate this.

The Army List for 1947 shows that Major A.S. Findlater
BEM RCOC was Deputy Assistant Director of Ordnance
Services in the Branch of the Master General of the Ordnance
between 1945 and 1947. Was this really the person who eight
years later tinkered around with cars, didn't have a proper job
and relied on his wife's income from journalism? The
Hurstpierpoint archivist has a record of Findlater in 1946 on
a government course in business administration. This car
mechanic was in the Royal Canadian Ordnance Corps, was
awarded a British Empire Medal, then became a Civil Servant
at the War Office dealing with guns that had come back from
an army of five million men during the war.

Anthony and Ruth Findlater lived at 52 Colet Gardens in
Hammersmith between 1951 and 1952, a few hundred yards

from Cussen's shop near Hammersmith Broadway. By the time they moved into their next address, 29 Tanza Road, Hampstead, in March 1954, Ruth Findlater had changed her name to Carole R. Findlater. I also found Carole listed as Carole Sonin (her maiden name) at 56 Parliament Hill, Hampstead in 1954 while she was living round the corner in Tanza Road. It was no distance from the steps of 29 Tanza Road to 56 Parliament Hill – looking across the street diagonally, you could wave to the upstairs occupants.

Gladys Yule and her husband lived at 24 Parliament Hill. She's the witness who said she saw the shooting of David Blakely outside The Magdala. Claude and Ivy Lusty also lived at number twenty-four. Then there's David Lusty at 43 Parliament Hill. I expect he was related to Claude and Ivy, Lusty being an unusual surname. David Lusty was one of two young fellows that gave statements to the police. They were twenty yards from the shooting and weren't called as witnesses.

This may sound like an Agatha Christie mystery unfolding, each player with a role to play leading to a pre-planned conclusion. But fifty years ago, the shooting of David Blakely was a perfectly planned operation carried out ruthlessly by experts who had to cover up the spying scandal of the century – Burgess and Maclean's defection to Russia. Ruth and Blakely knew too much, so the Establishment had one solution: eliminate both of them.

The characters playing a major role in Ruth's life and death had privileges and they had their privacy. They lived in a world where their background, their home, their family, their real work was a secret. They were masters in disguise – they knew how to disappear, change their names, disguise their addresses and their house names. They do not appear on electoral rolls at crucial times. They don't appear on service lists for longer than two years. I'll give some examples: George Ellis manages two years in the Air Force between January 1941 and November 1942, simultaneously managing his dental surgery in Sanderstead, then disappears off the Air Force list. But it was his outings close to home on the Surrey–Kent border that were incredible: Kath and Teddy Preston owned the White Hart Hotel in Brasted in Kent that Ruth visited after the war with Deborah Kerr. Kath Preston described in her book *Inn of the Few* how George wasn't 'brave enough to go to war'. But in 1940, she said he actually cycled night after night on his pushbike from Croydon to the White Hart – a round trip of thirty miles – risking the worst of the Blitz. Kath's daughter Valerie says, 'It was probably for the company he knew there, the people from Biggin Hill, the Battle of Britain pilots. It was a bit like a club. It must have been worth his while to come over.' What was George up to?

Antony Beauchamp, the photographer, is on the Army List from 1941 to 1942 with no further service record. Beauchamp was clearly in Intelligence. In his autobiography he described how he gathered propaganda with a group of journalists for the Ministry of Information, ensuring that British people reading newspapers didn't think our boys were forgotten in the war against Japan. It's called spin doctoring now.

David Blakely comes off the service list, disappearing from 1949 until 1951, then reappearing as a trainee at the Hyde Park Hotel, London. Did they all leave the services with flat feet? I don't think so. I believe their business was deception.

The Hyde Park Hotel was, and still is, at 66 Knightsbridge. Turning the pages of Anthony Masters' book, *Inside Marbled*

Halls, we learn that this grand hotel boasted the most glittering clientele in Europe, a *Who's Who* of royalty, politicians and celebrities. It was known as Westminster's alternative place of government as the Cabinet dined in the restaurant. Visitors, some of whom were members of the Little Club across the road, included Queen Elizabeth, Prince Philip, Lord and Lady Mountbatten, King Hussein of Jordan, Sir Winston Churchill, Lord Montagu of Beaulieu and Lady Docker.

I'm thinking about Blakely's job at the hotel as described by Robert Hancock. He wrote that Humphrey Cook, Blakely's stepfather 'decided that David should have a trade and arranged for him to become a trainee at the fashionable Hyde Park Hotel in Knightsbridge. It was here that Mrs Cook [Blakely's mother] had stayed before her wedding and the family were well known to the management. David was to receive fifty shillings a week from the hotel and an allowance of £5 a week from his mother.' Hancock understated the true nature of this famous hotel, failing to say it was one of the plushest in London, with the best clientele. Van Den Bergh continued the make-believe in his book preferring to focus on the forty-year-old women holidaying in London, whom Blakely mixed with, while their husbands 'remained at work in the North or West'. Yet Peter Wright, former Assistant Director of MI5, briefly mentioned in his book *Spy Catcher*, how MI5 commandeered a fourth floor suite in the Hyde Park Hotel as an operations room in the 1950s. This was no ordinary hotel.

I turned to the foreword of Hancock's book *Ruth Ellis, The Last Woman to be Hanged*. He wrote: 'Many passages [of the book] are based on the long and frank conversations I had with that sad, shocked man, Desmond Cussen, in the weeks that preceded Ruth Ellis's trial at the Old Bailey, and during the time she waited for her execution on 13 July 1955 at Holloway Prison.'

Forty years after Hancock's book was first published I feel sick, thinking of Cussen manipulating and feeding mis-information. Did all the stories published over the years stem from those conversations with Cussen in 1955?

Humphrey Wyndham Cook, described as the wealthy son of a wholesale draper, lived at 38 Upper Brook Street, Mayfair when he married David Blakely's mother Anne in February 1941. Upper Brook Street, parallel to Culross Street and off Park Lane was the favoured address of many Establishment figures. Cook was a neighbour of Lt Col Stewart Graham Menzies at number 23 who was Chief of MI6 between 1939 and 1952 and assumed the code letter 'C'. Captain Lord Louis Mountbatten, Prince Philip's uncle, lived at number 27.

Stephen Ward was a member of the Little Club and was in the Secret Service. It appears from my findings that he was recruited earlier than was thought and was into deception immediately after the war, targeting Ruth in 1950. In *An Affair of State*, Knightley and Kennedy wrote: 'Early in 1950 he [Ward] added another famous name to his list of patients, Bill Astor, a member of the enormously wealthy Anglo-American family . . . The relationship between Ward and Astor blossomed rapidly.' Lord Bill Astor served in Naval Intelli-gence, under Admiral John Godfrey, Head of Naval Intelligence during the Second World War. Lord Astor bought the building at 38 Devonshire Street, where Ward was set up with a consulting room and flat rent-free. Ward had actually practised at that address since 1949 – Lord Bill Astor and Ward were closely connected for at least fourteen years before the 1963 Profumo scandal which began at Cliveden, Astor's country residence. The scandal brought Ward's Secret Service career to an end. He committed suicide in July that year.

I am reminded of Knightley and Kennedy's words in *An Affair of State*: 'Ward's part in transforming Valerie Mewes into Vickie Martin had given him a lot of satisfaction. This was the first time he had played Professor Higgins and he had enjoyed transforming a girl from a humble background into the toast of London . . . Ward's search for someone as unusual and as enchanting as Vickie Martin, his first 'Fair Lady', was to contribute to his downfall.' Ruth was also one of his *first* Fair Ladies.

Ward didn't stop playing war games after the war – he was established in Intelligence, going straight into MI5 at the start of the Cold War. Having found this information I'll have to assume he wasn't working alone around the Mayfair clubs. Others from wartime Intelligence and Special Operations were recruited into MI5 and MI6 and moving in his circle. They knew how to mingle in the set that they wanted to infiltrate. Joe called it the fifth column. They put out lies and disinformation – for example, saying they're doing one thing but actually doing another. They knew how to get inside the minds of the person or organization they wanted to infiltrate. They knew about rumour-mongering, lying and how to control another person's actions and thoughts. They used their skills on Ruth. They tightened the screws until she snapped.

It seems that the British Secret Service and deception are features that link the characters in Ruth's story.

Ruth was impressed with the racing drivers who hung around the Mayfair clubs. She and Vickie often went to the Steering Wheel Club at 2a Brick Street, off Piccadilly. I'd no idea till now that Ward did too. Summers and Dorril confirm in *Honeytrap*: 'He [Ward] also frequented the Steering Wheel Club, nominally a watering hole for motor racing aficionados but also home to a much wider clientele, including the last woman to be hanged in Britain, Ruth Ellis, and her racing driver lover David Blakely. The film star Douglas Fairbanks Jr . . . was another regular, as were a number of MI5 officers.' Also Baron Nahum the court photographer and close friend of Prince Philip, Stephen Ward and photographer Antony Beauchamp, had an adjoining flat and studio at 2b Brick Street, from where he ran his photographic business known as Photo Craft.

The secret agents who frequented places like the Steering Wheel Club and the Little Club, would have practised their patter and blended in with the members. It didn't matter if they were photographers, businessmen or involved with motor racing; whether in the Malayan jungle or the Little Club, they knew how to camouflage themselves having woven and perfected their cover.

The Little Club, Ruth and Blakely's hangout, was also a safe place for high-ranking homosexuals to congregate. Like alcoholics, who were easy prey, homosexuals were open to blackmail and could be compromised and manipulated for information by the experts. Gordon Winter, a journalist who was a friend of Dorothy Foxon, and wrote to me in 1998, said 'Ruth was immensely popular with the gays that frequented the Little Club and they would sit with her at the hostess's table – she handled them brilliantly. I knew one elder gay known as a "mother hen" who used to bring his latest "chicken" [handsome young man who was underage] in and introduce him to Ruth, so that Ruth would assess them for him.'

On 9 July 1955 Ruth's solicitor Mr Bickford wrote to the Under Secretary of State at the Home Office, alleging a homosexual relationship between Anthony Findlater and David Blakely:

> I had an interview this morning with a Dr. Hertzel Creditor of 2 Daleham Gardens, N.W.3, who is prepared to support his statements on oath although most of them amount to theory or hearsay; but are, in my respectful submission, of value. Dr Creditor brought Carole Findlater into the world, he is a great personal friend of Mrs Ray Sonin and Mr Ray Sonin, the brother and sister-in-law of Mrs Carole Findlater. He knows Anthony Findlater and Carole Findlater well. Carole is about thirty or thirty-one years of age. Dr Creditor came forward, unsolicited, as he felt he was in duty-bound to do so. He knows well from conversations he has had with the Sonins that Carole Findlater, about two years ago, openly went off with David Blakely. Clinically, he recognizes Anthony Findlater as a homosexual. Mrs Findlater and Mr Findlater came together again. Later, Mrs Findlater made a remark to Mrs Sonin reported to Dr Creditor: 'Can you imagine anything more humiliating than to have my boyfriend stolen from my [me] by my husband.' Ruth Ellis told me some time ago that David Blakely had told her that when at school he was addicted to homosexual practices . . . [The doctor] thinks that the reason for the close combination of all three, in these extraordinary circumstances, was the relationship between them. This has

some support from . . . who tells me today that she had heard from Cliff Davis and others in the motoring world that Findlater was 'queer.' The relevance of this surprising and nauseating theory to the case of Ruth Ellis is that it explains the deliberate effort of the Findlaters to avoid making any statement which might possibly have the effect of preventing Mrs Ellis from being hanged. I am given to understand that Mrs Findlater has gone to Majorca and I know that my letter and phone calls in an effort to contact her have been ignored.

Ruth was hanged four days later.

Bertram Clive Gunnell, known as Clive, was a thirty-year-old car salesman. We learn this about his background at the trial:

Q. Bertram Clive Gunnell. Is that your name?
A. Yes
Q. I think your place of business as a car salesman is 12 Rex Place, Mayfair.
A. It was.
Q. It was at the end of this affair?
A. Yes
Q. How long had you known the deceased man Blakely?
A. About 5 years
Q. How long had you known Mr Findlater?
A. About 7 [years]

Gunnell emphasized that he no longer worked at 12 Rex Place. In Kelly's Business Directory there were no listings for properties between numbers 11 (Rex Hire Service) and 18. Didn't somebody check this out?

This same smart address behind Park Lane was mentioned at the magistrate's court. Findlater stated: 'On Saturday 9 April I was at 12 Rex Place, Mayfair . . . While we were there doing this [mending Blakely's Vanguard car] the accused telephoned.' In his statement he referred to the Emperor car he and Blakely were building: 'When the car was finished it was kept at 12 Rex Place, Mayfair which is where Mr Gunnell works.' Rex Place comes up again in the solicitor's papers, Bickford said: 'Blakely got short of money and Findlater found a job with a man named Simmons where he worked with Clive Gunnel (a Mayfair car salesman) another prosecution witness.' (HO291/237)

The only information available about Mr Simmons is (according to the rate book) that he lived at 12 Rex Place and paid the rates there between 1952 and 1955. He had a ground floor flat and basement with a garage, not exactly the car sales place we're led to believe. He was not registered on the electoral roll while he lived there, nor was he listed in the telephone directory. This is odd, as surely he would have needed a telephone for the garage and salesroom business he was allegedly running with Gunnell. Further investigations have shown that between 1952 and 1955 there was no commercial phone or street directory listing for that address. So how was Findlater able to receive a call there from Ruth the day before the shooting?

Christmas Humphreys asked Findlater on oath at the trial:

Q. On Saturday 9 April did the accused phone you in
   the morning?
A. Yes

147

Q Did you have any conversation or not?
A. No

What was the business being run from number 12 Rex Place? Findlater and Gunnell made statements at the magistrate's court concerning Blakely's whereabouts on Good Friday 1955. Their explanations are odd. Gunnell said:

> I learned that the accused had been telephoning to find out where Blakely was. If I had wanted him and he wasn't at the Findlaters [on Good Friday] I would have had no idea where to look for him. I would have given it up as hopeless. If he had made an appointment with me, had not kept it and I was worried about him, I would have telephoned the Findlaters first of all. After that I couldn't have thought of anywhere else. If the Findlaters had told me he wasn't there I would have been left wondering what on earth had happened to him and would have had no clue how to resolve my anxiety about him.

He said he had known Blakely approximately four years. That was crossed through to read 'five years'. Findlater, who had also known Blakley for about five years, was also questioned about Blakely's whereabouts on Good Friday evening – when he was giving Ruth the run around, two days before the shooting, pushing her over the edge, not answering her telephone calls and not telling her where Blakely was. Findlater answered:

> I do not know where he went when he left me. He did not tell me. I do not know whether he was going to

Egerton Gardens. If I had been asked at that stage where he probably was after he left me, I should have said Egerton Gardens, with the accused.

It is ridiculous. They both knew Blakely well. Why didn't they mention he might be at 28 Culross Street off Park Lane, the house provided for him free of charge by Humphrey Cook where he had lived since 1951 with his brother Brian, a nanny and Mr Desmond E. English? The house was owned by Mr A. Rothschild, a member of the banking family of which Victor Rothschild was an agent for MI5. Had Findlater and Gunnell forgotten their friend lived five minutes' walk from 12 Rex Place where they kept the Emperor racing car which Findlater and Blakely built? These men worked, drank and went to clubs together for four years but couldn't suggest Blakely might be at home!

They bluffed everyone with their double-dealing. Blakely's friends had kept quiet about the house because it would have ruined the story Blakely spun to Ruth: the one about being hard up; having to scrounge money off her to build the Emperor car; demanding free drinks and cigarettes at the club; and begging Ruth to give him a roof over his head in her one-bedroom flat above the Little Club. When all the while Blakely's home was a smart Mayfair mews house in Culross Street; on every street corner was lord somebody. Mr and Mrs Humphrey Cook lived at number four between 1952 and 1954 in a four-storey house like something out of *Upstairs Down-stairs*. Blakely, who was living in one of London's most prestigious streets, was putting on an act, giving the impression he was hard up. It was a ploy to detract from his wealthy background and away from the Secret Service people whom he was clearly involved with. He was leading a double life. His hard-up story and drunkenness was a cover.

It seems clear why Blakely was murdered. Being a homo-sexual, which was illegal, made him a target for blackmail. He was ideal for secret work, lying and being ruthless for fear of being found out. Like Ruth, he knew too much. He had information on activities which was of utmost importance to the Establishment. By 1955 with his heavy drinking, he was showing serious signs of stress. It would appear his cover was going to be blown.

I'll never forget Ruth's words in a statement she gave to her solicitors Mr Mishcon and Mr Simmons, the day before she was hanged: 'I didn't say anything about it up to now because it seemed traitorous – absolutely traitorous.' Now I see why Ruth lied at her trial – it was to do with national security. I'd say Ruth knew that Cussen was in MI5. She probably thought she was in the same 'club'. But she was never one of them. Like Blakely, she knew who was indulging in illegal activities in clubland. When she had produced enough information she was expendable.

Nobody questioned Ruth properly at the trial. What was the real motive behind her mad activity during that Easter weekend? Why was she chasing from the Findlaters flat in Hampstead thinking Blakely was having an affair with their nanny, to Penn village near High Wycombe in Buckingham-shire where Blakely was supposedly carrying on with Pam Abbot, a happily married woman. (Her name was recently released at the PRO.) Meanwhile Cussen assisted Ruth to stalk Blakely, winding her up and reducing her to a jealous, nervous wreck. Cussen was bent on destroying her. She was set up.

Blakely was buried in the Holy Trinity Church graveyard in Penn, the same graveyard where Donald Maclean was buried at a midnight service in 1975. Another well-kept secret. If Maclean was a traitor why was his body brought back from Russia and buried in the same churchyard as Blakely? It's extraordinary how everything is connected. Maclean's father, an MP and later a leader of the Liberal Party, had a house in Penn. Maclean's mother and brothers lived at Elm Cottage in Beacon Hill for about thirty years. The Griffith-Jones family lived in 'Drews' in Witheridge Lane, Penn; their son Mervyn assisted Christmas Humphreys, the prosecution counsel, at Ruth's trial.

I felt Donald Maclean being buried in the village was an important clue but it was difficult determining precisely what was going on there. But there were too many coincidences and connections to ignore. Here was a gathering of people with secrets. It seems likely that Blakely was involved.

I couldn't find a trace of Anne and Humphrey Cook at The Old Park in Penn until November 1953. What I did stumble on during my electoral roll searches, was an address for David Blakely between 1950 and 1951 – three years before his mother and stepfather officially moved to Penn. He lived at Albi in Witheridge Lane. I wouldn't have given it a second thought except it filled a gap – his whereabouts after leaving the army. Anne Cook was listed there between 1949 and 1950.

Mr Carden owned Carden Motors in Penn in the 1950s. He sold Blakely's HRG sports car for £250 after the shooting. He remembers Blakely:

David Blakely actually had a partnership at Sylicum Pistons Ltd for about eighteen months. He worked with someone called Bortolotti, an Italian chap. David's mother bought him a share in it. The job made it sound as if he had something to do. Not exactly a full-time job, more part-time. He was more or less provided for. Like Michael Keen, the man David took over from, they were both fed with a silver spoon. Keen was killed on the 20 August 1955, racing at Goodwood.

I saw him at odd times when he popped down at weekends because he had a flat in London. He was very much man-about-town. I met them [Ruth and David] in a pub near Aylesbury coming back from Silverstone. He wasn't mechanically minded but was a good driver. They belonged to the British Automobile Racing Club and various other clubs. I can see Ruth now with a gin in her hand. [Maurie] Conley, a little Jewish gentleman, used to come to The Crown pub in Penn. The Griffin in Amersham was David and Ruth's haunt en route for Silverstone – first port of call The Folly at Winslow, then The Griffin.

David Blakely at Albi in Witheridge Lane? That's new to me. There's less than a dozen houses. There's something wrong there.

Even more confusing was when I found Humphrey Cook in the 1950 telephone directory at a house called Granneys. He would have known the Rt Hon The Earl Howe, who lived opposite at Hatchitts in Witheridge Lane. He was big in motor racing, representing the RAC at race meetings. David Wooster ran a milk company in the fifties and knew the properties because of the milk rounds in the village. He said the Cook–

Blakely family, including their children, Brian, Derek, David and a daughter lived for some time at Granneys:

> That was definitely where the whole family lived, a large house in Witheridge Lane, the next house after Drews. It would have been 1949 to 51-time. It sticks in my mind that the name of the house changed for a period; then changed back to the original name Granneys. It struck me as odd as it was only a let. Why the devil would they change it?

12

A Shooting in Hampstead

About lunchtime on 11 April 1955, Bank Holiday Monday, I was cooking the dinner. There was a knock on the door. I turned the cooking down, nervous that Joe would come in and complain that lunch was ruined.

Standing there were my parents, with Andre and Desmond Cussen. I'd no idea what was going on and a terrible feeling filled my stomach. Andre came in with his wooden tuck-box that he took to boarding school filled with goodies. He was a lovely kid. He'd be ten-and-a-half. They hadn't brought any clothes for him, just what he stood up in. Pauline can remember that day, how the boys shifted bedrooms to accommodate Andre.

What happened that Bank Holiday Monday – the fact that Cussen came to our place – is significant to the whole story about Ruth and how she was hanged for murder. I've waited fifty years to tell this to the world.

I knew nothing of what had been going on with Ruth. Apparently she'd lost her job at the Little Club at the beginning of December 1954, moved in with Desmond Cussen at Goodwood Court in Marylebone on 7 December, stayed there till 8 February 1955, then moved in to Egerton Gardens, Kensington with David Blakely on 9 February.

I'd seen Cussen only once before but the minute he stepped through our door I recognized the untrustworthy face that I had seen at the Little Club. He acted sheepishly. Mother said: 'Can Andre go somewhere to play?' I told him to play with the children, not to come down till we called him, and not to get into any mischief. He went upstairs saying: 'Yes, Auntie Muriel.' The children thought it was great that Andre had come for Easter.

I made a cup of tea, wondering what had happened. I couldn't understand why Cussen had brought Andre round. I said: 'What is it, Mother?' She replied: 'Ruth's in the police station. She has shot David Blakely.' I said automatically: 'I hope it's not serious. Will he recover?' My parents stood awkwardly by the fireplace. Mother whispered: 'He's dead.'

I couldn't believe it. I wasn't skilled at reacting to this kind of thing. I immediately said to Cussen: 'Who gave my sister the gun?' As soon as I spoke he turned his head away. He sat awkwardly on a chair with his back to me. He didn't answer. I shouted: 'Who gave Ruth the gun?' I knew he'd been playing some sort of game between Ruth and Blakely. Mother said: 'We don't know.' I was told to be quiet.

I'll never forget Cussen's words that Easter Monday – more correctly his lack of words. The only words he uttered were 'cheerio' and 'I have to catch a train' when he left. I got the impression he didn't want anyone to hear his voice. There was something about that sly-looking sod; he had something to hide. All these years later I know what it was. More than any of us could have realized. Ruth was set up.

My thoughts immediately went out to Ruth's children Andre and Georgina. Those poor kids. What were they going to do?

Cussen's appearance at our home remained a secret. Throughout the court case nothing was mentioned about his connection with Ruth's family – it was as if we didn't exist. It was one of many facts that escaped the public's scrutiny. Anything my parents mentioned on their statements about him being a 'friend' was erased from public view. Nothing came out in the trial about him bringing Andre to us on Bank Holiday Monday. Cussen testified in court that the last he saw of Ruth and Andre was at 7.30 p.m. on Easter Day. He's a qualified liar.

On 11 April witnesses were called to Hampstead magistrate's court where the bench was specially convened, being a bank holiday. Ruth didn't have far to travel – the magistrate's court and the police station was one big building on the corner of Downshire Hill and Rosslyn Hill, a bridge out the back connected the two buildings.

The following sequence shows how Cussen could manipulate statements about happenings on 10 and 11 April, to give different meanings. Things were organized from the word go to make sure the case against Ruth stuck. The public was oblivious to the true circumstances of Cussen's involvement with the murder that took place at about 9.30 p.m. outside The Magdala. In his police statement Cussen said:

> She and the boy Andrea came to my flat . . . I drove them back to her room at 7.30 and that is the last I saw of her. I next heard from Hampstead Police that she was in custody. I later drove Ruth's parents and the boy to London Bridge station today.
>
> Statement taken down, read over and signed by R. Fenwick at Hampstead Police station. CCS600/2.

He's already forgotten he came to our place.

On 20 April Detective Chief Inspector L. Davies takes a statement from Cussen: 'He drove Ruth Ellis and son back to her room at about 7.30 and that was the last he saw of them. The next he heard of Ellis was when he was told by Hampstead Police that she was in custody.' CO201/5591

There's no mention of going to the station as previously stated. At the magistrate's court hearing on 28 April it becomes: 'I drove them back to Egerton Gardens and that was the last I saw of them.' There's no mention of Hampstead Police contacting him, if they actually did, or of him taking my parents and Andre to the station.

When Cussen appeared at the trial on 20 June Christmas Humphreys turned the question round, putting the emphasis on *her*, omitting my parents and Andre:

Q: That evening did you drive *her* back to Egerton Gardens?
A: Yes
Q: About what time?
A: About half-past 7.
Q: At 7.30 on the Sunday night, and that is the last you saw of *her*?
A: Yes

In the space of six weeks, Andre, the only witness to Ruth's behaviour on Easter Day was removed and Cussen's association with my parents had disappeared; 7.30 p.m. on Easter Day was definitely not the last Cussen saw of Andre or Ruth.

Andre was mentioned in Cussen's police statement dated 11 April yet none of the legal people delved into his involvement. Only Cussen and Ruth knew Andre was alone at Egerton

Gardens the night of the shooting. Ruth was in police custody, she'd been brainwashed and Cussen was confident he'd got her under control and she wasn't going to squeak. Andre, the only other threat to his cover, was hidden away. Cussen could say anything he liked.

I'd assumed the police went to my parents' on Bank Holiday Monday and told them about the shooting. They hadn't – it was Cussen. Afterwards he gave a statement to the police. A week later the police took a statement from my father. Why did they take so long? But the police did *not* come round to Haverstock Court to tell us about the shooting, as described in several books over the years. Nobody knew Ruth had a sister Muriel. You'd have thought the police would have checked out the whole family. Who stopped them? What beggars belief is how my parents sat through the court case, listening to Cussen's lies. But my parents were impressed by his man-of-the-world ways. They'd been bought off. Joe wasn't as complimentary. He thinks the court case was water off a duck's back to them: 'It was all where the next packet of fags was coming from and what Arthur would get at the end of it.'

Going back to Bank Holiday Monday, within half-an-hour Cussen had packed my parents off to Hemel Hempstead to stay with my brother Granville. He either drove or paid for them to go by train – they wouldn't have had any money. But before they were bundled off, they threatened me and told me not to speak to a soul. I was to look after Andre, not to discuss anything and not let him speak to anyone. If I were to open my mouth to anyone about Andre or Cussen coming on Bank Holiday Monday they would tell Joe about Robert and me. I was scared. Mother knew for years that her husband was Robert's father, but wouldn't accept it. Now, they were using it as blackmail. Nobody ever came. Nobody discovered Ruth's sister.

Today, it suggests to me that people involved with Ruth – Cussen, perhaps Ellis and Ward – knew exactly what happened with Ruth and me at home with Father. They knew we had something to hide and used that secret as blackmail that would ultimately play its part in Ruth's death.

Andre came downstairs after Cussen and my parents left and sat on my knee. He didn't say a lot except that he'd seen Uncle Desmond cleaning the guns in his flat the day before. He'd watched Cussen through the half-open doorway. He was an inquisitive kid, got into everything and understood everything but was no liar. He was innocent and intelligent. Then he added, quite naturally, that Uncle Desmond that same day drove him and his mother (who was in a state) to a forest to teach his mummy how to shoot. Cussen had one gun and gave another one to Ruth. Andre thought she was funny because she couldn't even shoot a tree and her hands kept shaking. I don't think he understood there'd been a murder.

The situation between Ruth, Cussen and Blakely just prior to the shooting was extraordinary. Cussen was in his flat at Goodwood Court, Ruth was in a service room at Egerton Gardens for two months with Blakely, paid for (according to PRO file) by Cussen. At the same time Cussen was with her every day – she saw him at his flat, and had French lessons there paid for by him, describing him to the French teacher as her husband. Somehow she also squeezed in seventeen days at the Rodney Hotel, Kensington, with Blakely. I don't understand why (if she really did) when she had a room in Egerton Gardens.

It's only now I've learned what actually happened on that Easter Sunday. After Andre's suicide in 1982, we cleared his bedsitter and found a tape that he had secretly made three months earlier in conversation with Christmas Humphreys, prosecuting counsel at Ruth's trial, at the Buddhist Society. Andre told Humphreys that on the day of the shooting his mummy forgot to pick him up from boarding school. When she met him at the station she was cross about something but not with him. She was in a state. It's peculiar because in the police statements they say Ruth was perfectly calm and composed at all times. Andre said the opposite – she was wound up. He told Humphreys that Desmond drove them later in the day in his black taxi. Cussen, in his statement two days before Ruth was executed, said he didn't own a taxi. But he had had one. It's a good way of getting round London unnoticed. He denied he drove to the scene of the crime in a taxi, but Andre knew he drove a taxi that day.

This is an excerpt from Humphreys' and Andre's taped conversation. They're talking about Andre not being questioned by the police:

CH: I see and once it had happened they didn't talk to you. Nobody came and took a statement from you? What happened to you? Did they take you away from home or what? Were you living at home at the time?

A: Do you mean at the end?

CH: I mean at the time of the murder. Were you living with her?

A: Oh yes she collected me from the station. I was at school in . . .

CH: Yes.

A: She was very annoyed and took me to Marylebone and went in Desmond's taxi to Egerton Gardens and she put me to bed and went off. She was mad.

CH: Well, when you say she was mad, your recollection is that she was what?

A: Very clear.

CH: Doing or saying what? Why are you clinging to the words here?

A: I am using the word mad now because I think it's simpler than saying she was psychotic. I'll use the word disturbed. Will that be better for you? She was disturbed. All right? Fair enough, she was disturbed at the station when we first met.

CH: Disturbed in what way? Women can be upset, so can we.

A: She was disorientated.

CH: Could you as a child form that opinion?

A: Yes, I can form that opinion. I know my mother. I know when she's had those episodes of disorientation.

CH: So you still think there was an injustice in that she was found guilty of deliberate murder when she wasn't.

There are crashes and bangs. Andre knocks his juice over. Humphreys sees the tape recorder in Andre's briefcase:

CH: Naughty!

Andre should have been interviewed by the police; he knew much of what happened on the day of the shooting. He'd seen two guns in Cussen's flat on Easter Day and Cussen teaching

Ruth to shoot. I told Mother what Andre said: 'Auntie Muriel, I was looking through the cupboard and saw two guns in a box. Then I saw Uncle Desmond oiling and cleaning them.' How can a little boy lie about something like that? My parents wouldn't listen. Mother said: 'You'll have to leave it. Andre didn't see anything.' My family did nothing.

Andre mentioned Cussen's taxi on the recording. On 6 July 1955 in a statement given to Detective Constable Claiden of Hampstead 'S' Division, Alexander Engleman, the Little Club doorman, told how he read in the newspapers that Ruth took a taxi to Hampstead on the night of the murder and thought Cussen might have driven her there in his taxi:

> One evening, I think at the beginning of 1954, when the club closed, Cussen was there and asked me if he could give me a lift home. I accepted and went downstairs with him. Outside the club I looked for his car, and he pointed to an old taxi which was parked across the road, and said 'This is my car.' I asked him where his other car was, and he said 'It's in dock, I've borrowed this. Jump in.' He went to the driver's seat and put on a chauffeur's cap then drove me to Goodwood Court, where I went in and had a drink with him. After a while I left him and came home.'

Claiden continues the report to Detective Superintendent Gill:

> Later on the 6 July 1955 I made enquiries of a number of friends of both Blakely and Cussen, but none could

remember Cussen ever having used an old taxi cab. It may well be that he did so when driving Engleman home but it would appear that it was an isolated incident . . . If within the next few days, Cussen is traced he will be interrogated in respect of the use of the taxi cab with Engleman, and again of the possibility that he drove Ellis to the scene of the murder . . . So far there is not a shred of evidence to show that Cussen did take her to the scene of the crime.

On 9 July Claiden left a message for the Home Secretary:

Re man named Cussen alleged to have driven Ruth Ellis to Hampstead on the night of the shooting. Cussen has been interviewed this morning and denies having driven Ellis to Hampstead on the evening of 10/4/55 in a taxicab or any other vehicle. He did own a taxicab from Feb. to September 1954. He drove it from Feb. 54 to June 54, and then lent to members of his staff to go on holiday. He sold it to his brother at Windsor in September 1954 and has not seen or used it since.

As I leafed through pages of police statements, it's obvious, even at the eleventh hour before Ruth hanged, that policemen from the sticks of Hampstead 'S' Division were still investigating the crime – the crime that was plastered over the newspapers. Scotland Yard experts weren't called in. But they weren't going to be – this crime would be pinned on Ruth at all costs.

Peter Grisewood, an investigating journalist, whose address is in my mother's address book, checked at a later date to see if Cussen had a brother. He found he didn't. He had a cousin.

Moreen Gleeson who has lived in Australia since the 1960s witnessed what happened prior to the shooting of Blakely. She first wrote to me in 1999 from her home in Western Australia. She told me how on Easter Sunday she saw Cussen come out of the bushes near the Findlaters' house in Tanza Road in Hampstead and he told her to clear off. He said to Ruth: 'I'll deal with this.' Moreen described in her letter what she saw and what action she took:

> I was in my early twenties and living in Netherall Gardens, West Hampstead. I had furnished rooms there. I worked in an office during the day and habitually walked each evening for exercise.
>
> On Easter Sunday around 9pm I was walking in a street and saw Ruth Ellis. She was standing near a fence with bushes near it. She was very upset and was crying. I remember Ruth as being very small and crying her eyes out. I could not possibly have walked by. I approached her and asked if she was alright and why she was crying. She said: 'It's my boyfriend, he's in there with another woman.' She indicated a house across the street. We chatted generally. I told her that things would work out and that she would get over him. She was wild eyed and talking abstractly. I told her to go home and perhaps talk to her mother. She said she didn't want to. I invited her to come home with me and to have a cup of coffee and a chat, but

she was crying again and said as if surprised: 'Oh I've got a gun.' Her right hand was in her right pocket. She opened her pocket slightly and I could see the glint of metal. I did not doubt it was a gun. When Ruth showed me the gun I was shaken. After all it was before television and we were not so blasé in those days. I tried to pursuade her to come home with me as I thought she was going to kill herself. I said: 'My God where did you get that gun, what are you going to do?' She said: 'I don't know.' She was quite hysterical. I said: 'Please come home with me, we can sort this out – a cup of coffee will help.' She said: 'No I want to stay here.'

When Cussen, as I believe he is named, appeared behind her I was frightened. He was definitely intending to take charge and I did not want to be involved with him. Ruth seemed to accept his presence so I left. I had assumed that Ruth was thinking of taking her own life and could not conceive that she would do so with this man looking after her.

I was young and inexperienced. I didn't know what to do. I walked the few hundred yards to Hampstead Police Station and saw an officer on duty at the desk. I told him what I'd seen and he said: 'Thank you very much.' As I left the room he was reaching for the phone. I thought he would find her. I went home and saw my neighbours Liz and Richard and told them what had happened. I told everybody I knew about my meeting with Ruth. I believed what I said had been given due consideration. I did not understand and had little sense of my own importance in the matter. Over the next few days someone told me that she had killed her boyfriend. I was very upset.

Of course I followed the case carefully and quite expected the police to contact me, but they never did. After her conviction and sentence and before her execution I went to Belsize Police Station [Hampstead] and spoke to an officer there. I told him what had happened on the night as I had strong feelings that she should not be executed. I expressed these feelings to him. I was told off and virtually ordered out of the police station. I then went to West Hampstead Police Station. I spoke to an officer there and repeated my story. I told him what had happened at Belsize Police Station. He rang them and at the end of that conversation he threw me out of the police station.

I had no luck when I asked my parents for help. I considered actually going to Holloway prison, but I did not know where it was and did not have the money for the fare. I remember asking around about what I could do but no one had any information for me, especially when I said the police would not believe me.

As a result of this I had a nervous breakdown. I could not get Ruth Ellis out of my mind and have thought of her throughout my life. I left the UK in the early 60s and travelled to New Zealand and Australia. I qualified as a nurse and then became a midwife. I have since retired.

I am still trying to fathom out why I was prevented from saying anything. I went to the police twice, and also asked a solicitor in Hampstead what I should do.

However after he had phoned the police he sent me away and would not help me. I cannot understand why the two people I lived with do not remember coming to the police station with me. I cannot tell if what I knew would have made any difference, but I do know I was prevented from telling what little I knew.

I read something about him [Cussen] in a newspaper during the 1960s or 70s. I was in Queensland and I think it was the *Courier Mail* and I dismissed the item as ill informed. I had been there and knew this was all wrong.

I was relieved to receive Moreen Gleeson's letter. Her evidence was ignored in 1955, but in my mind she held one of the keys to what really happened on the evening of 10 April.

Going back to that Bank Holiday Monday, I remember watching the children playing on the veranda. I was full of fear and had that awful feeling when anything you do or say is hopeless. I kept thinking to myself: I'm stuck here – I daren't open my mouth. If I'd been able to tell someone about my father then maybe somebody could have helped Ruth. But I knew nobody would believe me. My parents' threats about Robert were enough to silence me – it would have ended my marriage. I was a prisoner again. My parents played on my fears.

I didn't see Mother again till we went to visit Ruth in prison the day before she died. I was told nothing about the case. I remember asking my parents before they left if Ruth had a solicitor. She hadn't. I feared for her knowing that anything the police wrote down would be taken seriously. As usual I wasn't given a proper answer.

Before Ruth reached the police station that Sunday her fate was decided. Looking at her statement she recited, it's obvious it'd been rehearsed, she knew it off by heart. Completely brainwashed she was. Nobody asked why she gave such a practised statement. Didn't the police notice it was a performance? In the defence counsel document Ruth described her 'curious feeling of relief'. Ruth was interviewed that night by two CID men after they'd seen Blakely's body. She said: 'At the time all I could see was a lot of blood and I was talking more or less mechanically as though I were in a dream.' How much time did anyone spend trying to understand her state of mind? The police said she was calm and composed. She wasn't acting normally.

Who in their right mind would say, Yes I'm guilty, I shot him, knowing they'll hang for it. Which makes you think someone told her she wouldn't hang.

Mr Mishcon and Mr Simmons of Messrs Mishcon and Co were Ruth's solicitors – she had consulted them on civil matters for three-and-a-half years. But following the shooting Mr Bickford, who was with the practice of Cardew, Smith and Ross, appeared on the scene. Monica Weller wrote to Lord Mishcon asking how Ruth came to appoint Mr Bickford. Lord Mishcon replied on 3 April 2002:

> My memory is that Ruth Ellis telephoned from the Police Station after the shooting had taken place and that she was told that in the serious circumstances she should immediately instruct criminal lawyers. As I remember the next thing I heard was that Mr Bickford was acting for her.

There's no record on file of Ruth making that phone call, which would have been made late at night. Mr Mishcon's advice was ignored. No solicitor was present during her interrogation and the taking of the statement she gave to three police officers at Hampstead Police Station at 11.30 p.m. – Detective Inspector Gill, Detective Superintendent Crawford and Detective Chief Inspector Davies (*HO291/235*). Ruth was still without legal representation when she made her first appearance at the magistrate's court on 11 April. Legal aid and a panel solicitor were offered to her at the end of the hearing as reported in the *Hampstead News* of 14 April, though this offer is not evidenced in PRO documents. Mr Bickford, who was not a panel solicitor, appeared on the scene later on. He was a friend of Desmond Cussen.

Why didn't Ruth demand a solicitor immediately? There is no record on file about this.

Joe got involved when Ruth was locked up in Holloway prison. I think he'd always been a bit in love with her. He went with Mother after 5 May, when Ruth was transferred to a cell from the medical ward, where she'd been since the shooting. He described the worn-out winding steps, a little room, a narrow cot, and how Ruth stood with a warder beside her. It upset him more than he ever said: 'She stood there against the wall. She was well depressed. She'd always been flamboyant and jumping around. She wasn't like that in there. I wanted to ask her about the shooting but was told by the screw, No way. I couldn't ask anything about what she'd done. She was a rabbit in a hutch.'

Joe recognized Cussen from the day he visited Ruth in Holloway. He'd been waiting to go up to the tower and this chap came in. Joe said: 'Cussen knew your mother well from the way they spoke. That was the only time I met him to really know who he was. We didn't hold a conversation. I made one remark. He was smoking and I can remember him crumbling his cigarette. I said: 'Don't break it up. Leave the cigarette whole because the prisoners want them.'

Joe went to see Mr Bickford her solicitor at Holborn Circus. He recalls: 'I went to see Bickford to see how the case was going. "She said she shot him and it's an open-and-shut case." I went a second time. I only wanted to know how the case was going. I went up the stairs, Cussen was coming down laughing with Bickford. I couldn't understand why he should be there. I presumed Bickford was looking after his business assets.'

Having checked Cussen and Co. documents, it's unlikely Cussen was consulting Bickford on business matters. Just seven months before, in September 1954, he used the services of Arthur Dennis and Co. solicitors of Upper Brook Street, when he secured a loan on his two London properties.

Joe was sure they were involved. He got the impression that Cussen was friendly with him: 'I always thought it was Cussen who got Bickford for Ruth. I assumed but couldn't prove that Cussen was paying Ruth's bill and manipulating Bickford at the same time. Cussen was caught up in what happened at The Magdala and was a worried man and juggling to keep himself out of the trial.'

Now I know from official papers there was a conflict of interest. Bickford said in a statement to the Under Secretary of State, after the trial, when he tried to get a reprieve: 'Cussen was the first person with whom she put me in touch after I saw her on a number of occasions . . . I foresaw that there might be some eventual conflict of interest and in view of his close association with Ruth Ellis I advised him to consult another solicitor. This of course was before I knew he would be called as a witness for the prosecution as indeed at that time it seemed to me to be unlikely.'

Peter Grisewood's memorandum to Lord Mancroft is the only document at the Public Record Office throwing any light on how Bickford happened to represent Ruth. He wrote: 'A Mr Clive Clairmont, an acquaintance of Ruth Ellis's, Blakely's and Cussen's, told me a few days after the murder he rang up Cussen asking if there was anything he could do to help and asked whether a solicitor had been engaged. Cussen told him there was nothing he could do as he, Cussen, was attending to everything and paying for it. He had engaged his own solicitor – a Mr Bickford.'

Nearly fifty years on I'm picking through a tangled mess about that awful time. The truth and facts were hidden under layers of conflicting evidence. What could be easier than feeding the public the titillating story of how a model, later a hostess, shot her lover dead in cold blood.

This is a summary of how Ruth described, at her trial, the frenzied sequence of events between the end of March and 10 April, the day of the shooting. Ruth's miscarriage on 28 March was made worse by another fight with Blakely. On Thursday 31 March Blakely, Ruth and Findlater drove to Oulton Park near Chester where Blakely had entered the Emperor car on 2 April. Blakely didn't race it because it was written off during the practice. David moaned it was Ruth's fault. She was depressed and ill from the miscarriage and from a cold she'd caught and returned to London on 3 April with a high temperature. Cussen insisted she stayed in bed. In the week before the shooting Blakely was home late on Monday and

Tuesday evenings. He'd told Ruth he was seeing somebody about the Emperor. On Wednesday Blakely's mood changed, he talked about marriage and made plans to take Andre out over Easter. Blakely was selected to race at Le Mans on 9 June and gave her a signed photo of himself taken for the event: 'To Ruth with all my love David.' On Thursday the 7th Ruth booked theatre seats but he was late home again. They went to the cinema; during the film he told her he loved her. On Good Friday 8 April, Blakely left at 10 a.m., on good terms, to meet Findlater. He said he'd be home early. By 9.30 p.m. he hadn't returned so Ruth phoned the Findlaters, telling Anthony she was worried that Blakely wasn't back. Findlater said Blakely had left. By midnight Ruth was frantic. She phoned Cussen who drove her round to the Findlaters' flat in Tanza Road. She hammered on the door, but they wouldn't answer. She phoned the Findlaters from a phone box but they put the receiver down. Knowing Blakely was inside (his Vanguard was parked outside), in frustration she pushed the car windows in. At 2 a.m. the police came out. She returned to Egerton Gardens where she chain-smoked and spent another sleepless night.

On Easter Saturday Ruth went by taxi to Tanza Road, hid in a doorway and saw David and the Findlaters drive up. Later they drove off. Ruth went home, but later that evening Cussen drove her back there. Ruth was convinced David was having an affair with the Findlaters' nanny. She saw him from a distance, the first time since Friday morning. The Findlaters were having a party. Ruth was jealous. She remained there till midnight, distinguishing voices inside as Findlater, Gunnell and Blakely. She had not slept for forty-eight hours.

On Easter Sunday morning Ruth phoned the Findlaters and spoke to Anthony, knowing that he was laughing about her: 'I hope you're having an enjoyable holiday, because you've ruined mine.' In evidence she says she couldn't remember how she spent Sunday except she was with Cussen and her son Andre. She put Andre to bed about 8 p.m. at Egerton Gardens.

That evening Ruth picked up a revolver given to her three years before by a club person whose name she couldn't remember and put it in her handbag. She intended to find Blakely and kill him. She took a taxi from Egerton Gardens to Tanza Road arriving there at 9 p.m. as Blakely drove off with Gunnell. She dismissed the taxi and walked down the road to the nearest pub where she saw David's car parked outside. She said in her statement:

> I waited outside until he came out with a friend I know as Clive. David went to his car door to open it. I was a little way away from him. He turned and saw me and then turned away from me and I took the gun from my bag and I shot him. He turned round and ran a few steps round the car. I thought I had missed him so I fired again. He was still running and I fired the third shot. I don't remember firing any more but I must have done. I remember then he was lying on the footway and I was standing beside him. He was bleeding badly and it seemed ages before an ambulance came. I remember a man came up and I said: 'Will you call the police and an ambulance?' He said: 'I am a policeman.' I said: 'Please take this gun and arrest me.'

On 12 July, the day before Ruth was executed, she decided to tell her original solicitors Mishcon and Simmons how she actually obtained the gun on the night of the shooting, from Cussen at his Goodwood Court flat:

> We had been drinking for some time . . . All I remember is that Desmond gave me a loaded gun . . . I was in such a dazed state that I cannot remember what was said. I rushed out as soon as he gave me the gun . . . I rushed back after a second or two and said 'Will you drive me to Hampstead?' He did so and left me at the top of Tanza Road. I had never seen the gun before.

Between January and April 1955 Ruth's life was frantic, moving fast in parallel with political events. The screws were being tightened on her. No wonder the French teacher, Mrs Marie Therese Harris of 128 Ashley Gardens, who'd given her French lessons at Cussen's flat between 17 January and 23 February, gave up teaching her. She said in her police statement, Ruth was edgy and it was a waste of time: 'Ruth looked like a person on the edge of a nervous breakdown.' She also witnessed the awful bruises Ruth had received. She said that on either 20 or 31 January, Ruth was not at Goodwood Court for her lesson. Andre let her in, he was away from school, and they chatted about a problem she had with pigeons. Andre opened a chest of drawers. Mrs Harris noticed: 'Two guns, which at first I thought were his toys. He handled one, the larger one, then said: 'It's alright, it's not loaded.' Then he put it back and closed the drawer and I left the flat.' Mrs Harris wasn't called as a witness.

Ruth was pregnant again but had a miscarriage on 28 March – Blakely had kicked her in the stomach. It wasn't the first time he'd done it. He was all for Ruth one minute then beating her up the next. Meanwhile Cussen topped her up with alcohol. In his Plea for a Reprieve, Mr Bickford described her at that time as: 'Continually drugged by drink . . . ill and weak.' Ruth herself admitted to Mishcon on 12 July that she had: 'Been drinking Pernod in Desmond's flat . . . we had been drinking for some time.'

By the beginning of April the spy scandal involving Guy Burgess and Donald Maclean was at boiling point. We didn't know at the time but behind the scenes the pressure was on the government for a Public Enquiry and to come clean about Burgess and Maclean's defection in 1951. The newspapers, which had been on strike since 26 March, wanted to put out the story. Kim Philby's involvement with Burgess and Maclean wasn't known to the public then, but his name was being whispered in Whitehall. Anthony Cave Brown wrote in *Treason in the Blood*: 'Philby's part in their disappearance was unknown except to a small group of insiders in the secret circle. And that was the way it would remain for three years, until 1955. The press nibbled but got nowhere.' Blakely was murdered on 10 April. During the twenty-four days Ruth was in Holloway prison hospital under observation, Winston Churchill, who'd quietly resigned on 5 April, handed over to Anthony Eden as Prime Minister.

The month-long, national newspaper strike is referred to in *Clementine Churchill by Mary Soames her Daughter*: 'The strike meant, from a private and personal point of view, that we were spared the full pressure of press comment and speculation which would have been inevitable in these last few weeks, and which would have made life for Winston, his close circle and his government colleagues, that much more difficult. As it was, the programme as finally arranged took place with a measured dignity which did credit to everyone.' Interestingly the *Manchester Guardian* was the only national newspaper not on strike. The 11 April edition carried a tiny story about the shooting at the bottom of the front page:

> Man Shot Outside Public House
> A man was shot outside a public house in South Hill Park, Hampstead, London, last night. He was dead on arrival at hospital. Later a woman went to Hampstead Police Station to help the CID with enquiries.

Ruth made another appearance at Hampstead magistrate's court on 18 April and was remanded for seven days. The newspaper strike ended on 21 April and by 29 April the papers were filled with Ruth's story. I wouldn't have the papers in the house or the wireless on. I didn't want my children or Andre knowing about it. Everyone else knew about the model, Mrs Ruth Ellis, who shot her lover, a car ace, in the back. The newspapers and radio put out tittle-tattle disguised as first-hand evidence, crucifying her before she appeared at the Old Bailey. Those Intelligence men were expert at putting out wrong information. The story captured the people's attention. The shooting was crafted to look like a crime of passion. Only the Secret Service had the cloak-and-dagger skills to cover up the truth so deviously. On 11 May Ruth made another appearance at the Old Bailey. This time Melford Stevenson applied for more time to prepare the case. Nothing was prepared! There was an election coming up. The trial was conveniently postponed until 20 June giving the Conservatives time to win the General Election on 26 May.

176

To give an idea of timing, this item appeared in the *Sunday Pictorial* a fortnight after Ruth was hanged. 'News leaked out last night of a new witness in the Maclean and Burgess riddle – Mr Harold Philby OBE. He was the First Secretary at our embassy in Washington when Burgess was a Second Secretary. Donald Maclean had already left Washington when Mr Philby arrived. He resigned from the Foreign Office in September 1951, four months after the diplomats vanished. He lives at a red brick house in Crowborough, Sussex. Philby's mother who lives in a Knightsbridge flat said, "I cannot discuss my son's affairs. He resigned from the Foreign Office and I realized the news would leak out sooner or later."

By September, six weeks after Ruth's death, with the Foreign Office trying to keep the story quiet about Burgess and Maclean being Soviet spies since their university days, the story broke in *The People*. The Government didn't want another spy scandal involving Ruth and Stephen Ward and linked to Burgess and Maclean rocking the nation at the same time.

As I've mentioned before, Ruth's medical history was kept well under wraps at the trial. Winston Churchill knew quite a bit about Ruth. Lord Moran, Winston Churchill's personal physician, was always at his side and covered up Churchill's strokes in 1949 and 1953. He published his diaries in 1966, a year after Churchill's death. It caused a rumpus with the Churchill family because of patient confidentiality. This is the entry for 14 July 1955 (the day after Ruth was hanged) in Lord Moran's book, *Winston Churchill – The Struggle for Survival 1940-1965*.

Anthony Eden came at five o'clock to tell Winston about Geneva. 'He wants to put his visit to me in the papers,' Winston said. 'I went to the Other Club in the evening,' Winston continued. 'A quarter to nine till a quarter to twelve. Most of them had slipped away by then, but I stayed to the end. There was some good fun. I got home at a quarter to one, tired but not unduly tired.' I had a good talk with Lord Goddam [*Goddard*] about Ruth Ellis.

I [*Lord Moran*] told Winston that some of her clientele in Soho carried knives, and that on more than one occasion she had attended the Middlesex Hospital with flesh wounds inflicted on her in the practice of her profession.

How did Churchill's doctor know that? It's odd for someone of his position to come out with that. He was well up the ladder, she's down the bottom. They had access to information that nobody else had, but nothing was said about this in the trial.

This 'Other Club' mentioned by Churchill was founded by him. Amongst its membership of fifty were Harold Macmillan, Minister of Defence and Gwilym Lloyd-George the Home Secretary, and Colin Coote, editor of the Conservative newspaper the *Daily Telegraph*. Members met for dinner at the Savoy Hotel. During the fifties Jean Nichol, who was married to Derek Tangye of MI5, was the Savoy's public relations officer. Tangye's job, according to Anthony Summers and Stephen Dorril's book *Honeytrap* was to monitor 'the mood of people in influential circles.' Jean Nichol was 'an important link in the chain of his work'. Indeed she was. She and 'Baron' Nahum, the Court photographer, had their own club, the Friday Club, whose guests included Prince Philip and Stephen Ward. All these people seem to be extraordinarily interwoven.

Cussen had incited Ruth to commit murder. He wound her up and played on her jealousy till she couldn't think straight, till she couldn't stand what was going on in her life any longer, till she was out of her mind and relying on alcohol and *looked* as if she'd be capable of committing a crime. But Cussen knew she wasn't capable of carrying out the deed effectively. He knew she had been weakened by the recent miscarriage; that her eyesight was hopeless; and she wasn't in her right mind.

In the 1949 Acid Bath murder trial forensic scientists made sure everything went under the microscope. They set up a situation to check the firing of the gun where the murders took place to check if the gun could be heard. Was any check done to see if Ruth could hold a gun and fire it? No. The Metropolitan Police did forensics on the gun and on Blakely; not on Ruth. Why didn't they check the size of the gun, a Smith and Wesson .38 service revolver, in relation to a small woman with tiny hands, one of which was gnarled from rheumatic fever? There's no evidence in any file of fingerprints even being taken, or evidence on her fingers or clothing of having fired a gun. Why weren't samples taken from the deceased *and* the accused?

Why wasn't Lewis Charles Nickolls, director of the Metropolitan Police Laboratory, asked to repeat in court what he said in his police statement, that the trigger of the gun 'equalled 10lbs-pull, and requires a definite and deliberate muscular effort.' Instead he is asked: 'This is a revolver and of course different from an automatic, and you have to pull the trigger each time do not you?' Nickolls replied: 'To fire each shot the trigger has to be pulled as a separate operation.'

Joe has seen a Smith and Wesson; he had a friend who had guns over the years and before he died they had a conversation about the cowboy gun used to kill Blakely.

He fetched one. Knowing Ruth, the gun would have been impossibly large in her tiny hands. She was 5'2" and weighed seven stone. If she'd shot that big, heavy gun she couldn't have shot it more than once. She couldn't have thumbed the trigger guard back – the weapon's recoil would have knocked her arms backwards. A professional would know that and hold it with two hands at arm's length. Accuracy goes to pot except in trained hands. It says on the police report she shot Blakely three times from a distance and once close-up. With a gun like that you've got to hold it with two hands. If you're not used to shooting how the hell are you going to kill someone?

I went to the Crime Museum at New Scotland Yard. I've seen the gun. I've held it. The one they say was fetched from the crime scene. As I held that heavy thing I shook like a leaf. What must Ruth have been like? No way could she have shot that gun, not even with two hands. She was confused, drunk, suffering from the effects of her recent miscarriage and had poor eyesight. Her hand would have shaken like hell. With her tiny hands, one damaged by arthritis, she couldn't get her finger round the trigger, let alone keep on pulling it. It's like pulling three bags of flour in mid-air once the bullets are in it and you're really shooting. You'd have to train for two years with that gun to fire an accurate shot. A seven-stone girl and a deformed hand, she'd be no good with a gun, never.

A check was made on the gun's serial number – 719573. Smith and Wesson in America said it was one of two thousand British service revolvers issued on 1 December 1940 to the Union of South Africa. Why didn't the police ask a few questions? It wouldn't have been difficult to trace because people weren't carrying guns in numbers like nowadays, even the gangsters.

The evidence about the gun in the trial documents is difficult to understand. PC Alan Thompson of 'L' Division in south-east London was the off-duty policeman in The Magdala that evening. At the magistrate's court he said the revolver Ruth handed him was in 'proper working order'. Lewis Nickolls stated on 20 April that he received the gun on 12 April in working order. At the trial when questioned by Christmas Humphreys he repeated 'it was in working order. The barrel was foul and consistent with having been recently fired, otherwise the revolver was in clean condition and was oily.' And the two spent bullets in front of him had been 'fired from this revolver'. But in a police statement dated 25 April, Nickolls stated: 'During the course of firing in the lab, the cylinder catch broke, as a result of a long-standing crack in the shank.' (The cylinder catch revolves the barrel so that the next bullet is in place for the next shot.) When I pulled the trigger of the gun at New Scotland Yard it clicked. It didn't look broken, it looked in good condition. In 1955, the gun tested in forensics broke. I don't believe it was the gun used to kill Blakely.'

From the transcript of the trial, Christmas Humphreys questions Nickolls:

CH: Looking now at the revolver, was that in working order?

LN: On receipt it was in working order. I found the barrel was foul and consistent with having been recently fired.

CH: Did you find that the six spent cartridge cases which were in the cylinder were normal for that gun?

LN: Yes, they were, and they had been fired, and they had been fired from that gun.

CH: Can you help at all as to the distance from the body at which any of the bullets had been fired in respect of the wounds found in the body?

LN: Yes. I examined the clothing of the deceased man and I found that on the left shoulder at the back of the jacket there was a bullet hole. This had been fired at a distance less than 3 inches . . . The others are all fired from a distance.

What distance? One yard? Ten yards? Nickolls didn't say and wasn't asked. It was crucial when you consider Ruth's hopeless eyesight, coupled with the fact it was dark, half-past-nine in the evening. But Melford Stevenson, her defence counsel, incredibly had no questions. I realize it's what is *not* said that stands out. What Nickolls didn't say, more importantly, was that the absence of powder marks on the other bullet wounds shows the shots were fired from some feet away, out of arm's reach.

Dr Albert Hunt, pathologist in the Department of Forensic Medicine at the London Hospital Medical College, performed the post-mortem on Blakely. He was on the stand at the Old Bailey for about three minutes. Forensic evidence about the position of the bullet wounds, which should have formed the basis of the case, was glossed over, giving the expert witness no opportunity to elaborate. Melford Stevenson, Ruth's defence, had no questions. It's odd they didn't call Dr Keith Simpson,

Desmond Cussen and Ruth

Desmond Cussen's family home 'Dapdune', in Garlands Road, Leatherhead

Ruth in pub garden circa 1953

Dorothy Foxon with journalist Gordon Winter *(right)* at Dorothy's Club, formerly the Little Club, Knightsbridge

Alex Engleman, artist-receptionist of the Little Club where Ruth worked

What used to be the Little Club at 37 Brompton Road, Knightsbridge

Ruth and David Blakely *(far left)* amongst racing drivers and friends

Ruth and David at motor race meeting

The gun that was retrieved after the shooting,
now in Crime Museum, New Scotland Yard

The Magdala in South Hill Park, Hampstead, today

Hampstead Police Station and Magistrates Court

Melford Stevenson,
Ruth's defence counsel

Christmas Humphreys,
prosecution counsel

David Blakely's headstone in Penn churchyard, Bucks

Passport photo of Ruth's son, Andre, aged around 35

Polaroid photograph taken by Andre of his bedsitter and possessions

Sale Place, Bayswater, where Andre lived and committed suicide

The Paddock Club, Ottways Lane in Ashtead, Surrey where
Desmond Cussen and David Blakely were members

Muriel at Public Record Office,
Kew, looking through documents

Ruth's gravestone
in Amersham, Bucks

the Home Office pathologist, or one of his colleagues Mr Camps or Mr Teare to look at Blakely's dead body. Simpson mentions them in *Forty Years of Murder*. The Three Musketeers they called themselves. They were hauled in for big cases. They would have easily found it was a crack shot that fired those bullets into Blakely and not pinned it on Ruth. Instead they used Dr Hunt who was a world expert in stomach emptying according to Keith Simpson. Just who they needed for bullet wounds.

There were four bullet wounds in Blakely's body: one entered below the left shoulder blade, went through the chest, left lung, aorta, windpipe and lodged in the tongue; one entered the lower part of the back, travelled through the intestines and liver and out below the ribs; one entered through the left hip bone and . exited through the front; the fourth was a skin graze on the inner arm. Three bullets made holes in the wall of the pub, about twenty feet to the left of the main door and were within a confined area about twelve inches apart. They were not photographed by the police nor were they referred to at the trial. Two bullets were recovered from the shooting – one from Blakely's tongue was removed by Dr Hunt, the other from his ribs was removed by the ambulance man. A stray bullet hit Mrs Gladys Yule who was at least sixty feet away. PC Thompson removed six spent cartridges from the gun – two bullets were produced in court. What happened to the other four? A police car came with the ambulance. Did they cordon off and make a thorough search of the area? None of this is recorded. Ruth stated: 'The police car arrived and I walked over to it . . . I got in the car and waited till the policewoman arrived.' But PC Thompson said he drove 'the accused to Hampstead Police Station' in his car. Someone is lying.

A scientific reconstruction of the crime would have determined the positions of the people involved, indicating the angle of the shooting and when each shot was fired. This is what I think happened: Cussen drove Ruth to The Magdala. Ruth was incited to fire the gun Cussen had given her while the shots that actually killed Blakely were fired from a second gun. To the four people who said they saw the shooting, three of whom were not called as witnesses, Ruth *appeared* to shoot Blakely. In reality she could only shoot wildly. She was the striking blonde creating the drama in a carefully planned crime. While all eyes were on her chasing Blakely round his car before he gets shot, the witnesses failed to see the marksman across the road from The Magdala. To all intents and purposes Ruth *appeared* to shoot Blakely. In the state she was in, she probably believed she had.

I'll recreate the scene step-by-step from the moment Ruth said she dismissed the taxi at Tanza Road. I read these sentences in her police statement and knew she was lying: 'I took a taxi to Tanza Road and as I arrived David's car drove away from Findlater's address. I dismissed the taxi and walked back down the road to the nearest pub where I saw David's car outside.'

Why did Ruth take a long walk down the road when she could have followed Blakely in the taxi she was already in, if murder was on her mind? She could not have known where Blakely was going in his car, as she hadn't spoken to him for two-and-a-half days. Nor could she have seen where he was going. From the top of Tanza Road, the nearest pub, The Magdala, isn't in sight, it's a good twelve-minute walk. And it was dark.

Moreen Gleeson's testimony confirms that Ruth didn't dismiss the taxi as she described in her police statement. She and Cussen hung around outside the Findlaters' *before* Gunnell and Blakely drove to the pub. If Ruth's intention was to kill Blakely, and she knew he was in the Findlaters' house, she would have had her opportunity when he came out. She didn't need to go to the pub. But Cussen was there, waiting for the right position at the right time. Everything had been planned. Cussen made sure that Blakely and Gunnell had left the Findlaters' and were at The Magdala, before driving Ruth there in his taxi.

In Christmas Humphreys' opening speech he read Ruth's police statement. It was read out again in the judge's Summing Up. But she was not questioned about her arrival at Tanza Road during the trial. Did Ruth's barrister Melford Stevenson not see any significance in this? It was his opportunity to get at the truth. Or did he ignore it? At the Old Bailey on 11 May her defence counsel requested a postponement of the trial to prepare the case, yet in June, Stevenson did not ask what made her take a long walk to the nearest pub when she could have gone by taxi. Surely Stevenson should have made more of this, as these last moments were most important. Instead, he put forward his own summary to which Ruth could only agree: 'We have heard the evidence about your taking a revolver up to Hampstead and shooting him. Is that right?' Ruth answers: 'Quite right.'

The question now is, how did Cussen know that Blakely and Gunnell would leave the Findlaters' party and drive to The Magdala to collect more beer?

Lighting-up time on 10 April 1955 was 9 p.m. The shooting outside The Magdala took place in the dark – this was not pointed out during the trial. At approximately 9.15 p.m. two young men were walking down South Hill Park where it joins Parliament Hill. They were David James Lusty and George

McLaughlin Stephen. They stopped outside Hanshaws the tobacconist adjoining The Magdala. At the same time Mr and Mrs Donald Maclean Yule (an amazing coincidence) walked down Parliament Hill towards the junction with South Hill Park. They were about twenty-five yards from The Magdala. Four people witnessed what happened. Only Mrs Yule was called to give evidence. Her statements made between 11 April and 20 June were inconsistent.

At the first magistrate's court hearing on 11 April, Mrs Yule stated:

> Just after 9 pm on 10 April . . . when we were about twenty-five yards from the Public House, I saw a youngish man, dark haired, run out of the Saloon Bar door, *followed, almost on his heels* [underlined] by a blonde woman. I heard a shot fired and the man ran round a car which was parked outside 'The Magdala' and ducked down by the side of it. He went round the car and backed on to the pavement. She was shouting something at him when she was running after him but I couldn't make out what she said. When the man went down she continued firing the gun. By that time my husband and I were about twenty yards away, when I felt a searing pain in my right hand and I knew I had been shot. The woman was still standing between the man and the car, waving the gun. A taxi cab came along the road from Parliament Hill and I shouted and ran after it . . .

At the second magistrate's court hearing on 28 April, she had changed her story:

When I reached the junction of South Hill Park I should say it was about 9.30. I was talking to my husband and when I looked up I saw two young men coming out of the public house door and I saw a lady in front of them. I saw a motor car against the kerb in front of The Magdala. The two men approached the car. I saw a flash and heard a shot fired. I did not see where the flash came from. I saw a young man trying to get in the car through the door nearest the public house. He didn't get in and he ran round the car. The lady chased him. There was another shot. The man was then round the back of the car. He staggered round. He fell and there were two more shots. He was flat out then. Another shot went off. The flashes I saw all came from the lady's hand. I would not recognize the lady again. I can only say that I could see her hair was very blonde and she wore a light coat. After the last flash I felt a searing pain through my right hand. My husband stopped a taxi and took me to hospital, where my hand was attended to. When I saw these things happen and I was hit my husband and I were in the gutter at the junction of South Hill Park and Parliament Hill. I was standing still.

By 20 June at the Old Bailey, Mrs Yule was sure about what happened: 'I saw her on the pavement, and heard a shot, and then I saw her chase a man.' Miss Southworth, for the prosecution, asked: 'She chased him round the car after she had fired?' Mrs Yule replied: 'Yes.' She then heard more shots by which time the man had fallen. Miss Southworth asked: 'After the shots were fired at the man did you hear another one?' Mrs Yule replied: 'I heard two, and when he fell two more.'

If you've counted five gunshots, why wait for the sixth? The loud bangs and vibration from a .38 Smith and Wesson would make you jump out of your skin. But according to her statement of 11 April, Mrs Yule carried on walking to within twenty yards of the action, if it happened as she described it. Was someone else firing another gun? The ambulance and police car arrived within three minutes by which time Mrs Yule had already gone. There's no record of how the police came to take her statement on 11 April in which she said: 'A taxi cab came along the road from Parliament Hill, and I shouted and ran after it. I got into it and was taken by my husband to Hampstead General Hospital.'

At the Old Bailey, Mrs Yule was not questioned about this chance arrival of a taxi about which her husband, Donald Maclean Yule, gave a slightly different statement on 13 April:

A few minutes before 9.30 pm we decided to go for a drink at the 'Magdala' . . . On leaving my home we crossed the road and walked down the hill on the right hand side of the hill on the footway. Just before we reached the junction of South Hill Park and Parlia-ment Hill, I noticed a blonde, hatless woman, wearing a light grey suit and horn rimmed glasses, walking slowly up and down on the pavement outside the Magdala Public House. I also noticed a large motor car outside the pub. The woman seemed to be waiting for somebody. As we reached the junction I saw a man try the nearside door of the car, which was facing downhill. Then I saw another man trying the offside door of the car, that is, the driver's door . . . I then turned toward my wife and was speaking to her when I heard the sound of a shot from the direction of the pub. I looked in that direction and saw the dark haired man running along the nearside of the car, chased by the woman. His back was toward me and I heard the sound of another shot. The man was chased in a clockwise direction round the car and when they both reached the pavement again, almost opposite the Saloon bar of the public house, he seemed to face her. She fired at least a couple more shots and he fell to the footway. Almost immediately my wife cried out that she had been hit in the hand. I looked and saw that her right hand was bleeding profusely. At that moment a taxi cab came down Parliament Hill and passed us. I shouted at the driver and he stopped almost immediately opposite the 'Magdala.' We ran up to it and after a little argument, I persuaded him to take my wife and I to the Hampstead General Hospital. Just as I was helping my wife into the taxi, I recollect that I saw the blonde woman standing rigid on the pavement at the foot of the man lying there. I do not remember seeing a gun . . .

David Lusty and George McLaughlin Stephen both describe standing outside the tobacconist, next door to The Magdala, and seeing Ruth pursuing Blakely round a parked car. McLaughlin Stephen heard:

A series of minor explosions . . . I thought it was some sort of prank and that she was firing a 'cap' pistol. By the time I heard the fourth or fifth shots, I realized that the bangs were too loud for a cap pistol . . . The man stumbled as he ran round the car and when he had completed a circuit of the car, he fell face downwards on the pavement between the Public House door and the car. All the time he was running, the woman was pursuing at a distance of about two yards and firing continuously. After the man had fallen on to his face, the woman stood over him and I saw her fire the gun once; the gun was pointed at the man's body. After this, she fired again, but this time all I heard was a click, as though the gun was empty. I heard a man, who was standing beside the public house entrance, shouting, 'Look what you've done Ruth.'

Lusty described Blakely being chased by a fair-haired woman in light clothing, wearing spectacles: 'The woman had a gun in her hand. I saw the man run on to the pavement and then I heard the sound of a shot. As the man lay on the ground the woman stood over him and fired two or three shots at him. She emptied the gun, as I heard two or three clicks from the gun after the last shot . . . I just stood and looked, I was so surprised that I didn't realize what had happened.'

Clive Gunnell said he and Blakely left the pub together. Gunnell walked ahead, each was carrying beer for the Findlaters. Gunnell went round the front of Blakely's car to the locked passenger's door. At the magistrate's court he 'heard two bangs' about thirty seconds from the time he reached the passenger's door, which 'didn't sound like a revolver shot. They sounded more muffled.' At the Old Bailey he heard 'two bangs – shots I did not know then they were shots, and I thought they were something that had been put on the car at first.' He couldn't see what was happening on the other side of the car, ran round the back of the car and saw Blakely lying on the pavement and Ruth firing a gun. 'From the time I first saw that to the end of it appeared to me to be a second or two. Then it was all over.' When asked at the Old Bailey if he knew how many shots, other than the first two she'd fired, Gunnell said: 'No, I do not, more than one.'

Gunnell stood to the offside of the car towards the centre of the road, but said he didn't see Blakely being pursued round the car by Ruth waving a gun.

Where was Cussen during the shooting? The position of the bullet holes in the wall of The Magdala seemed odd – about twenty feet downhill from the main entrance. Was Cussen standing opposite The Magdala at this point? We've been led to believe by the witnesses that Ruth shot Blakely as she ran round Blakely's car that faced downhill outside the main entrance, between the small bar to the right and the large bar to the left. Four witnesses saw Blakely completing a circuit of the car, pursued by Ruth waving a gun. But there were three bullet holes in the wall of The Magdala, two of which were in line with the bullet holes in Blakely's body. These were twenty feet beyond the main door of the pub and the car. Neither the two young men outside the tobacconist, nor Mr and Mrs Yule on the right-hand side pavement at the bottom of Parliament Hill could possibly have seen the action at the far end of The Magdala. I have tested it. It's impossible. The pub at that point is on a steep downhill right-hand bend. Unless you stand outside the entrance you cannot see that spot.

This is my theory: Blakely ran beyond the front of his car, at least fifteen feet down the hill to the far end of The Magdala –

obviously escaping from Ruth who was brandishing the gun. For some reason he turned round, stumbled uphill in the opposite direction, collapsing on his stomach with his head level with Hanshaws. What made him turn? Did he see the marksman with a gun lurking near the bushes opposite the saloon bar? It was there, out of sight of the witnesses, that Blakely was fatally wounded. The marksman stepped out of the bushes when Blakely was clearly silhouetted in front of the lights of the saloon bar window. As Blakely turned, he was shot at long range in the back.

Ruth fired into Blakely's body as he lay on the ground. She's in full view of the witnesses even though it's dark. The marksman fires again, anywhere, giving the impression that Ruth is shooting Blakely. Meanwhile, amid the commotion, the marksman retreats through the bushes to his taxi in Parliament Hill – the perfect getaway car. He stops outside The Magdala, picks up Mr and Mrs Yule and drives off. A perfect murder planned by experts.

I know Ruth did not kill Blakely. The marksman was Desmond Cussen.

Ruth was admitted to Holloway hospital wing on 11 April according to official documents, and was under constant observation until 5 May. My parents said she was in the police station for two nights, in other words till 12 April – not how Holloway reported it. We'll never know the truth. Ruth's files for when she was in Holloway were reported missing around New Year 1964. Clerical staff said they'd last seen them two years previously. The theft wasn't reported to Scotland Yard until 1967. The Home Office file, PCOM9/1968, on the theft, was closed till 1999.

Dr M.R. Penry Williams, Principal Medical Officer at Holloway, in his report dated 3 May 1955 stated Ruth was in 'good health except for a genital infection of non-venereal type for which she has received treatment.' They played down her poor state of health making it look as if she knew what she was doing. There's a huge body of evidence, showing she was shocked, grieving and in a terrible state after her miscarriage on 28 March. She had a high temperature, which Mr Bickford referred to in his Appeal to the Home Secretary for a Reprieve, dated 28 June 1955, and was 'addicted to heavy drinking and was in a highly nervous and tense condition'.

Dr Penry Williams found: 'No medical condition which would be likely to cause the prisoner to be unaware of what she was doing or whether it was wrong at the time of the alleged offence.' She may not have been suffering from a 'medical condition' that made her 'unaware' and so on, but Ruth had been brainwashed by Cussen. Plus she'd had a miscarriage. If she was in her right mind she would have made a run for it if she'd killed someone. She was not in her right mind. She hadn't killed anyone.

The following disclosure of Mr Bickford's, in his Appeal to the Home Secretary, was important but wasn't mentioned in the trial. It said something about Ruth's health and Cussen's devious nature:

As she said to me on more than one occasion, 'He [Blakely] could have chosen any other weekend but that one to play me up.' She had had this recent miscarriage – Cussen saw evidence of this when he went round to Egerton Gardens to collect the linen – she was feeling ill owing to a cold which she had caught at Oulton Park races. She obviously should never have gone to the races in her condition but it is equally clear that she wanted to be with Blakely.

Why would he collect the linen? What man of Cussen's standing picks up dirty washing – unless it was calculated? Ruth had a miscarriage on 28 March, there was evidence of it on the bed yet the prison doctor said she was fine. Was Cussen destroying evidence of Ruth being unwell immediately before the shooting?

Evelyn Galilee, the warder who was with Ruth for her last three weeks, told me what Holloway was like when Ruth went in:

> There was a strange silence in the prison – it was hush-hush. One hundred-and-odd officers and nothing came up to us. I didn't even know she was in hospital. It had its own entrance so you never knew when anyone came in. She's probably there to keep the information down. Something funny has gone on. I did know she was in a very unhappy state, a bit despondent. Half a bottle of Pernod was brought in for her. Cussen wasn't the name I knew but the person that brought the Pernod in was the man that gave her the gun. He may have gone in with a *nom de plume*. At Holloway they would know everything about that man though. He should not have come in if he was going to be called as a prosecution witness. It's all irregular. What was going on? He must have been two-faced to get in under another name. Somebody did some planning.

194

I opened a letter dated 13 June from Mr Bickford to the governor of Holloway prison. On a day Ruth was not feeling well, a man with no name introducing himself to Ruth as a doctor, gets into Holloway, examines her and tells her he doesn't know who sent him:

Dear Madam,

Re Mrs Ruth Ellis

We feel we ought to call your attention to the somewhat extraordinary situation which arose yesterday when Mr Bickford called to see Mrs Ellis. As you are probably aware a psychiatrist by the name of Dr Whittaker had been to see Mrs Ellis on behalf of the Defence last week and when Mr Bickford arrived he was told that Mrs Ellis was being interviewed by a Doctor. He enquired whether the Doctor's name was Whittaker but there was some doubt as to this. He was asked whether he would prefer the interview with the Doctor to be postponed until after he had seen his client and he said that he would like this because he did not know who the Doctor was. He was then asked to go and see Dr Jagger, who, we understand, was deputizing for Dr Williams. Dr Jagger informed him that in accordance with the new regulations it was necessary that a Doctor from outside the Prison should be called to examine Mrs Ellis and that this in fact was what was taking place. Mr Bickford pointed out that he had not been informed of this and that in any event it was necessary to obtain Mrs Ellis' consent before she was examined.

195

Dr Jagger explained that she was in no way responsible for the arrangements which had been made and endeavoured to get in touch with you but unfortunately you were not then available.

Very shortly afterwards Mr Bickford was permitted to see his client after the Doctor had finished with her. Mrs Ellis informed Mr Bickford that a gentleman with a beard had just been to see her and he said he was a doctor and wanted to ask her some questions. She asked whether he had been sent by her lawyer and he said he did not know who had sent him. She eventually came to the erroneous conclusion that we had arranged the interview and thereupon answered all the Doctor's questions without reservation.

We still do not know the gentleman's name and have to assume that he was a properly qualified doctor since we feel that your Chief Medical Officer would not have chosen anybody who was not suitable for such a purpose. However, we are most perturbed that this interview should have taken place without our knowledge and approval and without our being able to see the Doctor or our client beforehand. We cannot think that this is the normal and proper procedure in such a case.

As you are aware we were given the opportunity of an interview with the Chief Medical Officer, who was most helpful. We do not think that it was right that the position was not put very clearly to our client, who we are sure would have wished to consult us before granting such an interview. We will, of course, have to mention the matter to counsel but, in the

meantime, we shall be glad to know the identity of
the gentleman who visited her and the results of the
interview at your earliest convenience.

But the bearded man visited Ruth again. How could this
unknown doctor just go into Holloway without identification?
Who overlooked security? Dr Dalzell, the bearded man, later
submitted a one-page report for the prosecution. The final
paragraph summed up his thoughts: 'There was nothing to
suggest at either interview that Mrs Ellis was suffering from, or
had been suffering from delusions, hallucinations or any other
symptom of mental disorder. In my opinion she knew the
nature of the act which she performed and knew it was wrong;
that she formed the intention of carrying out this act some
time beforehand, and that she was aware of the possible
consequences to herself.'

Mr Bickford, in his document in Support of Plea for
Reprieve, HO291/237, asked that the Under Secretary of State
disregard Dr Dalzell's report, saying that the circumstances of
that examination were unsatisfactory: 'Particularly because in
his report he suggests that Mrs Ellis felt she was "still justified"
at what she had done. I put that to Mrs Ellis and she was most
indignant and flatly denied ever having said such a thing.'

The Royal College of Psychiatrists' archives department said
Dr Alexander Charles Dalzell was medical superintendent at
Friern Hospital in North London: 'He joined the RMPA,
forerunner of the Royal College in 1941 and doesn't appear in
the membership list after the late 1940s.'

Dr T.P. Rees was the psychiatrist who had allegedly seen
Ruth at Warlingham Park Hospital and prescribed anti-
depressants. Where was he when he should have been giving

support? Instead they got a Dr Whittaker who didn't know Ruth. Dr Rees said after she died if he had known about the shooting he would have spoken up for Ruth's medical condition and she wouldn't have died. Maybe he didn't know, or was he afraid of a public embarrassment as in the Acid Bath murder trial where the prosecuting counsel Sir Hartley Shawcross and the judge Travers Humphreys made Dr Henry Yellowlees, the psychiatrist acting for John Haigh the murderer, look stupid. Or was he silenced like other witnesses? Was this why Mr Bickford said: 'Various specialists in psychiatry and neurology have been approached . . . all of whom with the exception of Dr Whittaker have found themselves, for various reason, unable to deal with this matter.' HO291/237

The crime was not investigated properly. It did not happen the way it was described in court. A reconstruction of the crime would prove Ruth did not kill Blakely.

13

No Defence

I didn't go to Ruth's trial on 20 June 1955. I wasn't allowed to because of Father, in case I opened my mouth. I would have shouted the truth. Joe didn't go either. Nothing registered with us that day. The place was depressed. Joe's feelings were that we had to live with what was going on – whatever we did would make no difference.

Mother didn't describe the trial to me. It would have broken her heart to speak out. She went with Father and Granville – and was on the verge of breaking down afterwards. All I remember of Father were the pictures of him marching out of court with a fag in his mouth. Joe still calls those involved at court, 'fake lying gits'. As far as I'm concerned the solicitors, judge, the Findlaters, Cussen, all had a hand in condemning Ruth. The trial lasted a day-and-a-bit. You only have to look at the time the jury was out – twenty-three minutes – to realize what defence was put up: none.

I've found out the true story about my sister and how her secret life led to her conviction. The people she mixed with were devious, unscrupulous liars. But Ruth also lied. In court. She admitted murdering Blakely to protect those wicked characters. No doubt they told her she wouldn't hang.

After Andre died in 1982 the police arrived on my doorstep.

They said: 'Are you Andre McCallum's aunt?' 'Yes.' The policeman said: 'Well he's committed suicide.' They walked off without saying another word. Chris, my eldest son discovered the
Humphreys tape, from which I've already given some extracts,
in Andre's bedsitter in Paddington, which had been sealed for
two weeks. There was still a smell of Andre's decomposing body.

Here are some more excerpts from the conversation between
Andre and Christmas Humphreys, the prosecuting counsel.
The recording was crackly – Andre hid the cassette player
amongst papers in his briefcase. Each time I listen to it I feel
sad for his wasted life. It's Humphreys' blinkered attitude, years
after the trial, that makes me feel Ruth stood no chance when
she walked into the Old Bailey. Nearly thirty years after his
mummy died, Andre thought he could get the case reopened,
obtain the transcript of the trial and find out facts. Humphreys
merely told him to forget his mother being executed, think
about cause and effect and, said, 'If you'd come to me a bit
earlier you could have had all the shorthand notes of the trial.
But they've probably been destroyed now.' Who destroys notes
from a trial like this? But in fact getting any records to do with
Ruth's case was near to impossible.

A: Did you choose the case?

CH: We had five. One after the other. And this was
the shortest.

A: And you had no doubts about it?

CH: I had no doubts about it. It doesn't matter
whether I doubted or not. The jury had no doubts.
The defending counsel couldn't help her.

A: And you're not concerned that there should have been other people involved who were guilty in some way?

CH: To me . . .

A: To you it was just one person and you wanted to sacrifice one person.

CH: No I did not.

A: You wanted to sacrifice one person to death.

CH: I did not. Don't be silly. Don't be silly.

A: You were the prosecutor and the person died. Is that not so? That is a fact.

CH: That is so, yes. The papers came to me as a senior prosecuting counsel as one of four or five murders in that section. I looked through and said, this is clear. There's no argument. There's no defence to the charge.

A: I agree there was no defence in the . . .

CH: In English law

A: I agree as presented.

CH: In English law one had to deal with a charge of murder, the wilful and unlawful killing of another person.

A: So you weren't concerned with the person who assisted her?

CH: There was no charge against anybody else in a conspiracy to murder. We were trying one person.

201

Prosecuting counsel and defending counsel are each doing their part and the judge is doing his. Nobody is concerned with an elaborate analysis of all the motives and troubles and so on and so forth.

A: There wasn't much time was there? It was very short.

CH: There was all the time needed.

A: All the time needed! It was one day wasn't it?

CH: What else was there to be said?

A: Open-and-shut.

CH: And so were the facts . . .

A: Do you believe in mercy?

CH: Yes, certainly, and the law is merciful. I was known as a merciful judge.

A: Yes, in certain circumstances. Yes, you made it quite clear that some people merited mercy. In this case I'm a bit unsure that you felt she merited mercy.

CH: It never came into it. It never came into my mind because, you must understand, how we play in parts as if on a stage. I have my part to play. Defending counsel has his. The judge has his. The jury have theirs . . . Mercy never came into it. It was never suggested. It was never part of it. There could be no mercy in what *seemed* to be cold-blooded murder in the sense she knew what she was doing. She did it.

A: She knew what she was doing?

CH: Well after all she picked up the gun and pulled the trigger. You know if you're pulling the trigger.

A: Are you sure?

CH: I don't know. Nobody suggested she didn't . . .

A: Yes but, the thing that concerns me is how much you can know. You're a person totally unaware of this event, miles away etc. How can you know what's going on in a person's mind? How do you know they're hardened and cold?

CH: You don't. You can only tell by what they do, think, say, look like and so on.

A: What they do? Not the facts?

CH: What they do, how they look, what they say and so on.

A: That's total behaviourism.

CH: I don't know what that means. I don't care tuppence about philosophy and all those things.

A: It's about psychology.

CH: OK, I don't care tuppence about psychology. It's the laws of principles that some people say regulate the conduct of the machine called the mind.

A: Well OK, Do you want to redeem yourself in a

small way by a few words? Should my mother have suffered the death penalty?

CH: Should you have suffered?

A: No. Should *she* have suffered the death penalty?

CH: Yes. Because she had brought herself into the condition where it would be the effect of what she did. She would know that when she walked towards that car what would be the result.

CH: I think I said to the jury, 'Members of the jury this is to all intents and purposes a plea of guilty.'

A: You said that to the jury?

CH: I may have done. I told them the facts. All of us regarded it as a plea of guilty. Melford [Stevenson] put up the only possible point of law to the judge . . . Can't you come back now to the law of cause and effect?

A: I think what we have been talking about is very important. Unless I understand it, it's very difficult for me to accept the law of cause and effect.

CH: Cause and effect are equal and opposites.

A: What is a cause? Is it that an event happens?

CH: Why does it happen?

A: Why does it happen? This is the thing I don't

understand. To me it's a complete mystery. I don't know why this particular event happened.

CH: Any event happens as a result of a vast amount of causes coming together at that point of time in that place.

A: But in this particular case there's no cause. Well I've never been able to find a cause.

CH: Yes there is. Right. We'll keep off your particular point at the moment because you've got complications there. The mind, after all, no one knows the whole of another person's mind. But science accepts that cause and effect are equal and opposite. Where there is an effect, there is an equivalent cause. Where there is a certain cause there is nothing on God's earth, in God's heaven, will stop the effect happening. Right. This is basic science. The wisdom of the world: We are responsible for what we do. We have produced the causes and there is the effect . . . We Buddhists teach each other and teach others to accept the consequences . . . We are the cause of everything that happens to us. There is no one else to blame. There is no one to complain about. We take what comes as a result of what we have created.

He didn't seem to have thought about cause and effect in the same way while prosecuting at a trial on 18 February 1955, four months before Ruth's. Six Teddy Boys went into the Blue Kettle café in Islington, stabbed a soldier in the throat and got life imprisonment. Humphreys talked then about execution being barbaric and that people not getting hanged was the way forward. He was prosecuting and against hanging. At Ruth's trial he helped to hang her.

On 20 June 1955, 'Christmas Humphreys and Mr M. Griffith-Jones and Miss Jean Southworth instructed by DPP appeared on behalf of the prosecution ... Mr Melford Stevenson QC, Mr Sebag Shaw and Mr Peter Rawlinson instructed by Messrs Cardew-Smith and Ross appeared on behalf of the prisoner.' Humphreys opened the case for the Crown:

> Mrs Ellis is a woman of twenty-eight, divorced, and the story which you are going to hear outlined is this: that in 1954 and 1955 she was having simultaneous love affairs with two men, one of whom was the deceased and the other a man called Cussen, whom I shall call before you.
>
> It would seem that, lately, Blakely, the deceased man, was trying to break off the connection, and that the accused woman was angry at the thought that he should leave her, even though she had another lover at the time. She therefore took a gun which she knew to be loaded, which she put in her bag. She says in a statement which she signed: 'When I put the gun in my bag, I intended to find David and shoot him.' She found David and she shot him dead by emptying that revolver at him, four bullets going into his body, one hitting a bystander in the hand, and the sixth going we know not where.
>
> That in a few words, is the case for the Crown, and nothing else I say to you, in however much detail, will add to the stark simplicity of that story.

Melford Stevenson, Ruth's defence counsel, was worse:

> It cannot happen often in this court that in a case of
> this importance, fraught with such deep significance
> for the accused, the whole of the prosecution's story
> passes without any challenge from those concerned to
> advance the defence. Let me make this abundantly
> plain: there is no question here but that this woman
> shot this man. No one is going to raise any sort of
> doubt in your mind about that. You will not hear one
> word from me – or from the lady herself – question-
> ing that.

And this was just the beginning. The pantomime continued
when he asked Cussen: 'I do not want to press you for details,
but how often have you seen that sort of mark on her?' Why
didn't Stevenson want to press Cussen to answer a question
about Ruth's bruises? What's so special about him? Humphreys
is the same. He asks Cussen: 'You'll not mind if we use plain
words. Were you her lover at some time?'

The old boy network! Justice doesn't come into it. They
achieved their result by manipulating words. No wonder the
transcript was locked away: the inadequate questioning of the
witnesses was there for all to see.

What chance was there for Ruth to be found not guilty
when she was up against high-ranking men? Was it their
addresses – and who they were – that protected them from a
grilling? Reading through the transcript and knowing what I
know now, I assume there was an unwritten law that exempted
the tobacconist, the car mechanic, and the car salesman from
being properly cross-questioned.

It's taken nearly fifty years for the transcript to surface, it being a closed file for forty-four years. There's more evidence to come out, in a seventy-five-year closed file. Why, if it was an open-and-shut case, was the closed procedure extended beyond the normal thirty years? The answer is not simple. There was a miscarriage of justice. Those at the top knew it. Was this to protect certain names?

Someone else tried to get the trial transcript. I met Ron Fowler in 1989. He kept a fish shop in West Byfleet, Surrey. Like many people Ron was obsessed with the story. Stimulated by *Dance With a Stranger* he wanted to know who was called at the trial, so tried to get a copy of the transcript. He received a letter from the Lord Chancellor's Department in 1989: 'I regret to say that the file does not contain transcript of the trial and therefore unable to assist you further.' Another senior person phoned and wasn't so nice: 'As far as you're concerned, Mr Fowler, that file lies at the bottom of the Thames.'

After Ron Fowler's failed attempt, his journalist friend Syd Gillingham decided to try. He was unsuccessful with the Crown Prosecution Service so phoned the Public Record Office in 1990, taping the conversation. By then it was well past the thirty-year closure rule. He asked precise questions and received confusing, contradictory answers. He simply asked for a copy of the trial transcript. The PRO official replied: 'That would have been in the public domain anyway' and stated there was 'no problem if one indeed exists'. He was cagey and fobbed him off as to why the transcript wasn't there, citing protection of relatives. After a rambling reply he said it was in a closed file under Long Closure.

Ruth's fate was confirmed when the judge sent the jury home at the end of day one. Whether she had shot him or not she was going to hang. She had to be got rid of. The judge, Justice Havers, spoke to Humphreys and Stevenson:

> Before you address the jury it would be as well if we had a short discussion as to the law, and the jury of course will not be interested in that. Perhaps we might release them. Members of the jury, there are certain matters which have to be discussed by learned counsel which you need not be troubled with, and in those circumstances you are at liberty to leave the jury-box now, and will you be back in your places tomorrow morning just before half-past 10. You will bear in mind what I have said: do not talk about the case to anybody, and do not let anybody talk to you about it, because if you do it will mean a terrible expense and waste of time and money, for we would have to have this trial all over again; so bear that in mind.

A discussion between the three men followed – transcript, pages 61 to 71. For nearly fifty years it's been in a closed file. It is plain that Judge Havers was searching for an excuse not to put a case of manslaughter to the jury. He said to Stevenson, 'I gather that you propose to address the jury on the question of provocation.'

Ruth's built up emotions were discussed: how Blakely didn't turn up on Good Friday when he said he would; Ruth was under emotional pressure; she was going out of her mind because Blakely didn't contact her; how Blakely would make an honest woman of her; in the same breath they said he lived off her and went off with other women. They discussed men's emotions, men's court cases, men firing guns and how there was no law stating that women and their emotions are any different to men.

With no jury present, Stevenson gets a new lease of life. Knowing the case is a *fait accompli* he discusses at length (unlike his near-silent performance in court) the question of provocation. A strange contrast with his court appearance.

The discussion ended when neither Stevenson nor Humphreys could find a similar case with which to compare it. The judge called it a day. Having picked his way through the legal jargon, Judge Havers found an excuse – the fact there hadn't been a similar case was enough to find Ruth guilty. He decided there was insufficient evidence to support a verdict of manslaughter and wouldn't leave the issue of provocation to the jury.

The jury returned the following morning. Judge Havers directed them that the evidence did not support a verdict of manslaughter on the grounds of provocation. Stevenson therefore couldn't address the jury without inviting them to go against the judge's ruling.

The judge found my sister guilty – he was judge, jury, defence and prosecution.

The more I read the transcript, comparing it to witness statements before the trial, the more I see the skulduggery that took place. Long Closure of the files covered up the truth, protecting those people who conspired against her.

PC Thompson, the policeman from 'L' Division who was in The Magdala that night, *did not* actually see the shooting. 'L' Division is based at Carter Street on the other side of London. Thompson was at The Magdala on his own on Easter Sunday, when most people were with their families, and in his own car, miles off his patch. Rarely would police constables, on their earnings, own their own car. He gave his statement to Detective Chief Inspector Davies on 20 April. He said he noticed a blonde woman wearing spectacles: 'She looked through a rippled-type glass window of the saloon bar near the door . . . I could not see her face clearly as she was very close to the glass.' If *he* couldn't see her clearly, what was Ruth hoping to see through rippled glass with her poor eyesight? Anyone knows you can see form but can't distinguish faces from the outside.

At the magistrates court PC Thompson stated:

> I noticed a fair-haired woman with spectacles looking through the saloon bar window . . . I saw the accused, when I was in the bar, through the left-hand window on the photograph below the word 'Wines'. I saw her face. I heard one bang, followed by the cry, and then I heard a succession of bangs. I did not count the bangs. The accused was looking down at the body of Mr Blakely. No shot was fired after I came out of the public house.

At the Old Bailey there were further subtle omissions:

Q: Shortly after that did you notice anything?

A: I noticed a woman looking through the saloon bar window . . .

Q: But some time after you first noticed them [Gunnell and Blakely] did you hear something?

A: I heard a bang outside the public house followed by a man's cry. I ran outside into the street and I immediately saw Mrs Ellis standing on the pavement with her back to the wall of the public house, and she had a revolver in her right hand.

PC Thompson's important statement at the magistrate's court, 'No shot was fired after I came out of the public house,' was overlooked at the trial. Thompson *did not* see who shot Blakely. He was *not* a witness, but listening to him being questioned by Humphreys, you'd think he was. Ruth's appearance at the window wearing spectacles is omitted. An argument about her poor vision might have influenced the jury into questioning her ability to kill Blakely. Humphreys' controlling questions avoid any seed of doubt being planted in the jurors' minds, that Ruth was anything other than a murderess.

Melford Stevenson, her defending counsel, said: 'No questions.'

Humphreys told Andre that you can only tell what is going on in a person's mind by what they 'think, say, look like and so on'. Nonsense. He'd already influenced the jury when he called Nickolls as a witness saying: 'My Lord, I will now call Mr Nickolls because he is anxious to get away.' He planted the impression in the jurors' minds that the case was cut and dried and that Ruth was worthless and guilty.

I bet she was sorry she peroxided her hair and did herself up for the trial. The papers went to town beforehand blackening her character. I realize now how much the public was conditioned by the media. Peter Rawlinson, now Lord Rawlinson of Ewell, was Ruth's junior defence counsel. In his autobiography *A Price Too High*, he referred to Ruth's appearance at the Old Bailey on 11 May 1955: 'The photographs of Ruth Ellis in the newspapers showed a young woman with bright blonde hair. That was not how she looked when I saw her in a cell in the Old Bailey some weeks before the actual trial . . . When I saw her, it was faded. She looked little like her photographs . . . We shook hands, hers a small, limp hand matching the listless face and hair from which the dye had faded.'

One person would have encouraged Ruth to peroxide her hair, the person who visited her every day – Desmond Cussen. From 'Brief to Counsel to Appear on Behalf of the Accused:'

> This man has frequently visited her in prison and is likely to be of assistance to the Defence if he is not attacked. He was frequently at the club during the material times and can confirm much of what she says. She told him a great deal of her association with Blakely but sometimes misrepresented the position . . . It is believed that the Police may suspect him of having originally possessed the gun. But the Accused is quite definite that this was not so and she certainly does not want anything to be said or done, which might involve him in any way . . . Efforts have been made to enable the Accused to have her hair attended to because it is now changing colour patchily as a result of continued neglect. All the necessary materials have been obtained and a request made either to allow her to have a hairdresser or for someone of the prison staff to apply the necessary preparations but the Governor has stated that she has no authority to grant such a request. An interview is being sought with the Governor in order to see what can be done: but it is submitted that it is of consider-able importance to the Accused that she should be able to look her best at the trial . . .

213

If Cussen loved Ruth, he would not want her hanged. He was a man of the world, knew about appearances and impressions and should have advised her knowing she would be judged by her appearance. But he didn't love her – he used her. Peroxiding her hair was part of the scheme to create a bad impression. For two months Cussen visited Ruth in Holloway, taking gifts, brainwashing her and keeping her quiet till the trial. Then at the trial he turned coat and gave evidence for the prosecution – some friend. When the trial ended he disappeared, his job was done. Ruth never saw him again.

Ruth kept her part of their agreement. She kept quiet. Not just about where the gun came from; more importantly about her secret role of intelligence gathering in London's clubland since 1950. Cussen's part of the bargain was to look after Ruth's son. He had the money to pay for Andre's private education. He'd negotiated a loan on two of his properties in September 1954. He had ready cash at exactly the same time as Andre started at St Michael's College in Hitchin. But Cussen wasn't interested in the boy. Andre never saw him again after his mother's death.

Tuesday 21 June 1955

Mr Justice Havers: . . . it is my duty as a judge, as matter of law, to direct the jury that the evidence in this case does not support a verdict of manslaughter on the ground of provocation.

Mr Justice Havers: Mr Melford Stevenson, I have in the matter of law ruled that the question of provocation, as a question for the jury, reducing this killing which would otherwise be murder to manslaughter, is not a matter which is supported by the evidence. In those circumstances, in view of the evidence of the accused with regard to intention, it does not seem to me that there is any issue left on which you could address the jury.

Mr Melford Stevenson: No, my Lord. I am obliged.

Mr Humphreys: In the circumstances, my Lord, I have nothing more to say.

Justice Havers directed the jury. Ruth wasn't sentenced to death. She was murdered by the Establishment. They could not risk a scandal to the new Conservative government.

14

The Last Hours

'No Mummy, no.' Georgina was so frightened when they came to take her away. She thought I was her mummy – Ruth and I looked so much alike. I loved her as a baby when she was with me – they broke my heart when they stole her away. I never forget them coming at midnight to take Georgina. I still see her arms stretching out for me, and hear her voice even now.

Pauline remembers the noise surrounding her being taken, even recalls Father by the front door: 'You thought we were still asleep upstairs but we were all crying.' Even my boys missed her. Pauline still 'sees' the pink rabbit she left behind.

My parents and Granville came and took her away but never explained what they were doing. Everything was done in a rush. They waited outside, probably thinking Joe would have a go at them. If only he'd got out of bed. I remember my mother holding her arms out for Georgina as I cuddled her in a shawl. She wanted me because I'd treated her well. I begged my parents to come the next day but they grabbed her and left. I never got over it. Those miseries don't leave you. It was like a kidnap. Our neighbours told me how they heard Georgina screaming that night.

George Ellis was granted custody of her. Days before Ruth died she gave him permission to take Georgina to Manchester. He'd told Ruth some story about a woman he wanted to marry who couldn't have children. She would have the child. I never believed him. I've never worked out why he didn't want her adopted. I'm not certain who took her up north, George or my parents. Either way my parents thought they were on to a good thing. Mother was told she could look after Georgina and Father would do the gardening up there. It didn't happen.

Georgina's version of events in her book of going up north were incorrect: 'I have no idea on what precise day or month my father acted and stole me away, but I suspect it was either at the end of 1953 or early in 1954.' Georgina didn't leave us till July 1955 – four days before Ruth died they took her away. George told her before he committed suicide in 1958 that she should have stayed with Auntie Muriel; she would have been happy with my children.

I don't show my feelings to people but when I'm on my own, that's when the past affects me drastically. You can't forget the horror of it all. But you learn as time passes to control your feelings. I cannot ever forget. When they took Ruth they might as well have taken a whole family.

My parents were in service in Hampstead in September 1954 and had Georgina with them. They tried keeping her quiet because children weren't allowed. But they couldn't keep her and brought her round to me. Andre was sent to the Roman Catholic boarding school in Hitchin courtesy of Desmond Cussen. I regret that – it had a bad effect on him. He couldn't settle without his mum and was always running away from school. He ended up a recluse and a wanderer; always looking for something. He thought he would bump into his mum. Imagine what you'd be like. Joe remembers Georgina was with us for a long period, we were going to keep her, the same as Andre. Joe said if all goes well, everything will be the same for him as it is for our children. If only it had worked that way.

When Georgina came to me she had nothing. She was so blooming excited when we walked to the park with my five children. I bought her patent leather shoes. They were brand new and cost five bob. I remember her looking at them and laughing. They fitted her perfectly. I found one of Marlene's best dresses. It was pink with a frill, had puff sleeves and lace round the edge all tied up with a sash. She looked super in it. Georgina had most of Marlene's clothes. She had dark curly hair and I'd put a pink ribbon in it. She thought she was in heaven. She was lovely when she was little.

Ruth wrote to me after the trial asking if I would look after her children. The end was coming. She'd already said her children would mingle with my family. I never kept the letter because of the children, they're nosy, but I remember some of her words. She wrote: 'Muriel, I've told Joe you could have Andre and Georgina for me.' She hoped I was coping OK, sent her love to her children and said: 'Take care of the children and your own. Lots of love. Ruth.' That was all. She'd arranged it with Joe as well. But my parents didn't care what she'd said, they wouldn't listen. They insisted Andre went with them. It's the last thing that should have happened.

Two days before Ruth died Andre went. The Labour MP for Kensington, George Rogers and his wife came into the picture and took him away. They liked to think they were helping out. But they were only interested in the limelight. Buried in a Home Office file at the PRO was a brief statement from Ruth to George Rogers, made during his visit to the prison on 29 June 1955, after she had been condemned to death. She had told him about 'matters she had not disclosed, but she did not want to as she did not want more scandal.' What were those dark secrets that went with her to her grave?

The MP was given permission by Mother to take Andre away on a holiday until Ruth had been hanged. What were they thinking about? He should have stayed with us, not gone off with total strangers. So two children I loved as my own were taken away. Inside a week the Rogers told him about his mummy. It wasn't for them to tell him, an eleven-year-old boy.

Mr Rogers brought Andre back to our place after his 'holiday'. He was crying his eyes out. Mother was with us. She politely asked Mr Rogers to go, not wanting any of his fancy talk. 'I have nothing to say to you.' Andre was broken-hearted, crying to me: 'Why didn't you tell me, Auntie Muriel, about what happened to my mother? I wish that you had told me.' Poor thing, he was so upset because he would never see his mother again. He cried, then we all cried.

My parents and my brother Granville had made some sort of pact with Cussen. But for some reason, two days before Ruth was executed, Granville started searching for Cussen. It was 11 July, the day that Ruth dismissed Bickford, her solicitor. Granville had collected names on a petition and taken it to Cussen's flat in Devonshire Street with a journalist. They couldn't get him out of bed. I remember Granville saying that Cussen eventually opened the door. Granville and the journalist looked round and saw a woman in his bed. They didn't know who it was. That upset my brother's attitude towards him.

On the evening of the 12th Granville went to Buckingham Palace with the journalist trying to see the Queen, hoping she could reprieve Ruth. They took armfuls of signatures done up in huge rolls of paper. They said at the Palace gate that the Queen had retired for the night. They wouldn't listen. My brother walked away disillusioned. He went out of his mind and lost faith in everything.

I don't know if Granville told Cussen about Ruth's solicitor Mr Bickford being dismissed, and how Mishcon and Simmons would be visiting her the next day. Knowing Granville, he did. But Granville's visit to Cussen's flat in effect forewarned him that Ruth might blow his cover. My own brother gave Cussen the chance to vanish the day before Ruth's death. When the police searched for him during the evening of 12 July, to question him about the gun, Cussen had disappeared.

Cussen lived at Flat 20 Goodwood Court in Devonshire Street, Marylebone. The number in the street wasn't mentioned in trial documents. But I discovered that the block is between 58 and 59 Devonshire Street ten doors down from Stephen Ward's consulting rooms at number 38. It appears that Ward moved in, in late 1949, about eighteen months before Cussen moved to Goodwood Court. Strangely, sometime around 1957, they both moved from Devonshire Street to places in Bayswater, within a quarter-of-a-mile of each other. Cussen went to the Lanterns Hotel in Craven Road, and according to Knightley and Kennedy's *An Affair of State*, Stephen Ward rented an apartment in Orme Square, retaining his consulting room in Devonshire Street until 1961. Ward and Cussen were no ordinary neighbours – Cussen seemed to be following Ward around.

Without Cussen visiting her in her last twenty-two days, without the brainwashing, Ruth was breaking down. Another couple of days and she would have told the whole story. I always believed that she told Mishcon and Simmons the truth about the gun because Granville told her about Cussen and the woman. With Ruth it was tit for tat. She'd been protecting Cussen when she should have protected herself. At 12.30 p.m. on 12 July she broke her silence, telling her solicitors: 'It is only with the greatest reluctance that I have decided to tell how it was that I got the gun with which I shot Blakely. I did not do so before because I felt that I was needlessly getting someone into possible trouble.' It was not the whole truth.

I'm going back to the day before Ruth died. I hadn't seen my sister since before the shooting and tried to put on a brave face, but was dreading going into the prison. It was a muddled feeling because I thought she wasn't going to die. I didn't know what I was going to do or say. Imagine, I would be seeing my sister for the last time. I shook and felt traumatized.

My sister-in-law, Vickie, looked after the children while I went to the prison with Mother. We left home early, nine in the morning, caught a train then got the tube to Holloway.

The newspapers reported who Ruth's visitors were that day. I was mentioned in some paper – they'd got it wrong. Evidently I was leaving Holloway prison with Mother and Father. It wasn't true, it was Granville's wife Kathleen, not me. I wouldn't have gone with Father – the secrecy was still going on about Robert. I was sneaked in. Mother took me in, still threatening me about keeping quiet or she'd tell Joe about Robert. She said: 'Don't ask questions, don't open your mouth. Ruth can't answer anything. The warders will shut you up quick if you do.' So I didn't.

Ruth was in a pyramid-shaped area at the top of the building. We climbed some winding stone steps that made me shudder, they were worn away by prisoners who'd tramped down them over the years. You could see the scratch marks where they had dug their nails in. It was horrible.

Ruth must have had a terrifically strong character to remain composed. I was more nervous than she appeared to be. Mother and I stood side by side. Ruth looked lovely. I'd never seen her looking so well. She'd put on weight because she'd been eating well. She was wearing a green overall. Her cheeks were rosy. She didn't have make-up on but she didn't need it – she had good skin. Two big warders stood there, one either side of her. They were fond of Ruth.

I wore a grey patterned dress with pleats, with a white collar and cuffs and had high-heeled shoes on. Ruth said: 'Do a twirl in your dress.' I felt silly but I did it for her. I longed to tell her to give in, change her mind and tell the truth but I couldn't. Why couldn't I ask anything? I wanted to mention her children, to tell her they were OK and well looked after. I couldn't. Mother had said not to. We didn't want her breaking down. Prison warders only allowed us to say: 'How are you.' She could talk to us. We were not allowed to ask her questions.

Ruth asked about my children. She never mentioned Georgina or Andre. It would have broken her heart. She asked about Martin who was two at the time. I said he had a dark complexion, inherited from the Russian side of Joe's family. She told us not to worry, that everything would be all right. She cheered us up. I believe she really thought she'd be reprieved even at that late stage with twenty-four hours to go. We were sad but had to bear up.

She didn't say goodbye.

I was choked. I wanted to cry but I fought back the tears. I'd learned to do it with the problems I've been through. I didn't dare talk to Mother because she'd start crying. She was in a state because that was her girl. I saw Ruth just that once. I felt so guilty I couldn't help her. Nobody phoned that day to reassure me about what would happen the next day.

On the morning of Ruth's execution the *Daily Mail* wrote: 'To her family she revealed no signs of the strain she was under. But when they had gone she collapsed and lay prostrate on her iron bed screaming, "I do not want to die."' I don't know if it's true but what woman wouldn't? She must have realized she was leaving her children.

Bickford wrote to the Home Office on 28 June saying: 'She'd done her utmost to tell the whole truth as far as she herself is concerned.' He added she posed and acted a part; he was right there, she should have been an actress. Like Joe said she was acting a part when she stayed with us at Domonic Drive.

At the PRO I looked through a box containing a scrapbook called Press Cuttings Ruth Ellis. I came across this article supposedly written by Ruth in the condemned cell. From start to finish, there was not a glimmer of truth. It was not the real Ruth.

'Today Ruth Ellis's Life Story Begins Exclusively In Woman's Sunday Mirror.'

'My Love and Hate' by Ruth Ellis

I was born in Rhyl, Wales, in the same circumstances as millions of you. I came from a happy home, with a sister and brother, and my parents were loving and understanding. My father was a musician with all the loveable qualities that music gives a man . . . My father travelled a lot and mother was the greater influence in my upbringing . . .

It was a curious thing about my hair. Until I was sixteen it was golden blonde. Then quite inexplicably I turned into a brunette. When I became manageress of the Little Club in Knightsbridge in 1953 I decided to become a platinum blonde. I did it on impulse. You know how it is – you look in the mirror one morning and decide that you must do something . . .

We moved to London when Daddy got a new job. Here something happened that was to influence my whole life. For a year I lay on my back in St Giles Hospital, Camberwell, with rheumatic fever. For a year I ate nothing but boiled fish . . .

My first serious date became my first love, my first taste of ecstasy and my first experience of absolute and bitter misery. I worked with a woman friend at the Lyceum. She was several years older than I and I knew she went to dances and parties with servicemen. One day she said: 'I've got a date with a Canadian tonight . . .'

We met at the Lyceum, I was excited, happy and looking my best. I liked my boy, Mac, from the start . . . Mac loved me devotedly, and when he was with his unit he would write not once but often twice a day . . . Then one raw November morning the telegram came. Mac was dead.

She said 'Daddy'. She didn't call him that. At that age we had a mother and a father. As for the wonderful man she was talking about – she knew he was wicked. Ruth wasn't alive when he went 'travelling'. Lying on her back for a year in St Giles Hospital with rheumatic fever! She was not there for a year. She talks of meeting Clare Andrea at the Lyceum – she met him down the dives with me. Nor was she a golden blonde. Her hair was always auburn. The bleaching was not done on impulse – it was part of the transformation.

The article continued: 'Now constantly watched Ruth Ellis reveals her experiences in a ground floor death cell.' She was *upstairs* in the condemned cell. Whoever wrote it forgot that all visits had to be supervised and recorded. When Mr Rogers visited her, the Governor of Holloway wrote to the Under Secretary of State at the Home Office: '9656 Ruth Ellis, Condemned to death.' She reported a visit that Principal Officer Griffin had supervised of 'Mr George Rogers MP to the above named woman on the 29 inst.' There's no evidence of a letter to the Home Secretary about a journalist's visit. Tony Van Den Bergh, co-author of *Ruth Ellis, A Case of Diminshed Responsibility*? told me he'd tried to get in but they wouldn't allow it. If the story were true it would have taken days of interviews. Like her police statement it was rehearsed. I don't believe she told her life story to anyone in prison. She wasn't allowed to discuss anything with anyone except for special people like the doctor and Judge Havers. You're in a little room with a grille and big warders.

I found four instalments of the *Woman's Sunday Mirror* story published between 26 June and 17 July 1955 – four double pages of useless words. How did the nameless journalist get in while she was constantly supervised in the condemned cell? Someone must have ransacked her room in Egerton Gardens for all the information, or got it before she went into prison.

There's a photo of her as a teenager in front of an aeroplane with letters OZ behind her shoulder. She's saying: 'It was in this mood that I met George Ellis . . . George had a pilot's licence. I enjoyed flying with him until he took me up one day and started crazy aerobatics . . . ' From that tiny picture, the plane was identified as an American Fairchild Angus, serial number G-AJOZ that flew from Biggin Hill or Redhill. The ATA (Air Transport Auxiliary) used them in the war. Billy Butlin, a member of the Little Club had two Fairchilds at Skegness.

There's a snap of George Ellis, looking like an ugly detective and one of Ruth with long dark hair standing in front of the St Ives Bay Hotel. The caption says it was taken on a long holiday to Newquay with George where they had 'champagne and caviar for breakfast. The hotel bill came to £100 a week.' That's make-believe. Eleven guineas a week all-in was the going rate in Cornwall, and you'd get full board, electric lifts and television.

The Hotel Bristol was and still is one of Newquay's best hotels, owned by the Young family since 1927. What Mrs Young remembers of 1950 turned the article inside out. She confirmed Ruth and George stayed at the Bristol:

> It would have been towards the latter part of the year – September. I remember because we didn't seem all that busy. They spent a lot of time in the sitting room and stayed four or five days, not a long time. My son estimates they would have paid ten guineas a week for full board including afternoon tea on the beach. Of all the people who came to the hotel she stood out. A memory I've always held is of Ruth in a black cocktail dress wearing black elbow-length gloves. She was the sort of figure you looked at. In my mind's eye she seemed older than twenty-three.

The chauffeur was with them and I thought how extraordinary it was. He came into the bar and it was like a threesome. I couldn't understand why he was with them all the time. The chauffeur was rather peculiar – he looked a bit suspect. The whole set-up was odd. It looked like Ruth and the chauffeur were having an affair.

The Ellis family used to come to us every year. George and his parents and George's sister, she came down. They were special people. His father was a dentist. Having known George for quite a few years when I saw him in 1950 I was shocked. His face had been slashed, fairly recently. He looked as if he'd been in a fight. That upset me. I was shattered. I never knew George had been married. I never knew he had a wife and children. He never brought them down.

It seemed like a bizarre *ménage à trois*. You can see George was spoofing – acting someone else. It is puzzling that George's birth and marriage certificates stated his father was a wholesale fish merchant; Mrs Young had been led to believe he was a dentist. Coupled with George's previous odd behaviour, the Newquay episode confirms in my mind that Ruth and George's marriage two months later was a sideshow – a cover. George was a minder-type, an organizer and an ingredient in the conspiracy.

I told Evelyn Galilee, Ruth's warder in the condemned cell, about the *Woman's Sunday Mirror* article, hoping she'd have something to say about it. I wanted the truth. She said:

There were times when she looked in the distance. Then, she'd look back. There was sadness there. I never asked. She never said. She wrote her life story? That's not possible. How did she get it out of Holloway? I was there. She wrote nothing like that. It wouldn't be allowed. We were there when she wrote anything. I can't see how it's done. She'd be under scrutiny. Everything she says or does is recorded in a special book – an officer gets it up to date. I would have seen it. Ruth's wing was called the CC wing. It's up the stone steps and the only visitors would have been the solicitor, the deputy governor or nurse; that sort of person and on the other side of the grille to Ruth. I believe I opened the door to the solicitors the day before she died. One was tall. One was short; thirty or forty mark. Everything, everyone goes in the book. In those years it was strict. A journalist couldn't have got to her during those three weeks. It wouldn't have been done before the trial. They seem to be making their own story for their own gain. There's got to be someone in higher places. There's so much fabrication. Why don't they get to the people who knew what happened?

And – Ruth would NOT write that story and admit what she's done. She WOULD NOT involve her family. Her little boy was uppermost in her mind. She loved him. I know Ruth said he had to be protected. She wanted to make sure he never found out.

It's not Ruth that's written that article.

Only recently, after reading the foreword in *Ruth Ellis, The Last Woman to be Hanged* by Robert Hancock, I identified the mystery author of the articles supposedly written by Ruth in the *Woman's Sunday Mirror*. Robert Hancock said he wrote them.

15

Death Sentence

I think Ruth just gave in. God knows, she must have felt something though when she was led to be hanged. Near to nine o'clock the two warders who guarded her that morning said goodbye. They didn't want to lose her. Her arms had been tied behind her back in the condemned cell. It's a cruel way to kill somebody. It was wicked what those people in authority did. They were murderers. People ask how I talk about this without getting upset. I've learned to control myself.

Poor Ruth, she listened to her own scaffolding being built. The governor of Holloway said it was previously used in December 1954 when Styllou Pantiopiou Christofi was hanged. Her gallows were knocked down and a new one was erected for Ruth.

I came across this question in parliament dated 8 December 1955. The Home Secretary lied in his reply to Mr Hyde:

Mrs Ruth Ellis (Execution)

Mr Hyde asked the Secretary of State for the Home Department if he is aware that the prisoners and staff in Holloway Prison were greatly disturbed shortly before the execution of the late Mrs Ruth Ellis, by the noise caused through hammering in the erection of the scaffold on which she was subsequently hanged;

229

and whether he will take steps to prevent inconveniences of this kind in future in all Her Majesty's Prisons where executions are carried out.

Major Lloyd-George: My Hon Friend is under a misapprehension. No scaffold was erected in Holloway prison before the execution of Mrs Ellis.

Mr Hyde: Is my Right Hon and gallant Friend aware that what he has just said will reassure those members of the public who were alarmed at a statement to the contrary sense made by the Bishop of Stepney, who visited Mrs Ellis shortly before her execution?

Wednesday 13 July 1955 was another sunny morning. I got up at seven o'clock to get the children ready for school. I hadn't slept at all like every night since the shooting. Joe was working in a shipyard but did come home that night wearing a black tie to see how I was.

I was wearing my housecoat and slippers ready to do the housework. My children had their cereal. That's all they liked in the morning and a glass of milk or a cup of tea. I had to take the milk out of the fridge the night before because the second-hand gas fridge we had that came off a boat used to freeze the milk solid.

It was hell trying to keep composed. I stood by the door as the children left, giving them their cod liver oil tablets, one in each mouth. They went to St Paul's Cray school over the road. I walked into the sitting room and switched on the wireless, to hear the nine o'clock pips of Big Ben, just as they announced that Ruth Ellis had been hanged. I didn't want to hear it. I was alone except for Martin, my youngest. I remember screaming out: 'Lord don't let Ruth die, let it be me.'

Evelyn Galilee, the prison warder who guarded Ruth in the condemned cell, was one of the last people to see her alive. She told me about Ruth's last few minutes:

> Prior to the 'drop' Ruth wanted to go to the toilet. I took her in. These thick padded calico knickers were brought and I was told they had to be put on her. It was against a woman's dignity. I said: 'I'm sorry Ruth but I've got to do this.' They had tapes back and front to pull. I blinded my eyes from them as she put them on. 'Is that all right?' she said to me. She was very calm. 'Would you pull these tapes Evelyn, I'll pull the others.' They had to be tight. It was in case anything came out. Ruth asked what they were for. I couldn't tell her.

I never believed what the papers said about Ruth being given a glass of brandy before being led out in her smock and canvas knickers to Albert Pierrepoint the hangman. As usual the newspapers, knowing nothing of what happened, made up a sensational story about Ruth being given a drink. Charity Taylor, governor of the prison, when asked by the newspaper men if it was usual to give a person a little brandy before being executed avoided answering and replied: 'I don't know.' Evelyn Galilee was there with Ruth. Fifteen minutes before the time, the deputy governor was at one end of the table in Ruth's cell, the chaplain at the other end, Ruth in the middle. Evelyn said she stood against the door gripping the heating pipes about to flake out:

The nursing sister came in with the kidney tray. She poured liquid out of a bottle, passed it to Ruth but she said no. The sister tried again saying, it will calm you. It contained knock-out drops. They didn't want a fight. She refused. I place my hand on the Bible and say she DID NOT have it. She refused three times. I kept thinking, please take it. But she didn't. They can say whatever they like on the autopsy report. It was made to appear clean and tidy for people to read, making people think it deadened the pain. The report was whitewashed for public consumption – to make it look human. Hang someone and they're human! Not to me it wasn't. It's all secret. You live in a twilight world. If he noted brandy, why didn't he note the knock-out drops? Just before Ruth went through the door she took off her purple diamanté glasses and put them on the table saying, 'I won't need those any more.' She was short-sighted and could have hurt herself if she didn't wear them.

Dr Keith Simpson the Home Office pathologist did the post-mortem on her. He reported she'd had a drink: 'Stomach and contents – small food residue, and odour of brandy.'

Evelyn Galilee repeated: 'Ruth did NOT drink any brandy.'

I've discovered the Coroner's report on Ruth's death is in another closed file, protected from public scrutiny until 2030.

One of the few people I spoke to on 13 July was my neighbour Mrs Hatch. She came to see if I was all right: 'Coo-ee, it's all over Muriel,' she called. I felt like dying. I felt like killing myself. Look at my mother, she tried to gas herself. Or so I always thought. Unless you have gone through this you've no idea what it's like. You can't describe it. It's something so ghastly. I went like an iceberg, as if it had been me. Nobody phoned me. There was utter silence.

I poked my head out on the veranda later and heard Mrs Hatch talking to Jean Turner. Our window boxes looked gorgeous that year and were full of snapdragons and fuchsias. I sat by the window, the sun poured on my face, and I stared into space willing *myself* dead, not Ruth. Martin woke me up with his crying.

What made matters worse was Ruth not having a proper funeral. She was chucked on top of four murderers in unconsecrated ground inside the prison walls. There was no final goodbye. Five women were executed at Holloway including Ruth: Christofi, Edith Thompson, Annie Walters and Amelia Sachs.

I didn't have a cup of tea. Nor lunch. I was busy running round the house shaking my head crying it can't be true. I felt trapped like somebody losing his reasoning. But I managed to get the children's tea when they came home. Chris was old enough to remember what went on. He knew in the morning that the hanging was going to take place but he hadn't said anything. He's deep and never talks about things, like his dad. He says what he wants to say, not what you would like him to say. The others came in, looked at me and said nothing. Chris told me how he'd heard about it at school; Joey said he'd read it in the papers. Chris was coming up for eleven, Joey was ten. In the same way Joe got shouted at by uncouth people near the river, slinging remarks like 'Your sister-in-law's a murderer,' my children got it at school. The kids that day said: 'This is what your auntie got. Hung.' They went through hell. The other kids said: 'We shouldn't really play with you because your auntie is a murderer, she shot somebody.' Then the string and hangman's knot and scaffolding came out.

Pauline doesn't remember anything unusual. Her first real knowledge was when she was a teenager. 'I can remember you giving me the newspaper clippings to read. I said "bloody hell" and kept it to myself. It wasn't until years later I was able to talk about it. I remember my first job at the Royal Bank of Scotland in Mayfair, nobody knew until I left seven years later. They called me a dark horse after they'd read a clip in the paper and associated the name.'

I'm getting emotional now. The children remember their Auntie Ruth with her clippety-clop shoes, her stilettos. She'd bring them sweets and see her two kids. But my children never spoke about her after what happened. Their Auntie Vickie told them 'not to mention Auntie Ruth to your mum.' I never told them their Auntie Ruth had been hanged, just so they wouldn't say anything to me, especially not with poor Andre there. Pauline said that Joey wasn't aware of it until he came home from school that day. As he passed Mrs Hatch's house, she grabbed him saying, 'you're staying with us tonight'. She was a good woman, old Ethel.

Joe can't bring back much about the day Ruth left us. He says her life and death didn't really affect him, but when he came home that evening I knew he was upset. He wasn't a man for cuddling. If he saw me upset he wouldn't touch me. He'd say: 'There's nothing you could do and that's it.' He kept quiet but I know he was upset. He remembers the article that reported Ruth as she walked out to be hanged 'as though she were going for tea or something'. It shouldn't have been printed.

Ruth had ambitions but when she got involved with Blakely they were crushed to bits. She told Mother that all she wanted was to get enough money to put down on a house and get a normal job. She told me about her dreams too: how she was determined to escape our abusive childhood and how she wanted to work hard any way she could. But from 1950 she was living on borrowed time – she'd been led into an even more dangerous world. Getting involved with George Ellis and Stephen Ward was the starting point; Blakely was the final straw. Then she was fixed, good and proper, by Cussen. He got her hanged.

The magazine called *Today* came out every Tuesday. In 1961 they wrote about Albert Pierrepoint: 'He had a disarming smile.' He was given the privilege of killing people which in my mind makes him the biggest criminal of them all. He did a whole batch at the Nuremberg trials. He went round the world killing. Ruth was led out and stood on top of the trapdoor. He interviewed her beforehand to find out her weight to get the drop right. They tied her ankles together with rope. Windows were covered; the door was secured. Pierrepoint came out and put a hood over her head. He put a loop of rope round her neck. It was covered in chamois leather so she wouldn't feel the burns. She wouldn't have time to feel the burns, would she? She stood trussed up like this. As soon as it came up to nine o'clock, he pulled the lever. There would be a terrific vibration that shakes the chamber and Ruth would have jerked upwards and downwards for a few seconds till she was dead. It's evil. Ruth's death was quick. We died a thousand deaths. Nobody knows what her final words were.

I found this in the *Sunday Pictorial* letters column. It was from Mr H.W. Critchell of Brixton, a hangman in London for eight years:

At 9 o'clock last Wednesday morning Ruth Ellis was hanged. That's that. You extracted your pound of flesh. All was over and would soon be forgotten. HOW WRONG YOU ARE. That same morning there were at least ten people waiting to witness or carry out the execution of Ruth Ellis. There was the Governor, the Padre, the Sheriff, the Hangman, the Death Watch etc. All would have been greatly relieved had a reprieve been granted. No such miracle happened as Ruth Ellis 'hit the rope'. These ten or more people, looking down the pit at that ghastly spectacle suspended from that rope, received a severe shock to their systems. It is the living that suffered by this devilish, uncivilized practice. I write this in good faith. I have entered that pit and shamed myself many times. I am thoroughly ashamed . . . No medicine can ever help me. I still suffer.'

Robert Hancock wrote the following in *Ruth Ellis, The Last Woman to be Hanged*: 'In Hemel Hempstead her father started to play a lament on his cello and her mother, unable to cry, went upstairs to pray.' That July morning Mother and Father were actually by the gate at Holloway prison while they were hanging Ruth. My mother loved her. Afterwards they came down to my place with Granville. They asked if Mother could lie down on the bed and took her upstairs. She was tired and distraught and was crying. Granville had to identify Ruth's body at Holloway because Father refused. He couldn't get away quickly enough. He must have felt so guilty. That was his punishment for what he did to his girls. For forcing Ruth out to get money for him. Some newspaper, I think the *Star*, reported that my father, a street musician, was outside the prison that morning playing 'Abide with me' on the cello. It's typical of the lies that were put out. My father's never been a street musician; it was big orchestras for him. Reporters believed anything they were fed. He hadn't played the cello in years since his illness. AND he wasn't religious. He'd never been to church in his life. He'd say: 'When you die, you die and when you're dead there's nothing else.'

It wasn't till years later, just before he died, that Granville described to me what Ruth's body was like when he identified it: 'Muriel, I want to tell you this, it's been on my mind. I want to be truthful. I told you Ruth looked so beautiful. She didn't. It was a terrible mess. Her face looked lovely but it had been put together. Her head was lopsided. Her neck was twisted. They'd tried to push it together.' They asked him if he'd like to look at the rest of the body which was covered with a sheet. He told me how hanging doesn't just break your neck it affects the rest of your body, it goes to pieces. It's only the skin that holds it together. When she went everything went into those canvas knickers they put on her. The bones moved, the heart moved. All the guts, the liver, everything gets mashed up. Even her private parts come out.

Evelyn Galilee told me what she'd heard at Holloway on that July day in 1955: 'It was a vicious drop. Whatever the autopsy report said about it all being all right, clean break and everything – it wasn't all right. It was horrific. She was such a doll-like creature. I could see her as she was. Then I could see her broken body in my mind.'

Amongst documents at the PRO I found this letter dated 27 July 1955 from Mr Douglas Glover MP to the Home Secretary: 'I supported capital punishment but the next of kin having to identify the body is barbaric. It is surely bad enough for any family to know that one of their members is being

237

hanged, but after the law has taken its course to demand then that the next of kin shall come and see the body seems to be quite dreadful.'

Mrs Hatch was supportive to me after the hanging but it wasn't long before the malicious calls started. One regular was from somebody who asked if I went to bed with anybody at the drop of a hat. Then in the newsagent's where I'd get sweets for the children, a group of women sniggered, 'Served her right for killing that lovely young man,' to my face. As I went out I said: 'Are you the judge then?' I never went in there again. I'd go to the hairdresser's and she wouldn't do my hair. One day I was walking along with two of the children. A lady stopped me and said: 'You have two lovely kids.' I had Martin and Marlene with me toddling along. 'But isn't it a shame that they had an auntie that was a murderer.'

I couldn't face going out for weeks after that. Pauline went on errands with a list and did the launderette because we didn't have a washing machine. She told me the lady there felt sorry for us. In the end she told Pauline to go and play – she'd do the washing. Eventually, so I didn't have to face people in the shopping centre where we lived, I took a train to Bromley. People wouldn't know me there. I got as far as the teashop in the town but turned round and got on the next train back. I was so frightened. It took ages to get out and face anyone.

The children were teased at school. I told them not to worry and it wasn't Ruth who was to blame. I tried hard to cheer them up. If we went to the park I shielded them so nobody could make fun of them but Chris and Joey would fight their own battles. We coped for ten years. Eventually we moved because there were so many filthy mouths about.

At the end of June 1955, with fourteen days left until her hanging, Ruth had decided that 'Mr Bickford was to blame for everything that had occurred and no longer had any confidence in him.' HO291/238. She said she wanted to see Mr Simmons of Victor Mishcon and Co. urgently. But Bickford, instead of instructing Simmons to visit Ruth straight away in Holloway, wrote to him suggesting that Mr Mishcon should write to the Home Secretary about her. The more I scrutinized the document, the more I realized Bickford was wasting time. He dilly-dallied until 11 July, before finally writing to Simmons saying Ruth wanted to see him urgently. With twenty-four hours left, what could Mr Simmons effectively do to help her? Nothing. I can only assume Cussen was manipulating Bickford behind the scenes.

I found a memorandum amongst PRO documents, dated 20 March 1973. It refers to a request made by Jonathan Goodman, general editor of the 'Celebrated Trials' series, to publish Ruth's statement made on 12 July 1955 in his forthcoming book *The Trial of Ruth Ellis*. His request was refused by the Home Office.

The document didn't seem important originally. Now I can see the plotting that went on. Mishcon and Simmons must have rushed round to see Sir Philip Allen, the civil servant at the Home Office, straight after seeing Ruth that day. Allen noted their discussion and *wrote* to Mishcon, as if there was all the time in the world. An anonymous Home Office official stated on the memorandum: 'A careful perusal of all 66 sub numbers does not, however, reveal when, why or how they came to be in possession of the note.' Somebody was obviously scared and playing for time. Ruth's statement on 12 July 1955 was instantly put under wraps. What was going

239

on? It looks like Ruth had to go. Nobody was going to rock the boat.

I began collecting every bit of information relating to Ruth's death when I realized she had been framed in the last years of her life. I had to have answers to questions. Document number HO291/237 explained how Mishcon and Simmons visited Ruth on the 12 July to make 'an alteration to her will and certain other legal documents'. I didn't know she made one. Where is it? More importantly, what was the alteration?

I wrote to Lord Mishcon and asked him those questions. On 28 November 2002 he wrote back but couldn't or wouldn't answer the questions:

Dear Madam

The events about which you have written to me occurred nearly fifty years ago and any papers in this office relating to them would long since have been destroyed. Most of them would in any event be covered by professional privilege. The sole question upon which in these circumstances I can comment upon is that relating to whether or not the late Ruth Ellis made a Will. My recollection is that she did and that the sole beneficiary named in it was her son. I am afraid that I cannot be of any further assistance to you.

Lord Mishcon

I know Ruth is with me, pushing me to find the truth. Papers destroyed! Joe told me all solicitors know wills are lodged publicly. The PRO said: 'Probate records for England

and Wales, from 12 January 1858 to the present day, are held by the Probate Service, Principal Registry Family Division in London.' On 24 December 2002 the Probate Registry at Castle Chambers in York wrote to Monica Weller:

> In the Estate of: Ruth Ellis
>
> A search has been made in the estate of the above-named from the beginning of 1955 to the end of 1958, and on information given we can report that no record has been found.

All the way down the line I've been blocked.

I thought about Ruth's property. She must have accumulated stuff, clothes and so on. I'd always been suspicious when Mother said there was virtually nothing left in Ruth's flat. An expensive black evening gown that Father bought for her was still in the flat. Mother found Ruth's red jacket that she'd bought to take to Le Mans (she never got to France), a pair of beige trousers and a white hand-knitted pullover, a shirt-waister dress, an empty Christian Dior perfume bottle, a bent ring, a satin dance bag and a black velvet coat. The rest, including a cassette player and tapes, had disappeared. Where did it all go? I wouldn't have thought it was destroyed. It was more likely to be in the hands of the police, or so I thought.

Ruth taped the men in her flat. And she was desperate enough to ask mother to retrieve the tapes. But somebody else got them away quickly. I suspected back in 1955 that Cussen had taken them or destroyed them – he had had the opportunity. Now the PRO files show that Cussen took them to Bickford for safe keeping straight after the shooting: 'Instruc-

241

ting solicitors have tape recording of a conversation between the Accused and Deceased on Christmas Day 1954 and the Accused and Cussen on 10th January 1955. These recordings do not appear to have any real significance so far as the trial is concerned but may nevertheless possibly be of interest to counsel.' (HO 291/237).

Why did Cussen give them to Bickford if they were harmless, and why was Ruth so agitated about them? The tapes were not returned to my mother. In 1977 extracts were broadcast on the radio. I was furious. My solicitor wrote to Mr Bickford's executors demanding their return. We didn't receive a reply. (This letter is in the Appendix.)

I read journalist Peter Grisewood's memorandum at the PRO. It was sent to Lord Mancroft on 21 February 1956, nine days after Burgess and Maclean surfaced in Moscow, the first time they'd been seen in public for five years. Grisewood queried the police investigation at the time of Ruth's case and the Home Secretary's refusal to grant a reprieve. He stated that Cussen took all Ruth's clothes to Bickford along with Ruth's tapes for safe keeping. Grisewood said: 'He [Bickford] had all Ruth Ellis's clothes in his possession and would have to return them to her family but was arranging to have them photographed first. I was disgusted by what I heard and saw . . . After this I left and severed all connection with Mr Bickford.' What right had Cussen to do that? Nothing was returned to Mother.

Some time after Ruth passed away I heard the story that Tony Van Den Bergh had Ruth's handbag in his possession and her compact which he'd given to his daughter. It played 'La Vie En Rose'. How he got it I don't know. He made money out of Ruth, issuing bits of paper about her to the press. When he

242

interviewed me he said he was a friend of Blakely and that they talked together in the Little Club. He also said he tried to get off with Ruth at the club but she didn't want to know. Perhaps that's why I felt he had a vendetta against her, because she said 'no'.

Three months after Ruth's death there was another tragedy. After Ruth was arrested, Betty, my youngest sister, was silenced. My parents wouldn't let her speak to anyone. She wrote to Ruth in prison saying she wanted to see her but my parents wouldn't allow it. When Ruth died she wrote to me saying she hated living in Hemel Hempstead. I felt from the tone of her letter that my parents weren't doing enough to help her. She couldn't stand being boxed up in a small place after being in big places and was going back to London. She wanted to live with us but Joe wouldn't agree and said I had enough to do. She never got to London.

Pauline remembers Betty's flowery shirtwaister and high-heeled shoes. They'd play snakes and ladders and get on well. She was a big sister to them. When she came round she'd sit the children on the draining board and give them a good wash even though they didn't need it. Pauline and Marlene loved her.

It was October 1955. I'd been cooking Sunday dinner when Granville arrived with my father. Granville said: 'We've come to let you know Betty's died.' I burst into tears. Father didn't seem worried. He never shed a tear and just went. He was always kicking her out to a hostel in London where they kept young girls. I expect he thought it was one less mouth to feed. He must have eventually felt some remorse. The day before he died of lung cancer some years later, Mother told me he'd said pitifully: 'What have I done to my girls?'

Betty was ill for three months and had a bad asthma attack in front of them brought on by the shock of Ruth. The doctor told us that she shouldn't have died. I often wondered what the poor thing really died from. She was eighteen. On the day of her funeral we waited ages for the priest to arrive at the cemetery. We assembled round the coffin, Mother and Father were opposite me with Granville. Mother had some flowers and told me to throw one in. As the priest said earth to earth, there was a whirlwind-type thing that shot vertically past me. It was no imagination. It makes me feel cold to this day. That's when I thought there was something in the hereafter.

Imagine being a mother and losing two daughters in three months. It doesn't bear thinking about.

Joe went away to the Persian Gulf soon after Ruth was hanged. He couldn't stand the misery of it all plus the fact this was his only way of earning money. He was away a year. I had no money for three whole months, lived off my family allowance, I was in debt with the rent and Ruth's hanging was another cross to bear. When I got a lump sum of eighty pounds from Joe I paid off the man who came round with ladies' and gentlemen's clothes in his suitcase. I'd pay for my children's clothes week by week. They had barathea blazers and were the best-dressed children at school yet half the time I never had tuppence to rub together. It took me six months to clear the rent but by the time Joe came home I'd even bought a new double bed, distempered the bedroom, bought new curtains and a black satin cover for the bed. Money went further then. It seemed my luck had changed. But Ruth was always in my thoughts.

16

The Antony Beauchamp Mystery

All the grieving in the world won't bring Ruth back but it doesn't stop me thinking about her. What saddens me is no one cared enough to find out the truth in 1955. But then it was so well concealed. I'd call it a work of art how the Little Club escaped scrutiny after the shooting. The real action went on amongst top people there yet nobody wrote about it – it was as if it didn't exist. But I found one article in PRO files from *Reynolds News*; I vaguely remember it, it was a bit like *Titbits* magazine with beauty queens and naughty vicars running off with women and a bit of socialist stuff and run by the Co-op movement *for* the people. Those in authority must have rubbed their hands when this story was printed. In my mind it confirmed that the club was untouchable.

REYNOLDS NEWS 26 June 1955

Lonely, jealous men at the bar . . . and murder began at
The Unhappy Little Club
By John Knight

Everything was in character. Except one thing: some of the people . . . last night in the Little Club, up the staircase in the Brompton Road, there were anxious looks on the staff's faces. For Ruth Ellis, the ash blonde of 28, who slew her lover by shooting him down, was manageress there. She was sentenced to death. And the club is bravely turning its music higher, laughing louder to live down that dreadful story. It was there, at the Little Club, that the unhappy love affairs of Ruth Ellis started. And many more which are not on record. Murdered David Blakley met her over the narrow bar. So did director Desmond Cussen. Lonely men drifted up the stairs into the lets-be-madly-gay atmosphere and found romance – which never survived.

The on-and-off-smile

Ruth Ellis's brittle, flashing smile deceived so many men who thought they could buy friendship and, maybe, affection for a drink. But her smile, flashing on and off, and the long procession of men who eventually found that they had been made fools of by the mock radiance, spread discontent along the bar. Quarrels often sprang up. Jealousies. David Blakely, even though he lived with Ruth in the 10-guinea flat above, watched his woman like an animal. The manageress of any club has to be the most social of creatures. Most play the part with some reserve so that the customers aren't led to expect too much.

Ruth Ellis often overplayed her hand. Then came the let-down and bitterness . . . while Blakely brooded in the background.

Audience for the bores

It was a club of unhappy people. A well-known racing

driver would go there only when he lost a race. Another visitor was found later in a gas-filled room.

The Unhappy Little Club . . . On many nights I have sat there and seen have-been and never-will-be celebrities trying to be so gay. The girl with the fair hair was always among them, talking, smoking, drinking. They were flattered by her attention she gave to their platitudes. The bores, the drunks, the little people realized that at last they had found an audience for their bragging. Ruth Ellis, as manageress, confided in me two summers ago: 'If only some of the members here knew what I thought of them . . . But I have to be charming to them all . . .'

Too charming, perhaps. Too insincere. That's what made it the Unhappy Club. For people eventually saw through the smile. But Ruth Ellis is gone. It is becoming plain Little Club again: happy if pretentious.

The journalist was writing about a kindergarten. In reality it was a place where conmen, spies, call them what you like, congregated. And where they recruited anyone who could be compromised – homosexuals, prostitutes, drunks. The Little Club was their way of life. The Little Club seemed to be run on Her Majesty's service.

John Knight who wrote the article must have been blind or gagged. Like all the newspapers – one followed another with fiction about Ruth, putting you off the trail. 'A club of unhappy people!' Surely he knew about the top people who frequented the place when Ruth was manageress, and the place upstairs where the girls went with men. Surely he wasn't sitting at the bar night after night for a ham sandwich; he was there to pick up stories. That is where it was happening. His article covered up a world of secrets. Miles from the truth it was, exactly what the powers-that-be wanted.

Stephen Ward's best friend was society photographer Antony Beauchamp. He was a Little Club member, another shady character Ruth knew – she and Vickie Martin were photographed by him. Ruth probably believed everything he said was gospel – her favourite word.

Who was Beauchamp? There isn't much of a family tree: just Beauchamp's birth certificate in the name of Antony Entwistle (he changed his name in 1939) and an autobiography published after his death. He said in it that he was brought up at top London addresses but gave no details about his childhood or the school he attended. At sixteen, having been set up in a studio by his assistant, Pandora de Melgar, he was moving in top society circles. First he photographed Vivien Leigh. But his favourite model was actress Frances Day. Secret PRO files opened after sixty years revealed she was an associate of Oswald Mosley at that time, a Nazi sympathizer. After the Second World War Beauchamp was photographing beautiful women like Marilyn Monroe, Elizabeth Taylor, and Greta Garbo. He even wormed his way into photographing the very private Charlie Chaplin who had Communist links at the time.

He must have been the luckiest man in the world. In 1949 he had married Churchill's daughter Sarah – a nice ticket into Whitehall and the White House. He travelled backwards and forwards to America in the late 1940s and early 50s, and mixed with people like Winston Churchill and President Roosevelt. You could not have a bloke in a better position. Could his presence at the Little Club, he being the Prime Minister's sonin-law, be one of the reasons the club wasn't investigated after Blakely's murder?

He photographed so many politicians and celebrities, that he should have gone down in history. But none of the long-established photographic organizations have archives about him, other than the Royal Photographic Society which has a brief reference to his autobiography. Without my copy of this rare book and the one-sentence references to him in biographies about Churchill, nobody would have known he existed. It's as if there's been an effort to wipe his name off everything.

Where did Beauchamp come from? According to his birth certificate he was born in New Romney, Kent, on 17 April 1918. In those days, living in the sticks you didn't know much about London or travel, unlike nowadays. Yet sixteen years later Antony Entwistle is running his own business off Park Lane and acting the aristocrat. Making a big jump and getting into photography in the City of London from a background of New Romney – it's a bit like Joe being born in Bow in the 1920s and becoming Prime Minister of England. Next, and still not eighteen, Beauchamp called himself a consort for the London debutantes. It seems he was bluffing his way into everywhere. He made friends with Robin and Jean Beauchamp Duff and their mother Margaret Duff who lived in 'Franchise', an elegant house in Burwash, Sussex. Jean and Robin must have been exceptionally wealthy and liked Beauchamp a lot, because in 1939 they set him up in a ground-floor flat and studio in Cleveland Row opposite St James's Palace in London. He said he borrowed his new professional name, Beauchamp, from the Duffs.

Beauchamp's photographic career suddenly accelerated with the outbreak of war in 1939 when he was commissioned to photograph Mary Churchill, Winston Churchill's youngest daughter. Then he wormed his way further into the Churchill family by arranging to photograph her elder sister Sarah. So Beauchamp aged twenty-one, a man with no education as he admits in his autobiography, had acquired a prestigious address, and within weeks, in his words 'busied himself as a cadet at Sandhurst trying to learn how to become an Army officer'. Thanks to his benefactors Robin and Jean Duff, Beauchamp was perfectly positioned in the heart of the British Establishment.

Most people my age remember listening to Ben Lyon and Bebe Daniels on the wireless. After the war they did a series on the BBC Light Programme called *Life with the Lyons*. The family played themselves including their son Richard and daughter Barbara. She was Vickie Page's best friend. Vickie Page was a friend of John Steel, the ARP warden from Leatherhead, who had been in the Home Guard with Desmond Cussen.

Mr Steel said Barbara Lyon and Vickie Page met up in clubs and studios. Barbara appeared in films and made some records. Vickie was making her mark in films and dancing in the early fifties. In 1956 she became pregnant by Antony Beauchamp. When Mr Steel heard about it he decided, 'That bastard's going to pay.' He went to solicitors to get things moving. When he mentioned Beauchamp's name it was: 'No, sorry old chap. I'm awfully sorry we can't take it on. They all knew he was Churchill's son-in-law. There was no point going to the papers, Churchill would have put a stop to anything like that.'

On 26 February 1957 Vickie Page gave birth to a baby girl, Carey-Ann. By coincidence at that time Vickie lived in Egerton Gardens, exactly opposite where Ruth had lived. Carey-Ann says her mother loved Beauchamp passionately but could not have him: 'I got the impression that they were having an affair. My mother did say that he paid for the nursing home where I was born in Hampstead.' Carey-Ann revealed that Vickie was introduced to Beauchamp by his best friend Stephen Ward: 'Apparently she quite liked Stephen as a person. She named my younger brother Stephen after him.' Vickie Page died in South Africa in 2002.

The Lyons family were regular visitors to the Little Club when they were in London and while Ruth was manageress. Richard Lyon used to go with Raymond Nash, side kick to Peter Rachman, the East End slum landlord who bought up properties, charged huge rents and put the strong arm on when the tenants didn't pay up – he was famous in the early sixties, in the Profumo and Christine Keeler affair as Mandy Rice-Davies' protector and lover.

All these people were interlaced with another, well before the Profumo scandal.

A first-class 1950s photographer, John Chillingworth, described Beauchamp as a 'Charming, ageing somewhat dandy figure who had a West End portrait studio and may possibly have shot fashion pictures for magazines like *Tatler*.' But after thorough research there is no record of any photos Beauchamp said he took for *Tatler*. Renowned Hollywood photographer Bob Willoughby, describes Beauchamp photographing Elizabeth Taylor:

> My one and only experience with him was when I was a young photographer, and to keep food on the table worked as an assistant to several photographers in LA. One of them gave Beauchamp my name. He

hired me to work as his dogsbody when he went to Palm Springs to photograph Elizabeth [Taylor]. He also hired my lights . . . He was apparently on assignment from *Pageant* magazine at the time. This was 1951. She wore a bathing suit, which he ignored, and wrapped her in voile . . . *Pageant* used my photograph instead of his, which of course he took credit for. Never heard from him or about him again. The photos I've seen are not much . . . I know he was married to Sarah Churchill at the time, and that he killed himself . . . how much of the latter is true, I'm not sure.

Many photographic assignments that Beauchamp mentions in his book coincide with other events: Guy Burgess was Second Secretary at the British Embassy in Washington between August 1950 and April 1951 and living at Kim Philby's home in the city, while Beauchamp was toing and froing between America and England, darting from the east coast of America to the west, photographing famous stars, all on the off chance. None were official commissions, he just 'happened to be there taking pictures in the spring of 1951'. At that time Burgess was being manoeuvred out of America, back to England, before he and Donald Maclean defected to Russia.

Beauchamp originally met Sarah Churchill in 1939 when everything was in turmoil at the beginning of the war. Was he biding his time while nobody was watching him? When agents were put in they used to lie low, sometimes for years, before they were needed. He changed his surname from Entwistle, which was run-of-the-mill, to Beauchamp, to improve his image. When you're in that game you have to adapt and adopt the lifestyle. In 1948, he met up with Sarah by chance in the foyer of a Park Lane hotel – the first time since 1939. Sarah Churchill, when she was acting and under contract to London Films persuaded her boss, film director Alexander Korda, to send her to Beauchamp to be photographed. Beauchamp wrote: 'I could never understand why, because I felt I never even began to do her justice.' Interestingly, it has been well documented that Korda was renowned for helping the British Secret Service.

It was a perfect cover being married to Winston Churchill's daughter. Beauchamp was a great asset. He was in the right position, moving amongst exactly the right people and knew exactly what was going on. It doesn't seem possible that the man from nowhere was right next to our greatest man, Winston Churchill, gaining entrance to his home and probably knowing everything that was going on.

He was in society to do a job. And it wasn't just photography. That was a sideline to conceal the undercover things he was doing. But it was photography that got him into the Churchill family. Is this why Churchill, in Mary Soames's words from her diaries, 'remained resolutely hostile towards him'. Had Churchill sussed out his tricky-dicky son-in-law?

In 1957 he committed suicide. On 19 August, *The Times* announced the death of Antony Beauchamp, who had died the day before from an overdose of Tuinal tablets. Was the strain of playing a part showing? Beauchamp couldn't go round bluffing indefinitely. Somebody no doubt was watching him from the wings and by 1957 he was in trouble.

In *The Times* report on the inquest following his suicide it said the coroner handed Beauchamp's mother, Vivienne Entwistle a large brown envelope and asked: 'Has there ever been anything of that kind about him before?' She replied: 'No.' Reporters and the public were refused admission at the beginning of the inquest. *The Times* wrote: 'After repeated protests to the Coroner's Officer, six journalists were allowed inside. The remaining journalists and members of the public were not admitted until after the second witness had been called.' Who was the first witness and what was in the envelope? Something about Beauchamp was being covered up.

I suspect that Antony Beauchamp, the man from nowhere, who by 1939 was perfectly positioned in the heart of the British Establishment, used photography as a front for spying activities. He was in the right place at the right time before the Second World War and during the Cold War, and had significant links to communist and Nazi sympathizers. I believe Antony Beauchamp was a double agent, who has never been publicly uncovered.

He was cremated on 22 August 1957. The short list of mourners gave more clues about his secret life. David Thomson was an MI6 agent and friend of Kim Philby; Jack Deane Potter was the Indian Army official reporter and on special operations with Beauchamp in Burma during the war; Lady Jane Vane-Tempest-Stewart was a cousin of Lady Margaret Vane-Tempest-Stewart who was befriended by Kim Philby when he was infiltrating the upper classes in 1940.

Ruth's death may have protected individuals like Beauchamp. It helps to make clear why such a complicated story was woven around Ruth – the trumped-up murder charge was to protect people at the heart of the Establishment.

17

More Deaths

Not long before my father died in 1967 he phoned to say he had a bad cold. I realize now how pathetic he was. He was a chain-smoker. He contracted cancer of the left lung, went into hospital, didn't have any treatment and died. Despite everything he had done to Ruth and me, I made up my mind not to hold malice against him. But I didn't have the normal feeling a daughter should have – he'd put me through hell which I'll never forget. I didn't go to his funeral. I paid for a rose tree to go where his ashes went.

Mother, with Ruth hanged and Betty and Father dead, had every reason to commit suicide. But she didn't. She carried on working. Then two years later I received a telegram from Bennets End Hospital, near Hemel Hempstead, saying she was very ill and would I come and see her. It was springtime 1969. She'd been there for a fortnight before the staff found my address. I asked the nurse what had happened: 'Well, she had a bad chest infection and was very ill,' is all she'd say. Mother couldn't tell me – she couldn't speak.

After a few weeks the hospital asked me what they should do with her. I wanted to take her home. The nurse disagreed: 'I wouldn't try that because she's still a bit upside-down, not really knowing what day it is.' I kept asking what happened and I kept being told it was a bad chest complaint. As Mother smoked a lot I put it down to that. I went to see her neighbour who lived in the flat upstairs a few weeks later. That's when I learned the truth. She said she'd smelt gas coming from below and sent for the police and an ambulance. They broke Mother's door down to gain entry. Her bedroom, where they found her, was next to the kitchen. She was unconscious. They reckoned she'd been ill for two weeks before she got gassed. I was surprised her friend hadn't been down before because Mother was friendly with her; she did her washing at one time when the woman went to work.

I don't know why the doctors and nurses didn't mention she was suffering from gas poisoning. I didn't ask because I wanted to get her out of the hospital quick. I'm doing my best to describe something we had no suspicions about initially. But when we learned the truth from the neighbour, we thought she'd tried to commit suicide. Thinking about it now I'm not sure. So many sudden deaths: Blakely, Ruth, Andre, Vickie Martin, Linda Justice, Antony Beauchamp, George Ellis and Stephen Ward, five of which were suicides, in such a small circle associated with Ruth, seems very suspicious. My mother's attempted suicide, if that is what it was, adds to this list.

When it was plain she wouldn't be returning to her flat, I cleaned it ready to hand back to the landlord. I searched the place with John Sherwood the taxi driver, who'd hired a van to take Mother's belongings away but I couldn't find anything – no documents, papers, letters, bank statements, all the usual bits and pieces you'd expect to find. All I found were a couple of photos and a little strongbox containing half-crowns to pay for her newspapers and electricity. It was odd because Mother would have made payments for Andre's education in the past but there was no record of anything. (Knowing how hard up they were, I was surprised to see that according to PRO documents my parents had a solicitor in Pall Mall – M.A. Jacobs and Sons.) But there were no legal documents lying around. Somebody had tossed everything out, just as most of Ruth's possessions had gone missing from her flat in 1955.

Mother was moved to Tringham Ward in Brookwood Hospital in Woking close to our house. Months went by. I'd wheel her out into a rest room or round the shops but I could tell she didn't like it there. She was deteriorating. She'd forgotten her English and gibbered in Flemish as she had as a child. She couldn't even sign her name. We thought she had blanked her mind out. Then something peculiar started happening. People we didn't know, strangers, were ringing up trying to see her in hospital, pestering and saying they knew her. Eventually the Divisional Nursing Officer of the Psychiatric Nursing Division wrote to me on 4 March 1975:

> . . . The staff at ward level will do their best to ensure that no unauthorized visitors are allowed to see your mother. The Hospital Secretary has asked the staff in charge of the switchboard to ensure that any telephone calls are answered by the Charge Nurses and if they are not available the calls will be re-directed to myself. We have done our best to keep the number of people concerned in this as few as possible . . . I could not agree with you more that any unnecessary attention or publicity would be most undesirable for your mother and we obviously cannot allow this to happen.

Somebody must have had Mother firmly in his mind, perhaps a journalist. Like Ruth, there was a lot she knew and never told anyone. For years my parents and their solicitor, and Mishcon, Simmons and the Home Office were the only people who *officially* knew of Ruth's statement that she made the day before she was hanged, about where the gun came from. Is this why people wanted to get at my mother?

Then there was another scare with Mother. It was 12 February 1977. I received a phone call from the sister in Tringham Ward saying Mother had been missing since the early afternoon. Remember this is a woman who could hardly walk unaided and got out of breath with bronchitis. Early on Sunday morning I sat up hoping some news would come through. We'd had the worst frost for ages. The thought of Mother wandering outside was unbearable. At eight-thirty on the Sunday morning the police were called. My sons Martin and Chris went to the hospital grounds and helped them hunt for her. After hours of searching with sniffer dogs the police retired for the night. She could not be found. Then Martin happened to glance at a fenced place with locked gates which housed the pigs. He heard a whimpering. He immediately climbed the high fence and found Mother naked behind the pigsty lying on a dry patch of grass surrounded by ankle-deep mud. Her legs were curled up on her tummy, her head completely lifted off the ground. She had no mud on her. Her slippers were paired up away from her on the hill. We believed it was deliberate: she must have been picked up and taken outside. They carried her in on a stretcher, put her on a machine to defrost her and admitted her to St Peter's Hospital after being thawed out. Mother must have had some constitution to survive that. The story got into the *Woking News and Mail*.

She clung on for another two years. On her last day in April 1979, I asked her to make a sign: 'Let me know you know it's me.' She sat up straight, looked at me with her beautiful violet eyes, she looked normal, then she laid down and died. She was eighty-three.

In the years following Ruth's death, my son Robert had lived with my parents in Hemel Hempstead then returned to live with us at our home in Woking. When Joe lost all his money Robert came with me to a council flat in Woking town centre. When we finally moved in to the bungalow I am in now, Robert thought he was in heaven. I only wish I could have told him that I loved him and that I was his mother. But it was all such a big secret. Up until he died he thought I was his sister. He was heartbroken about Ruth. If anyone spoke about her he would get on the defensive, saying: 'Hang on a minute, you seem to forget Ruth was my sister too you know.'

Robert suddenly became ill in October 1995. He was ill for two weeks and looked like something out of Belsen by the time a doctor came to see him. He was sent straight into hospital. Robert walked the wards all night in agony but was given nothing for the pain. By this time he had twenty doctors round him who could not fathom out what the problem was. They talked about blood clots on his lungs. At eight o'clock the following morning the hospital rang saying, 'Come quickly, Robert's dying.' Just a fortnight it was, from start to finish. He died on 31 October 1995 in St Peter's Hospital in Surrey.

On the death certificate it stated the cause of death as ischaemic enterocolitis and superior mesenteric artery thrombosis. The Coroner, M.J. Clement Burgess thought Robert had been neglected and said to me: 'Wouldn't you like to do something about this?' All I hoped was the doctors would learn from it.

On his headstone we put the words, 'The Champion'. He'd learned how to box and won all the bantam classes. He could even knock out someone bigger than himself with his punches. He had such drive and determination to be as good as anyone else. Even during the week before his death, with all the pain, he repeatedly said that Ruth did not kill Blakely. He and Andre were pals and talked together. He knew that Andre had seen Cussen cleaning guns in his flat before the shooting. Andre had also told him that Judge Havers, the judge at Ruth's trial, had been sending money for Andre's upkeep. So sure was he about Ruth's innocence, it made me wonder what else he knew.

18

Ruth's Son Andre

Andre wasn't like other children somehow. Not after his mum passed on. He changed. He was the sort of kid you couldn't make out if he was feeling anything. I loved him, poor little thing. He was a sort of eccentric person and wouldn't talk much. He only had my kids to play with. I remember it was soon after Ruth passed on that he was playing with a train set on our balcony. He would go away and leave it, then come back and fiddle with it again, then put it in the larder. And take it out. It was getting obsessive but I just let him do it. I would never interrupt him – I'd just move away, I knew he didn't know what he was doing. If it took his mind off it, that was OK. Imagine what it was like for that boy to know his mummy was hanged from the neck?

By the time he was twenty he was locking himself away in a blacked-out bedroom at Mother's place in Hemel Hempstead. With only candles for light he'd write notes, hundreds of them you couldn't make head or tail of, then stick them on the wall. His mum's death was definitely playing on his mind. It took years for him to face the fact that she'd died. I told Mother she should fetch a doctor because they couldn't do anything with him. My parents were the last people on earth to be looking after kids. I told them: 'He can't live like that for ever. You'll have an insane person on your hands.'

It's like flashbacks from a horror film as I put it together fifty years later. That's how I think of Andre – flashbacks of sadness. One day here, the next he's wandered off like he had done since he learned to walk. I found a word that described his behaviour as a youngster, in Mother's address book. Opposite the entry for G. Hoare in Drayton Gardens, London S.W.7 she'd written down Mr Stroud, the Boys' Welfare Officer at County Hall in Hertford. Underneath, it just says *absent*.

I wondered if they blabbed at that boarding school who he was. Is that why it was intolerable for him? I don't think so now. Only one person at the St Michael's College reunion remembered Andre. Jim Donovan wrote, without knowing that the boy who 'always remained on the edge of the play-ground . . . and for whom special arrangements were made' was Ruth Ellis's son. In his words, Andre was 'I regret to say one of those, who could not, or would not, easily integrate . . . perhaps entranced by some introspective view in his own mind. Because of this rather insular behaviour, Andre did not make any friends and despite the occasional invitations from his fellows, he remained very much a loner who did not care to join in play. In hindsight I suppose, his increasing, although self-imposed loneliness led to an occasional, becoming more frequent, absenteeism . . . My memories remain of a tragic, delicately fragile, and definitely strange boy who apparently preferred being a loner.'

Chris and Joey recognized him on the Internet – he is on the right in a photograph of year nine boys at St Michael's College in Hitchin. He's looking pale and sombre, more like a leftover of Ruth's life. The worst thing they did was send him there. I saw him when he'd run away twenty times. He'd always come back to me.

Sitting here surrounded by pictures of my family, I'm remembering Andre. Those memories are rotten things but at the same time I don't want to forget. I remember Pauline reminiscing about how they played together as kids, cowboys and Indians and skating on the frozen canal: 'We were a rough-and-tumble crowd, apart from Andre. He'd join in to a certain extent, but not completely. Maybe he didn't want to get too close.' That's how he appeared to my children when he stayed with us in school holidays. Joey's memories are of a ticking off from Auntie Ruth for swiping Andre's sweets from his tuck-box, instructing him to leave them alone because they were for Andre when he was at boarding school.

Joe thought more than he said about Andre. His memories are of him in his early twenties: 'I can picture him sitting there at the table in our kitchenette. We tried to get him to come to live with us. Having five children, one more wouldn't hurt in the least. But you just couldn't get into him. He was vague. He was a good-looking kid with a nice face, the same sort of build as my own sons, nothing half-starved. A few years later he's committed suicide.'

I can only see sadness as I trace a few features in Andre's life. The tatty letter, almost fifty years old, dated 6 July 1957 and signed by Roger Killeen AA, the headmaster of St Michael's College. He was an Assumptionist. Very strict they were. Father Killeen was a bully of the highest order, as some old boys testified. God knows what he did to Andre. Nobody enquired. Something made him run away. Killeen tells Mother: 'You will be pleased to learn that your grandson Andrew will be accepted for Form 1 in the College next September, subject to the condition that you intend to maintain him at the school for at least five years . . . Incidentally your boy is now entitled to wear the "promotion stripe" denoting senior status.' The next thing, about five years after Ruth passed away, the headmaster wrote to her again. This time it says they can't have her grandson any more because he keeps playing truant. Andre hated that school. When he ran away for good he hid himself in his bedroom at Mother's place. He bolted the door on the inside. He wouldn't eat. I don't remember him going to school again. He wandered about. I have a strong memory of the monthly visit I made to Mother's in Hemel Hempstead. I see the small boy I loved so much. Then I imagine him at our place sitting next to his mum while she reads to him. I see the mixed up young man he'd become. I thought he was going mad. I was cross with my parents, they had done nothing to help him: 'You can't leave him like that. He needs a doctor.' Fancy letting a child get like that. He should have been with me, the only one he confided in, his Auntie Muriel. But my parents kept him for a reason – they were getting money. By the time he saw someone the damage was done.

I knew Andre obtained purple hearts from the doctor. He was swallowing them like sweets, to keep his mind going. He carried a hard briefcase and kept his blue pills in there, sneaking his hand in to retrieve one while he walked along. In the end he'd take more than one at a time. He couldn't stop. If he had, his life wouldn't be worth living.

We'd moved from New Eltham to a detached house in a tree-lined road in Woking in Surrey. Our address was 24 Paxton Gardens. We'd had enough of the slanging we'd been getting about Ruth. Shout across the street they would: 'That's the sister of Ruth Ellis.' Robert was back living with us. And Joe had made lots of money in his marine engineering firm, building ships for Saudi Arabia.

It was the end of March 1971. I'd been to the kennels. I'd already got two Afghans and I came back with two mongrels. I was trying to keep them quiet when two women who'd worked at Holloway prison turned up – the governor Charity Taylor and Officer Griffin. The dogs got to the door first. Robert served tea on my best tray with brass handles. One of the women said the building Ruth was in at Holloway was being demolished and that they wanted Ruth reburied. I was embarrassed with the two old girls sitting there with cups of tea and I'm explaining how worried I was about the dogs. I bet they thought I thought more of my dogs than anything else. They told me they hadn't classed Ruth as a murderer – they thought that she was a wonderful girl and the hanging shouldn't have happened. I was to give her a private burial; her son wasn't to know. 'Just bury her,' they said. They knew what Andre was like. I wasn't to tell anyone – newspapers, friends or relations. I said I couldn't move Ruth without telling him, he was after all, Ruth's son. She would never have forgiven me.

I contacted the Home Office as instructed and insisted Andre should be told about the burial. A Mr Wilson contacted him. I was relieved they were doing one thing my mother had wanted: to bury Ruth in the family plot in Hemel Hempstead with Betty. A couple of days later reporters were on the phone at four in the morning saying my sister's body had been exhumed and buried in Amersham. The Home Office had handed over Ruth's body to Andre who decided his mum should be buried near to Blakely's burial place in Penn. However the Rev. Muspratt wouldn't allow her in, so her body went to Amersham instead. The Home Office should have phoned me, not left me to find out via the press. She was my sister. I couldn't believe Andre had spilled the beans to the press.

I'd forgotten until recently about this episode in 1977 when I went with a vicar to Ruth's grave in Amersham. As you go out of Paxton Gardens in Woking, the road goes in a circle and Jean Bowers lived up one end. We never chatted, just said hello if we passed. Then she moved. The next time I met her was in Amersham years later, but I didn't recognize her. She was the manager of The Griffin Hotel there. Joe was a millionaire by then and I went with the vicar, Reverend Jack Bramley in our chauffeur-driven Volvo car to visit Ruth's grave. I don't know how I knew him. He'd just heard about Ruth and me and found my phone number. Somehow he knew Mr Bickford and received letters from him which, in his words, made him think more highly of him. Rev. Bramley had been a padre in the Navy during the war. We went to the grave and he told me to put words on Ruth's stone like 'Gone to Rest Now'. I told him I would put 'To Ruth from her loving sister Muriel and her son Andre'. I felt suspicious of why some old vicar should rake up something that was no concern of his. Afterwards he took me for lunch-in-a-basket at The Griffin. I can't understand how he came by *the* original photo of Ruth and Blakely standing in front of the Lotus Engineering bus at the races – the one that appears in all the books about Ruth. He gave me the photo as a present.

Jean Bowers was reminiscing recently with a friend of mine about my arrival at The Griffin with the vicar:

'I remember the car pulling up in the car park. The chauffeur was dressed out in grey uniform. It was incredible, like royalty arriving. The next thing Muriel came in with a vicar in a dog collar, followed by the chauffeur. I vaguely recognized her but it was out of place. We chatted for the first time, and Muriel explained what she was doing. She told me Ruth Ellis was her sister. I'd no idea. It was Ruth's birthday, she was putting flowers on the grave. It's an extraordinary coincidence she should come in a chauffeur-driven car with this vicar into our pub, not only that, this chauffeur was our barman at one time.'

On 1 April 1971 at five o'clock in the morning, Ruth's body had been removed from Holloway prison by the London Necropolis Company. Thirty years after Ruth's midnight reburial, I've discovered details about that night in the churchyard. Andre was there, and a vicar, but it was kept from me. Mrs Bowers' memories made it all come together:

I was relaying the story of the chance meeting with Muriel in 1977 to one of our old regulars, Henry Washington who was the organist at Amersham Crematorium. I remember the conversation that day about the burial: 'Oh yes I can remember when her body was brought here,' he said. He wouldn't have known it was Ruth Ellis but knew something had happened in the middle of the night in the church-yard and somebody was buried. They'd have parked the hearse in the main road because there was no back entrance. Everything had to go through the memorial garden in the front. Henry gave us the details but he's up there in Heaven now.

Burying her in the middle of the night because they're too ashamed! But it must have been odd seeing the coffin arriving in the pitch black, the funeral car parking out the front and men walking amongst the rose bushes with a coffin to bury. If it wasn't so serious it could be an Ealing comedy.

Six months after Ruth's exhumation Andre put a headstone on the grave. It said Ruth Hornby and her dates, 1926–1955. She was never a Hornby. She was christened Ruth Neilson and became Ruth Ellis. Eventually I spoke to Andre on the phone: 'The stone is lovely Andre but if only you'd put Ruth Ellis. Why do you want to hide her? When anybody comes to visit her they won't know where she is.' That upset him. Some while later, shortly before he died, in a state of depression, he smashed it up.

In the taped conversation between Christmas Humphreys and Andre in 1982, when Humphreys discovered their conversation was being recorded, the old boy's voice immediately changes. His speech quickens, he stops lecturing about cause and effect, starts talking about psychiatric help for Andre, a new room that he'll pay for and a job he'll help him to find. I didn't think he meant it until I found this letter dated 6 March 1982 from Humphreys:

THE BUDDHIST SOCIETY

58 Eccleston Square London SW1V 1PH
Tel 01 834 5858

Dear Andre

I had news of you last night from Dr Biddulph and hope that you will keep in touch with us. I am always at the Society on Mondays and generally on alternate Thursdays as you will see in the Middle Way [*Journal of the Buddhist Society]*, so come and see us and have a meal after. You need the company of friends and something to occupy your mind, such as study. So come when you can,

Humphreys

In view of patient confidentiality I was unable to find out any details about Andre's consultation with Dr Desmond Biddulph.

Here is more of the conversation between Andre and Humphreys:

Andre: It's the loss-ness of everything. My mother went off and I was very much bonded to her. When she went off I had no father. When she went I wasn't a fully formed person . . . I never developed past sixteen or seventeen . . .

Christmas Humphreys: Would you accept expert help . . . A psychiatrist?

A: Yes, certainly. I have no objections.

CH: It would mean going once a week, maybe for months.

A: Yes, if you feel this would help. Yes, certainly. Because I'm getting tired . . .

CH: What I mean is that you needn't worry about the fees. Are you taking unemployment money I suppose?

A: I am getting . . .

CH: Well you could get it on the National Health . . .

on the other hand you might want secrecy and so on and so on. I do know a man who's good.

A: Yes, that's a very important point.

CH: Well, he's a man who is a keen Buddhist. He's a very fine psychiatrist. Incidentally also a homeopath. It's a lovely mixture. We know him very well. He would be interested if you would let me have a talk to him about you . . . He being a doctor would be as secret as I am. He would never know about this trial because he's young. He would have only vaguely heard. But I will tell him something of the background.

A: How much will you tell him about my mother?

CH: That's for you to say. When the time comes I must tell him everything I know simply of the trial. You may then go on if you like and I shall say it is probably because he thinks perhaps all the events weren't brought out at the trial etc. etc. But it would be right that he should know, not vaguely about your parents. He will want to know about the case because he will feel as any human being feels like myself. That the enemy is . . . That would be his starting point . . .

CH: How many friends have you got who know the truth about the past?

A: I did have quite a few but I had to give them up. I found I couldn't bear it. I found I had one or two.

CH: That's terrible. Who knew about the past? None of them any use to you?

A: How do you mean?

CH: Well none of them is trying to get you medical help or anything else to cheer you up?

A: No. They seemed to say, well that's life and that's it. Non-interference.

CH: Well, are you quite clear that I may have a talk with a chap? I assume it would be once a week. I may even see him tonight when I get home. I'll say I want half-an-hour with you about a patient . . . Well now. Listen and apply your mind to this. Are you willing for me to talk to this chap? Of course it will be entirely secret. He's a doctor. I'll say I've got a patient for him. I'll tell him briefly: 'Have you ever known of something like this before?' And of course he'll smile and say six in the last five years. And I will say: 'What would you do?' He'd say I shall want to see him maybe once a week, once a month. And you'd go, would you?

A: Yes . . .

CH: I shall tell the doctor then. Nobody knows. McCallum. Is that your father's name?

A: You know a lot. You want to know, do you?

CH: No, no. Was your mother Ellis or . . .

A: No, no. That was that awful man. He was my step-father. McCallum is my father's name. His first name is Clare, without the 'i.' This is very peculiar the way you've got this out of me . . . I wouldn't tell anyone else these things.

CH: Where did Andrea come from?

A: My father.

CH: Oh, I see. What I mean is no one is going to associate you by name . . .

CH: Well, shall we take the next step? Look if you can for somewhere to move and allow me to pay for the move. Because a move is expensive.

A: I beg your pardon?

CH: Well, to move to a new home means moving furniture . . . If you get a chance to move into another room, take it. And if the money worries you would you allow me to help you? . . .

I re-read the transcript of their long conversation. Humphreys was clearly aware that Andre knew more than anyone realized about Easter Day 1955. One sentence stands out. Humphreys says he will tell his psychiatrist friend about the trial and will explain that Andre 'thinks perhaps all the events weren't brought out at the trial'. I've often wondered why Humphreys didn't report this discussion to the appropriate authorities. He kept what he'd heard from Andre quiet.

Three months later Andre, who had seen Cussen cleaning guns and teaching his mother to shoot on the day of Blakely's murder in 1955, was dead. He was thirty-seven.

Andre is still, in my mind, the boy who'd turn up un-announced at Paxton Gardens in Woking. Like a ritual he'd walk on the other side of the green, looking from a distance to see if we were in. He'd phone me late at night – I'd talk to him quietly for hours. He often said his mummy visited him. It was always in the corner of the room, she'd be holding her arms out as if to say come to me. Two years previously, he said he was going to die. He didn't mention suicide.

When I think about his pathetic will dated 18 September 1981, it comes flooding back: how he said he loved me, my darling little boy. If only I could have done more.

> I, Clare-Andre McCallum of Flat 3, 21 Sale Place, London, W2 IPX hereby revoke all former testamentary dispositions made by me . . . I request that my body shall be buried in the same burial plot as my mother Ruth (Reference Number 256B) at St Mary's Cemetery, Amersham, in the county of Buckinghamshire . . . I request that the burial plot (256B) be returfed as soon as is proper after the funeral . . . I give all my real and personal property whatsoever and wheresoever (including any property of which I may have a general power of appointment or disposition by will) . . . testamentary and memorial expenses absolutely and subject there to balance to my aunt MRS MURIEL JAKUBAIT . . .

It was 1982. Andre phoned my daughter Pauline the night before she went abroad. He'd asked to see her. She explained she couldn't make it and asked him to phone me. I was out with Marlene and her children at the London Dungeon. Two weeks later there was a knock on the door. Two policemen were standing on the doorstep. 'Mrs Jakubait?' I replied yes. 'Are you Andre McCallum's aunt?' 'Yes.' 'He's committed suicide.' That's all they said and went.

I've said how his life was a series of flashbacks. The next thing I'm seeing are hundreds of flies as we opened the wardrobe in Andre's room. My sons saw bits of decomposed body. Flesh from Andre's hand was in the bedside drawer. A bit of flesh from his arm was beside the bed where he'd been kneeling. The authorities took most of the body to the morgue but hadn't scraped everything up. I saw some bits of Andre but Chris made me wait outside. We took everything we could but burned his bed. Everything was crawling with maggots. Pills were scattered over the bed. The police hadn't taken them. On the death certificate they called it 'Glutethimide overdosage'. Another suicide, I suppose the police thought. That's good enough for them.

God knows when Andre moved to Sale Place in Paddington. It looked like some scruffy boarding house to me. He had a large middle-floor room when we first visited, but his landlady asked him to move to the attic room – her daughter had passed some exams and needed a bigger room to study in. So he's pushed into Flat 3, a room the size of a gent's hanky. She said she'd lower the rent. His bicycle and everything he owned was crammed in next to a sink and hotplate. The bike was brand new; where it came from I don't know because he didn't have any money. He'd never mentioned it in his letters apart from saying he'd been knocked off it in London. Amongst his few belongings (it looked as though he'd cleared things out) I found a Polaroid snap that Andre had taken of his room, showing his few belongings before he died. You can make out dates he'd circled on his calendar, for the month of June: Tuesdays 3rd and 10th; Thursday 25th. He was still planning for the future. There was no picture of his mum; she was in his mind, not on the wall.

It's a mystery why nobody noticed that Andre hadn't been around for two weeks – that's the time he'd been lying there dead according to the death certificate. A rotting smell and black flies emerging from under the door alerted somebody eventually. I phoned the landlady to say we'd cleared the room. She said: 'Good. I can let it now.' Chris found the tapes including the Humphreys one. He said I should keep them safe. And Andre's will. He left £30. I used that for flowers at his funeral.

At the morgue the police said: 'Can you identify your nephew?' I said yes, he had a scar above his eyebrow. When they pulled the sheet back they said: 'Yes you're right. That's all you need to see.'

Andre didn't want to be cremated; he wanted to be buried with his mother but I was advised to cremate him because he was decomposed. On 28 June 1982, the Jakubait family assembled at St John's chapel, Woking. We had a church service and went back to collect the ashes in a little coffin with silver handles and a plaque. On 6 July I did as Andre wanted. I buried what was left of him near his mum in Amersham. The vicar took seven pounds fifty and told me to stand somewhere. The gravedigger dug out a square in Ruth's grave, pushed Andre into it, leaned on his shovel while the vicar babbled a prayer. I couldn't understand a word. He said: 'That's it. Thank you.'

At the Coroner's Court on 19 July 1982 I said Andre was my nephew and we were close. The Coroner asked if I knew why he ended his life. I said: 'His mother died. He was very depressed. He was afraid that I would die first and he'd have nobody from his mother's family any more.' That was the truth. Andre's death didn't go down nicely on the certificate as 'took his own life'. Paul Knapman, the Coroner, wrote: 'Killed himself'.

Humphreys paid for Andre's funeral. As a last resort I wrote to him at the Buddhist Society in London, telling him Andre had committed suicide and I didn't know where I'd get the money from to bury my nephew. By the 1980s Joe was having financial problems, his customers weren't paying their bills. Humphreys had condemned Ruth at her trial. He was still condemning her twenty-seven years later when Andre taped their conversation. Ruth's death killed Andre. The next thing there's Humphrey's cheque in the post written out to the chapel for the whole amount, four hundred and ninety one pounds and fifty pence. It was decent of him. He told me never to mention it to anyone. I swore I wouldn't. I didn't, till now. Humphreys died a year after Andre. He was eighty-two.

I have every right to say there's no wonder he paid out money for Andre. He probably felt guilty for what he'd done to Ruth. Just like Judge Havers who sent money for Andre's upkeep every Christmas. Why? It's because there was a cover-up all the way through the trial. It's all too quick for a hanging. Someone else, I never discovered who, paid for Ruth's headstone that Andre organized, the equivalent of five hundred pounds today. It could be interpreted as an act of compassion for an innocent victim. Some would call it a guilty conscience.

Ruth's passing made me feel completely distorted. But I coped. I've put it down to not being too clever. I was always told that I didn't understand things so I wasn't affected. Maybe that's how I remained sane. God knows what it was like for poor Andre.

19

Albert Pierrepoint, Executioner

Ruth's hangman Albert Pierrepoint was another participant in her death who couldn't just walk away from it. Twenty-four years after her death he finally tricked me into meeting him. It is only when he held his hand out to shake hands with me in a Knightsbridge hotel that I realized what a devious little beast he was.

In 1974 I wrote to him. It had taken nineteen years to muster up the courage. I wanted to get things straight in my mind and put my mother's mind at rest – even though she couldn't talk, I knew she would understand. I thought he would be able to tell me what my sister's last words were as she stepped through the door to her death. I wanted the truth.

I wrote to the newspaper that published an article about him, asking them to pass my letter on. I received a reply quickly. On 17 November 1974 he wrote using his publisher's address, Harraps in High Holborn. He told me Ruth said nothing. This was the first letter he wrote to me:

Dear Mrs Jakubait,

Many thanks for your kind and understanding letter, I am sorry indeed, at this stage, I am unable to give you the full details concerning your sister Ruth. If this letter should go astray the press could have a field day, so we must keep any correspondence strictly confidential.

277

As I put my hand on the bible, what I am able to tell you in this letter will be absolutely the whole truth. I was in London last week, sorry I didn't receive your letter a little earlier.

I have seen some brave men die, and in my mind, anyone who walks bravely without a falter, into the unknown, in my opinion they were heroes. I was never concerned what crime they had, or not, committed I always tried to show them dignity, which I think was of great help. Now for the information you wish to know, which I sincerely hope will not cause you any further distress, first of all I have always placed Ruth in the above paragraph, without any doubt. She died as brave as any man, and she never spoke a single word, but one thing I do remember, and have never mentioned this to a soul, as I was the last person to see her face to face, she just pucker[ed] her lips as though she wanted to smile, in the few seconds we had, I painfully accepted her smile. I hope these few lines will give you, and your mother, some satisfaction 'God bless her.'

As you are aware, a great deal of publicity has been given to Ruth and myself, which has never come from me, the press can be very cruel at times, if they don't know things they will soon guess and nothing we can do about it. Sorry at present we have not a forwarding address as we have sold our bungalow, and have been living in an hotel for a few weeks. In a few days we are leaving for a few weeks holiday in Spain, and should be home about early January.

I make frequent visits to London, if you wish the next time I am in London, and you are available, I will send you a line and probably we can meet and have a further chat. If I use the name of Fletcher, you will understand, as I am very cautious.

Yours very sincerely

A Pierrepoint

P.S. I receive hundreds of letters but never feel as though I should acknowledge them, but I think you are a special case. Hope you can understand my feelings, and don't feel too bitter against me. AP

Between 1974 and 1979 I received nine letters from Pierrepoint. Anyone reading them and not knowing the background might have assumed I was having an affair with him. It was the way he wrote them. If they'd fallen into the wrong hands imagine what the press would have made of them. Joe didn't interest himself in any of it.

Pierrepoint occasionally wrote under the name A. Fletcher and asked that if I write to his home to sign myself Jack. He wrote in a very familiar way. In one he asked me to meet him at Euston saying he'd be wearing a dark suit, grey trilby hat and carrying a slim document case. I was not to mention Ruth in any letters; this time I was to say it was from Mrs Jakubait. I answered one or two letters purely to say I could not meet him. I never turned up at any of the meeting points, Surbiton, Ewell, Guildford or Woking stations, that he suggested.

He told me to phone him at home using another name, between half-past-seven and half-past-eight at night on a Tuesday or on a transfer call. Or I was to write to the publisher, all cloak-and-dagger, and was to address the envelope to Mr Fletcher, not Mr Pierrepoint. This letter arrived in his own handwriting:

If you have to write to Harraps again, please use my correct name, the lady who I had arranged with to re-address my mail, has now left the firm, and left nothing to the successer regarding my mail, that's the reason your letter was delayed. I am just writing this short letter, as my wife has just gone to bed, I never get her involved, in fact, she doesn't know about the letters. Will write again soon.

Yours sincerely

A. Fletcher. AP.

This went on for five years. Every time there was any media recognition of Ruth, Pierrepoint would be on to me in a flash. But that wasn't all. While he was corresponding with me I was invited to appear on Kilroy-Silk's television programme about capital punishment. The Mayor of Woking's car was hired to take me to Shepherd's Bush studios, a little flag was waving on the front. The programme went out live, without a rehearsal, so there was no time to practise what you were going to say. Kilroy was discussing hanging. I gave my opinion about serial killers and child killers. Kilroy said: 'I'll go and ask Albert Pierrepoint.' He was sitting in the audience a few rows in front of me but I didn't recognize him – we'd only communicated by letter. Kilroy's words to him were: 'Do you think that everyone you hanged deserved to die?' Pierrepoint replied: 'Yes.' I spoke firmly to Kilroy and the audience, referring to the letters Pierrepoint had written to me: 'That is not what he told me.' Pierrepoint made me sick because by saying that, he'd included Ruth.

He was excited I was there, and was enquiring: 'Where is Muriel?' As everyone left he put his arms round me, trying to get friendly. He was a peculiar little man, nothing like the five-foot seven he said he was in his letter. More like five-foot two. He made me feel creepy and reminded me of my father – just as wicked. I was not having any of it and made a fast exit. The horrible little hangman wore a black leather glove on his right hand ever since his ring finger was operated on in 1977. As far as I was concerned it was his punishment for pulling the trigger too many times. Then in May 1979 he wrote asking if he and a friend could come and take a photograph of him standing next to Ruth's grave in Amersham. I didn't reply.

I'll do my best to describe this bizarre episode bearing in mind it all happened quickly. It was July 1979. I had decided to go shopping in London and met my daughter Marlene in Harrods. She bought curtain material and we both had our hair set in the salon and had lunch in their restaurant. I went from poor to rich. From a pound a week in Herne Hill in south London to shopping in Harrods. Joe had been under contract to Kuwait Bechtel Corporation, then moved on to building patrol boats for Saudi Arabia, was working from sunrise to sunset and earning the money. We were living in style. He came back to West India Docks on the Thames doing ship repairs. Anyway, it would have been a nice outing to Knightsbridge, but as we came out of the side entrance of Harrods a stranger came up to me saying: 'Hello Muriel.' He knew who I was. I replied: 'What do you want?' There was a crowd with him all with cameras and photographic equipment. He said he wanted me to meet somebody, a famous man, and asked if I would mind coming with him. I had no idea what he was talking about and told him I was out shopping with my daughter. It turned out that this man had telephoned our home and Robert told him we were in Harrods for the day.

We went into this posh place almost opposite the side entrance to the store. It was dark and I remember there was an old-fashioned folding screen, the type people used to undress behind. A red light was flashing on and off. The table was dressed beautifully and a banquet was laid on. Everything in the room was done out as though they were expecting something to happen.

Then Albert Pierrepoint was introduced to me. Marlene who was sitting next to me at the table was speechless – it spoiled our day. He'd been positioned behind the screen so nobody could see him. Everything was black and scary. It was one big set-up. He held his hand out: 'Oh my God, you're like your sister. You're like two peas in a pod. I want to put your mind at rest. She died like a warrior.' I said politely: 'I'm sorry. I cannot shake hands with you. But I'd like you to know that I don't hold malice against you because it was your job. But you hanged my sister.' Pierrepoint's publishers had pulled a fast one on me. They'd laid on a press conference and huge meal for the newspapers. All to do with some members of parliament who were trying to bring back hanging. He used me to get publicity for articles about him.

I was told I would be given a lift home because someone was going my way. They bundled me into the car with two reporters. Pierrepoint sat in the front with the driver. Marlene caught her train back to Marlow. As we passed through Surrey they'd obviously forgotten we lived close by so I pointed to our road. But one of the press men said: 'We're taking you down to Ruth's grave in Amersham because Albert [Pierrepoint] would like to see it and be photographed near it. We've got a cream tea organized for you.' I felt like an outsider. In those days I was on the nervous side and what they had done shocked me.

I did not know what the hell was going on. They tried to make conversation but I told them I did not feel like talking.

We reached Ruth's grave. Pierrepoint turned to me and had the audacity to ask me to go for a walk. He said he wanted to talk to Ruth at the grave and say prayers. He should have prayed for *all* the ones he had killed. He maintained he didn't want to hang Ruth. He thought it was wrong and knelt down and asked for forgiveness. We all turned round and looked at him, the photographers took pictures from a distance and it was very weird. He said he was really sorry. I don't think he felt guilty or had any feeling whatsoever. Perhaps he was consoling himself. Or perhaps it was just good for business. Apologies made no difference to me.

The reporters tucked into their cream teas in a little café in Amersham High Street. They had been eating all day long. I felt sick just watching them because they had got me there under false pretences. A big publicity stunt at my expense. I bet the *Sun* readers who read the two-page article on 17 July 1979 said how awful, how could she have tea and a chat with the man who hanged her sister. That is what it must have looked like. They did not know the half of it – how the horrible man and his cronies tricked me.

What a wicked man he was. I would not have wanted my husband doing that job. Imagine going home at night and the only contact you have had with a person is weighing and measuring them, then killing them. Apparently he killed four hundred people. The last letter he wrote was dated 20 November 1979, four months after the *Sun* article. I never heard from him again. They say that when Pierrepoint died in 1992, he died peacefully. If that is the case, as far as I am concerned he did not have a conscience.

20

Conspiracy

If my father had not had a stroke in 1940 he would not have been sent to Leatherhead Hospital and maybe I would not have made the discoveries I have. My research around Leatherhead unearthed information about Desmond Cussen. I've collected every piece of information on him, but it has not been easy.

I may have sounded dim in earlier chapters. But I'm undoing the damage inflicted on me as a child. Nothing will bring Ruth back but I know she would have been happy with what her sister did for her – exposing the criminals that conspired against her. And proving she was innocent of the crime she was murdered for.

Mrs Joan Winstanley and Miss Elizabeth Riley were house-keepers at 44 Egerton Gardens, where Blakely and Ruth stayed for a short while immediately before the shooting. Nine days after Blakely's murder, Mrs Winstanley told the police that Ruth originally called at the house on 8 February 'as a result of an advertisement in the *Evening Standard*'.

Robert Hancock, in *Ruth Ellis, The Last Woman to be Hanged*, wrote: 'The next morning, 8 February, Ruth bought an early edition of the *Evening Standard* and took a taxi to No 44 Egerton Gardens . . . The house consisted of fourteen furnished rooms and was managed by a resident housekeeper, Mrs Joan Ada Georgina Dayrell Winstanley.'

I found the reference to the *Evening Standard* was not true. Mrs Kirk was the owner and landlady of the property. The telephone number under her name was Kensington 1974. Neither Miss Riley nor Mrs Winstanley was listed in the directory. I checked every classified ad in the *Evening Standard* for 8 February and two weeks either side. None of the ads tallied with the Egerton Gardens property.

Why did Mrs Winstanley mention the non-existent ad? Why didn't the police check this detail? During cross-examination at the trial Humphreys was more interested in how Mrs Winstanley took Ruth and Blakely tea and toast in the mornings. Melford Stevenson had 'no questions'. Mrs Kirk and Miss Riley were not questioned by the police.

You only have to look at the timing of events to see that the truth surrounding Ruth's move to Egerton Gardens on 9 February 1955 was carefully overlooked. Ruth said that on 6 February: 'David started beating and kicking me so severely that I was a mass of bruises from head to toe.' On 7 February Cussen took her to Middlesex Hospital to get treatment for the bruising. According to Bickford she blamed David's behaviour on his jealousy because she was staying at Cussen's flat. Twenty-four hours later she is looking for a new flat. And on 9 February she moved out of Cussen's and in with Blakely who had just beaten her up. What sort of man sends a woman, who he is fond of, out for another beating? The answer: the sort who has a job to do. It is part of the conspiracy. The shooting took place on 10 April; the rent was conveniently paid in advance by Cussen up till the 11th.

Undercover operations is what Cussen was in. And Cussen became involved with Ruth for one reason. The Little Club gave him perfect cover for his real job. He was with British

Intelligence and keeping track of double agents working for the Soviets. He may have decided that Ruth and Blakely knew too much. The police should have tracked Cussen down on 12 July 1955 after learning he had supplied Ruth with the gun. The hanging could have been postponed. But they were not going to find him, someone was protecting Cussen. Ruth was in a position to embarrass the government with her information about people in high places, just like Christine Keeler in the sixties.

Mr Bickford, Ruth's solicitor, tried to contact me after Ruth's body was exhumed. His letter dated 9 May 1973, sent via the *Evening Standard*, didn't arrive till 1977:

> Dear Mrs Jackubait [sic],
>
> I have been trying to find you – would you mind contacting me please. My home tel. Number is 603 6062.
>
> Yours truly
>
> John G.A. Bickford

I've no idea why it took FOUR years to arrive at my house in Woking, but the envelope looked as if it had been opened. I phoned the number and spoke to Mr Bickford's son and told him about the letter. He said: 'My father's dead. What he had of this case is finished with. Don't phone again.' I can only think the contents were detrimental to somebody – it was in their interest to keep it under cover until Bickford had died. I gathered Bickford wanted to tell his story to me. No doubt he was feeling guilty. After all, he held the case back. According to a closed PRO file which my solicitors Bernard de Maid and

Co. were able to look at (for the Appeal that I wished to bring to overturn the murder verdict) Bickford made a statement to Scotland Yard. In the early 1970s he was recalling what Cussen told him in 1955: how Ruth lied at the trial; and how he (Bickford) had concealed that information. A police investigation followed. No further action was taken regarding Cussen.

Cussen went to ground immediately after Ruth's execution and was not available for police inquiries. I'd been led to believe by my mother and brother Granville that he was living in Australia – and this seemed to be common knowledge at the time. But in fact between 1955 and 1957 he was still living at 20 Goodwood Court; between 1958 and 1959 he was at the Lanterns Hotel, Bayswater; and around 1962 he moved to the Atlantic Hotel and remained there till approximately 1964.

I have mentioned that Cussen's signature on business papers dated 29 May 1964, at a London hotel, was the first clue to making discoveries about Ruth's secret life and Blakely's death. Cussen gave his address that day as Flat 543, Atlantic Hotel, Queens Gardens, London W.2. Mr Casserly owned the Atlantic Hotel then. He agreed to be interviewed:

> I bought the hotel about fifty years ago and we created bedsitters in the late fifties. Three big houses came on the market. We gutted them out, renovated them and made a decent living. It was much more residential in those days. Things changed when tourism arrived.
>
> Desmond Cussen was not a great mixer. He led a straightforward life, like clockwork. Went out in the morning same time every day, came back at half-five

and would be at the bar every evening having a large whisky. I never saw him intoxicated. There were always a few of us in there and we'd serve Des and chat. But he never dined here. No inkling whatsoever of when he'd eat in the evening. Very private. In the morning I don't know what he had.

Number 543 was on the lower ground floor and was a bit more than a bedsitter. He had it on a permanent let, registered under the name Desmond Cussen, signed the visitors' book and never moved out all the time he was with us. He stayed for a good two to three years. I couldn't give you the exact dates because all the records have gone out the window. As far as I know he was around London prior to coming to us. He could eat in his flat but there was no sign of ever eating there. He would have paid six or seven pounds a week, paid his rent regularly and occupied the room on his own and had his own front door with a key. He had his privacy. If he had visitors I wouldn't have known but we had the chambermaids who cleaned the rooms every day so we would know if there were any shenanigans going on. There was never any evidence in his room of what he'd been doing. He was very tidy. He had his radio.

He lived very nicely by the look of things and was a dapper man, he had his moustache and was smart and upright and wore a yellow cravat with a black spot on it. He smoked quite heavily. In the bar he'd use these smart lighters, the big Ronsons. I never took any notice of him going out in a car but in the back of my mind I think he had one.

Nobody ever called for him or asked for him. A loner he was. The Atlantic wasn't the sort of hotel where you would be guaranteed privacy, definitely not, but nobody asked questions about him. I was under the impression he had one shop at Marble Arch. Somewhere around there – a kiosk. All I can say is he was a tobacconist.

We used to advertise the Atlantic rooms in a club in Craven Road called The Lanterns. Connected with that we were. That's how Desmond came to us, through The Lanterns. It was owned by a well-known building society at the time. At that time it was difficult to get a licence. What you had to do was get twenty-six members' names and it formed itself. They'd pay half-a-crown a head and were allowed to drink twenty-four hours because they were resident. It had a residential club licence. Desmond was well known there because I had a brother who was running the place.

We had top police coming to stay here. Detective chief superintendents would be here – don't know their names. My grey matter is terrible. The Richardsons came and tried to drink in the bar. The police never came to see Des. They wouldn't have had access to his front door and we hadn't fitted an intercom for him to let them in. So it would only be by arrangement.

I know Profumo was supposed to have registered in the hotel. I never saw him myself but it would have been in the late fifties, early sixties. I had a night porter that was not a hundred per cent. You're talking about when clubs like Churchills in the West End were going and there were all the club girls. Christine

Keeler and Mandy have been back here for drinks. They'd come in the evening. I went home at ten o'clock. The night man would sign them in. There was a certain amount of money in the book but the night man took us to the cleaners. I can mention only his first name – it was Addie – because his daughter is still alive. Of course the thing about it, we weren't running a brothel but they were entitled to bring a guest to the room. 1958 is the furthest it would go back. Stephen Ward regularly stayed at the hotel around the time of Desmond in the early sixties. He was never seen in the bar at the same time as Des and was a one-night person. Not a long let. There wouldn't have been anyone of concern staying at the same time as Des but anyone could have come into the bar.

Tom Kelland, a gay man, secretary to Winston Churchill during the war was at the Atlantic for seven to eight years. He left everything of his to me. He had one friend who was in the Secret Service on the British side. He knew all about Burgess and Maclean and their escape to Russia.

Des gave a week's notice before he went to Australia. I wasn't surprised. I just had to get another tenant. I don't know how it came about that we heard about Ruth Ellis. But I recognized him on the TV later in Australia. We all said: 'There's Des Cussen, he's supposed to have been connected with Ruth Ellis.' I didn't know there was any connection.

From 14 May 1947 Cussen gave his address for his Cussen and Co. shares as c/o 52 Kingsway, Sydney, NSW, Australia. He had plans of going there then. The British government had tie-ups with the Australian Intelligence Service at that time.

I bring in George Ellis now because it is these shady characters, acting as if they are someone else, that are part of a secret jigsaw which nobody else has put together. They are the guilty ones. This was in the *Warrington Examiner* on Friday 23 September 1955:

DENTAL OFFICER RESIGNS

Warrington Education Committee has accepted the resignation of Mr G.J. Ellis, Principal School Dental Officer, his engagement to end on 5 November. He has been granted three months leave with full salary from 5 August. Mr Ellis is the former husband of Mrs Ruth Ellis who was executed earlier this year for shooting her lover.

In 1958 Ellis was again in trouble. This story appeared in the *Liverpool Echo* on Wednesday 9 July 1958.

Dentist Fined – Drunk Outside House

After being told he was being taken into custody for drunkenness, a dentist was alleged at Stockton Heath yesterday, to have replied: 'You do, and I will have the Lord Chief Justice on you – he is a friend of mine.' The man George Johnson Ellis, of 135 Walton Road, Walton, near Warrington, pleaded guilty to being drunk on June 18 and to conduct likely to cause a breach of the peace.

The Little Club was renamed Dorothy's Club, after Ruth died, by the next owner Dorothy Foxon. Peter Nolan who managed the club for eleven years, knew George Ellis then:

You'd see George Ellis spasmodically. He'd come and go. You wouldn't see him for weeks then he'd arrive 'a little bit under the weather' if you know what I mean. Sometimes he'd come in alone, sometimes with medical people but more times than not under the weather. Apart from liking his drink he was a quiet man, a difficult man to work out. With a grand-fatherly look. He had a protruding scar from the eye to the middle of the face type-of-thing. Being in the medical world you'd have thought he'd have got it done properly by a specialist in return for dentistry work. I asked if he'd been in a motor crash. All he'd say was: 'Shall we have another drink?' If anyone started talking about Ruth he'd get up and go. What was the real attraction between Ruth and him? She was so much younger.

When he came in at the end of July 1958 he was very concerned. And he was sober. He was wearing his fifty shillings tailored suit. Dark suits normally he wore – well dressed. It was early evening time. I re-member because the club was quiet. I think it was a gin he had at the bar. He said: 'Peter, I want to have a word with you.' He talked and talked and was heavy into Ruth. Said he was going to Jersey. I asked: 'How long for?' He said: 'Indefinite.' He said he would like some flowers to go on Ruth's grave. He gave me five pounds. I did as he requested but she didn't have a grave so I put the flowers outside the pub near Holloway prison.

The next thing – bang – I got the *Sunday Empire News* two or three days later, to read that the previous day, 2 August 1958, George Ellis, hanged himself from his bed in a Jersey hotel. I was more than surprised since I'd just seen him during the week. Did he commit suicide? Did he die with a secret we don't know about? I've always thought of that. People go to the grave with things they don't tell anybody. I wouldn't have believed he would have committed suicide. Why did everyone associated with 1950s clubland clam up? Little people got prison or killed off. Big ones got away with it. The family of the one that was shot never came out of the wilderness.

George Ellis said the Lord Chief Justice was his friend. That was Lord Goddard who had no regrets about Ruth's trial and hanging other than she was a woman. On 26 July 1958 Lord Goddard wrote his resignation letter to the Prime Minister. Three weeks after George's arrest was reported in the *Liverpool Echo*, George was dead. Did he feel guilty about how Ruth was used? Would he be forgiven by sending a bunch of flowers, like Blakely used to? The press cutting shows he'd been shouting his mouth off. He's another one up to his neck. Peter Nolan commented, did he commit suicide or was he caught up in something big?

Even George Ellis's death may not be what it seemed. The Saturday 2 August 1958 edition of the *Jersey Evening Post* reported that the body of a visitor named George Ellis was found that morning at 'Le Chalet Hotel, Corbière, where he had been staying for the past few weeks . . . according to the dead man's passport, he was born in Manchester on 2 October 1909, and his home was at 135 Walton Road, Warrington.' There's something wrong there. The paper claimed Ellis was in Jersey for a few weeks yet Peter Nolan saw him in London a couple of days before his death.

Following the inquest, the *Jersey Evening Post* of 6 August carried the headline: 'Witnesses tell of money troubles and drinking at inquest on former husband of Ruth Ellis.' It reported: 'The deceased was a guest at the hotel from the 10th to the 17th July and from the 22nd July until his death.' London to Jersey flight tickets dated 10th July and 22nd July were found in Ellis's room. According to the paper he returned to England on 17th July before flying back to Jersey on 22nd July.

Could Peter be mistaken about when he saw Ellis? 'No. There are some things you never forget. When I nipped down to Knightsbridge tube to pick up the Sunday paper, I got the shock of my life reading the banner headlines, how George Ellis, Ruth Ellis's husband, had committed suicide the day before. I'd only seen him two or three days earlier, on the Thursday or Friday [31 July or 1 August]. I remember how that night he asked me to join him for a meal at the Normandy Hotel and Restaurant across the road that backs on to Knightsbridge Green. George had new fivers on him, he always had plenty of cash. I remember telling him to be careful with his money.'

Valerie Preston, whose parents owned the White Hart Hotel in Brasted confirmed George's movements at this time:

> I was the last one to see George at the White Hart in 1958. It could have been a Thursday or Friday, round

about twelve o'clock. We were quite busy with the luncheons going on. My parents had gone racing and George turned up anxious to see them. I didn't have a lot of time to spend with him as I was in the office. Then a matter of days later we heard he'd gone over to Jersey and hanged himself. It was an awful shock for my parents because they hadn't seen him. They'd known George since 1932 when they first came to Brasted and George set up his practice in Sanderstead. George used to fly them from Redhill to Le Touquet in France for lunch.

A passport was found in George's hotel bedroom, odd when you don't need a passport for visiting Jersey. Was the body really that of George Ellis? The *Jersey Evening Post* reported Ellis was penniless and unable to pay his [£35] hotel bill. They didn't mention that he had enough money to fly twice to Jersey within the space of a fortnight. Not something you'd do if you were hard up. Peter Nolan spoke of him being flush with money. It doesn't make sense. It wouldn't take a detective five minutes to see something fishy was going on. Did Ellis commit suicide or was his death faked by the Secret Service?

We parked outside Sevenoaks library in Kent in the spring of 2003. I wanted to know about Whites the chemist – I'd seen the name in *The Climate of Treason* by Andrew Boyle. Sevenoaks library housed over fifty years of local papers. Mr White ran a chemist shop in Westerham, the town where Ruth and George stayed for a week before their marriage on 8 November 1950, at the Kings Arms Hotel. Mr White made the front page of the *Sevenoaks Chronicle*. On 23 September 1955, about the same time as the government published the White Paper about the defection of Burgess and Maclean, the *Chronicle*'s headline read: 'A Little More White Light on a Darkroom at Westerham – final local chapter on the great Maclean spy story.'

Mr White apparently loaned his upstairs darkroom to Donald Maclean to print his photographs, before Maclean defected to Russia in 1951. He'd drive down from Tatsfield – everyone talked about it. He was doing that at the time George and Ruth got married and stayed at the Kings Arms. Mr White's story was kept under wraps for over four years.

His shop was three buildings along from the Kings Arms. An enormous black statue of Churchill towers over the square on the other side, he's still keeping his eye on things. Mr White was forty-ish in 1950, an eccentric with a beard and long hair. He left snakes in his shop at night-time for security. Peter Finch, a Westerham resident, recalled how Mr White was a smart man wearing pinstriped suits when he first arrived in the town: 'But he completely changed. He became a hobo. It was a transformation. He resided in Croydon or near there and went home every night, often late. He often spoke to me about his undercover work during the war. The shop was run-down, he started collecting junk, keeping old chickens that ran about in the road – not what you'd expect from a chemist. Despite what he looked like, with his long hair, he went regularly to Chartwell for tea with Lady Churchill. Nobody could get to the bottom of him.'

Mr Waterhouse, who was the chef after the war at the White Hart Hotel in Brasted, frequented by Ruth and her boyfriend also knew Ruth, had further evidence about Maclean's visits to Westerham. Mr Waterhouse became the chef at the Kings

Arms in 1950 when Westerham Brewery took over the hotel from its previous owner. Apparently Maclean used to have Sunday lunch there and he described how Joe Jenner, Winston Churchill's chauffeur, would go in afterwards and say to Mr Waterhouse: 'You've had Donald Maclean in for lunch today.'

Valerie Preston recalls both Maclean and Burgess visiting the White Hart Hotel: 'They used to come regularly to the hotel at weekends for meals. That would be after the war. If they mixed with anyone else, I don't know who it would have been.' Her mother Kath wrote in *Inn of the Few*, 'We did not know anything about them but they struck us as rather an odd couple, one was so smart and well dressed and the other untidy and bleary-eyed.'

Joe told me that a couple of miles east of Westerham, towards Sevenoaks, was a secret underground complex of bunkers stretching for over six miles, called Fort Halstead. It was built in 1895 by the British War Office to defend London. When Woolwich Arsenal in London closed down, many workers transferred to Fort Halstead. It was a high security armament research establishment and it was there that top-secret work on Britain's nuclear weapons programme began. In December 1949, Dr Klaus Fuchs, the physicist who had fled Hitler's Germany and became a British citizen, confessed to passing secrets to Russia about Britain and America's atomic weapons. In *The Crown Jewels, The British Secrets at the Heart of the KGB Archives*, authors Nigel West and Oleg Tsarev confirm the atom spy's involvement with Fort Halstead: 'Fuchs reported [to his Soviet contact] that other bomb facilities were being constructed and a production unit was planned at Fort Halstead in Kent, twenty-five miles from London, under the direction of Dr (Lord) William Penney.' In February 1950

Fuchs stood trial and was sentenced to fourteen years' imprisonment.

The village of Brasted, just along from Westerham, is in the valley and Fort Halstead is about three miles away up on the hills. Valerie Preston says, 'Personnel from there frequented the White Hart when my parents owned the hotel. All the boffins were up there [Fort Halstead] like Commander Powell, he took up residence with us, and Penney, he was quite well known.' William George Penney (later 1st Baron of East Hendred) was director of the Atomic Weapons Research Establishment at Aldermaston in the fifties and was one of the architects of the British nuclear bomb programme. He also worked at the Los Alamos Laboratory in the USA from 1944 to 1945, working on the Manhattan Project, developing the atom bomb. Dr Fuchs the A-bomb spy, passed secrets from Los Alamos to the Kremlin. Commander Powell was known for his work on the photography of nuclear processes and won the Nobel Prize for physics in 1950. Ruth must have felt very important moving in this circle of such high-powered people at the White Hart Hotel.

I believe the following apparently unconnected activities between 1950 and 1951 all link up in some way: George's dental practice in Sanderstead; his drying-out in Warlingham Park Hospital; Donald Maclean's house in Tatsfield; Ruth and George's stay at the Kings Arms Hotel in Westerham; their wedding at Tonbridge. I suspect Fort Halstead was the link to Donald Maclean, Guy Burgess, George Ellis, Stephen Ward, my sister Ruth and their secret activities.

Seven months after I first wrote to the actress Deborah Kerr about her association with Ruth and their visits to the White Hart Hotel in Brasted, a letter arrived from her office. Miss Kerr who is now in poor health asked her assistant Miss Yates to write the following:

> She [Miss Kerr] has instructed me to tell you that she does remember Ruth Ellis and Stephen – and the pub in Kent – but her recollections of that era are vague and she can no longer recall that time in greater detail.
>
> If it is of any help she can date that period to within two years: 1945/1946. She met her first husband, Tony Bartley (now deceased) in May of 1945 and married him in November of that year. They lived at Mayfield in Sussex. In November 1946 Deborah and Tony left the UK to live in America and did not return to England.

It was one of the few moments during my research that I couldn't help feeling relieved. For months I had suspected that Ruth's boyfriend in the foursome at Brasted was Stephen Ward. Now I had proof of their relationship, a relationship nobody knew about outside that secret clique of RAF pilots, homosexual spies and atomic weapons bigwigs. The Establishment kept it covered for fifty years.

Ruth had known Ward for nearly ten years at the time of her death. It seems obvious now that Ward transformed her specifically to blend in with the circle of top people at the White Hart. My sister would have loved the glamour and, of course, the money. She wouldn't have realized she was gathering information, probably thought she was just socializing. She was recreated as a peroxide blonde to blend with the Little Club clientele for the purpose of intelligence gathering. By then she may have realized the purpose. But there could be no going back.

I now suspect Ruth's husband George Ellis, also closely connected with the White Hart, was a 'sleeper' recruited at university, as were Burgess and Maclean; his cover could have been his Sanderstead dental practice convenient for Brasted, where the special people were congregating, and Fort Halstead. The question is – was he working for the British or the Soviets? Or both? It is likely that he went to his death (or disappearance) with a guilty conscience about Ruth, if he used her as a cover. He did not display this publicly, but had asked Peter Nolan, manager of the Little Club, to put flowers on Ruth's grave.

Looking at the evidence, it is plain that Cussen was a perfect spy. He knew how to make himself invisible. Like Beauchamp nothing is down on paper about him. Cussen's only claim to fame is what he said in court (half a story), one signature on a Cussen and Co. business document and the convincing story he gave Robert Hancock prior to and following Ruth's hanging.

He was on the electoral register at 16 and 20 Goodwood Court from late 1951 to 1957, then disappears; he reappears at The Lanterns in Craven Road around 1958 or 1959; he's at the Atlantic for over two years up to 1964. But there's no mention of him as Desmond Cussen on electoral registers at either hotel – odd because Mr Casserly knew him as Cussen at the Atlantic.

Certain names stand out on the electoral roll. Mr Casserly emphasized in his interview that a Harry Harris lived at both The Lanterns and the Atlantic. Harris was on the voting list between 1959 and 1961 at The Lanterns but not at the Atlantic later. I hoped to learn more about Harry Harris but Mr

Casserly was not forthcoming. Was Harry Harris a member of the 'well-known building society' that Mr Casserly referred to? I don't think he meant you could get a mortgage at The Lanterns!

In the Acknowledgements of Van Den Bergh's book *Ruth Ellis, A Case of Diminished Responsibility?* he thanked a Mr Harry Harris. Could this be the elusive Desmond Cussen's undercover name?

Discovering that Cussen was at the Atlantic Hotel between 1962 and 1964, in time for the Profumo scandal, confirmed he was up to something. That's why he chose to disappear off the electoral roll in the name of Desmond Cussen – he was undercover. Thinking about it now I'd imagine he was on the voting list at Goodwood Court for a reason, taking his time and perfecting his cover of the tobacconist businessman.

When the names Stephen Ward, Christine Keeler and Profumo popped up I thought it was no accident Cussen was living at the Atlantic. It was deliberate – he was on location again. Was he watching Stephen Ward? Spies among spies. Is that why he and Cussen were not seen in the bar together? Did Cussen know that Ward was snooping for the other side? Cussen had done his stint with Ruth at the Little Club, had a break somewhere like those spies do to avoid blowing their cover, then on to the Atlantic Hotel for his next job.

Mr Casserly said: 'There was never any evidence in his room of what he'd been doing.' Cussen was there over two years. Normal people leave things lying around. With Cussen there wasn't a clue about his identity or what he was doing. Mr Casserly spoke of Cussen going to his 'kiosk' at Marble Arch every day. What kiosk? According to company documents, he didn't have premises there. Between 9 September 1947 when

Desmond Cussen became a director of Cussen and Co., and 31 May 1972 when he resigned his directorship, there is no mention of a kiosk at Marble Arch in official documents. So where was Cussen going every day? His so-called shops were in Hammersmith, Stepney, Barnet, Peckham, Finsbury Park and at Lower Marsh and Falcon Road, SW11.

Cussen squirmed on his seat that Easter Holiday Monday fifty years ago, while Mother explained how Ruth was in custody for shooting Blakely. He could not look me in the eyes. When he looked at me he was looking at a reflection of Ruth. We were identical. He was a guilty man.

From 1950 to 1951, David Blakely was living in the house in Witheridge Lane in Penn, that had been strangely renamed Albi. What all the authors missed in their books about Ruth was the activity in Penn village between 1949 and 1951. Writers focused on Mr and Mrs Humphrey Cook when they lived at The Old Park in Hammersley Lane in 1955 when the shooting happened, mentioning in passing that they moved in in 1953. Granneys, the rented house that Mr and Mrs Cook and David Blakely inconspicuously resided in between 1949 and 1952, was kept well under wraps. The defection of Burgess and Maclean was being planned during that same period. David Blakely was conveniently released from National Service at the end of 1949, having served a matter of weeks. At the beginning of 1950 he went to Penn where the Cooks had been installed since 1949 at Granneys, changing its name to Albi. Albi was a nice little sanctuary. Another safe house?

I can see they had a special job for that so-called waster David Blakely. You only need to look at the dates: by 1949

Donald Maclean was under suspicion for passing secrets to the Russians. He'd left Cairo in May 1950 having been found guilty of serious misconduct while serving at the British embassy. He recuperated in London from his 'breakdown' and was dried out from his drinking problem, then stayed with his wife Melinda in a hotel in Sevenoaks, Kent, from September, before returning to the Foreign Office in November 1950. He moved to the house called Beacon Shaw in Tatsfield a month later.

MI5's 'B' Division kept Maclean under surveillance in London. According to Nigel West's *A Matter of Trust*, a warrant was obtained from the Home Office 'to tap Maclean's telephone at his home in Tatsfield, on the North Downs'. The Secret Service watchers waited for Maclean to make a move. West said that the watchers 'believed that extending the surveillance operation into Surrey would alert Maclean'. After his departure to Russia 'much fuss was made over the fact that surveillance on the diplomat was limited to London and as soon as he had climbed aboard his train home in the evenings the watchers turned in.'

Maclean's journeys from the Foreign Office to his Tatsfield home were more complicated than West described. I have evidence that he travelled home on the 706 Green Line bus that went past George Ellis's front door on Sanderstead Hill. Pat, a resident of Tatsfield remembers: 'I used to get on at Stockwell [south London]. Nine times out of ten Maclean was on it. We reached the village at six thirty – the coach passed the corner by his house. He'd clout everybody on the head with his briefcase as he got off. I lived half-a-mile further on. Now and again a couple of them would get off. A medium build fellow, probably forty and the better looking of the two.'

While Maclean was under surveillance in London, Blakely was hand-picked from the army and placed in Penn. I cannot believe that I am the first to make this connection particularly as the Macleans owned the house in Penn for thirty years. Surely the Establishment knew it was one of Donald's known haunts – I'd merely stumbled on it by accident. MI5's casual surveillance of Maclean, confined to London, struck me as odd. It almost signified that they helped him defect to Russia.

I'm no expert. But from what I know now, it's clear that Maclean would visit his mother. I believe Blakely was in Penn at that time, waiting and watching Maclean. Blakely, like Maclean was involved in homosexual activities. He was the fall guy ruthlessly carrying out instructions from his MI5 pay-masters, in fear of his sexual preferences being revealed. Nobody could connect a thing, yet the place it seems was a Secret Service hideaway. With Blakely's knowledge of these events, time was running out for him.

The concocted story put out about my sister, a blonde model with two children, who murdered her lover in a fit of jealousy, was a titillating smokescreen. Ruth had provided a safe cover for the Secret Service people at the Little Club in London and another clique of them in Penn. They used her looks, created by Stephen Ward and Antony Beauchamp, and her character for a purpose, for pillow talk and to listen to influential people's secrets. By Easter 1955 it was time for Ruth to be removed because of what she knew. Her hanging meant she could not expose the Establishment's dirty game.

When I began my research I stumbled over a couple of mistakes in official documents. Then I found more 'slight' inaccuracies. I looked at them together and it implied a web of intrigue. I have followed a trail of suspicious addresses, non-existent businesses, incorrect initials on official documents enabling characters to change their identities and mislead anyone who dares to look for them. I've looked at birth certificates, death certificates and company documents. I knew in the end, that nearly going blind over electoral registers would pay off but when I started my quest for the truth I'd no idea how.

When that snake Cussen came to our maisonette on 11 April 1955 I knew Ruth's story was false. Only now as I approach the end of my book do I realize the extent of his deception and the conspiracy that led to Ruth's death. In the winter of 2003 I learned something extraordinary from Bob Wallis, an eighty-nine-year-old retired dentist from Leatherhead. As I read the account he gave to Monica Weller about the Paddock Club in Surrey, I saw evidence of Cussen's long-term friendship with David Blakely, which has not been made public before; and proof that Cussen lied at Ruth's trial:

> The Paddock Club was hidden at the end of a hundred-yard gravel drive, off Ottways Lane in Ashtead village, just north of Leatherhead. The club was in a big Victorian detached house with nine bedrooms, curiously called The Hut. I only knew it as the Paddock Club. It was very isolated. The house was let to Captain Bill Sulis. He kept ex-racehorses, lived in the house and ran the club from 1948. I was a dental officer in the RAF, demobbed in 1946 and joined the club soon after, about '48 or '49, and was there for about six years. The very best people frequented it from London when there were parties on. It was a bit of a risky club.

Some members came from the RAF, Army and Navy. I know Diana Dors went there, she was talked about and was ordered out. Desmond Cussen and David Blakely were frequent visitors and already members when I joined – they were well-known drinking members and came to all the parties. Nobody introduced them, you drank at the bar, you talked to everybody. I was casually acquainted with them.

The racing driver, Blakely, wasn't there as often as Cussen – sometimes one would be there, sometimes both. Blakely would turn up in a super racing car, typical post-war one, red, single-seater with a rounded front. To have a racing car like that at his age he was pretty well heeled. We all talked about our experiences in the forces. I don't remember Cussen ever talking about his. He was a quiet sort of guy except for one year, about 1952, he turned up at a Christmas fancy dress party as a cowboy. This was the guy that got the gun in 1955. We were all amused because he was hauled in by the police on his way home, and was dressed as a cowboy with a six-gun and wearing a stetson.

Mr Wallis was extremely helpful with his frank statement about the Paddock Club. Others who I suspect knew about the club, for their own reasons did not provide information. There's nothing about it on record, no documents, nothing in local history publications. No one else who lived in the lane, other than one lady, knew, or admitted to knowing the Sulises who lived there between 1948 and 1958. It's as if the Paddock Club in the distinguished Victorian house oddly called The

Hut, never existed. In Nigel West and Oleg Tsarev's book *The Crown Jewels, The British Secrets at the Heart of the KGB Archives* is a glossary of Soviet Intelligence code names. It states that Winston Churchill's code name was Peer, President Truman was Sailor and the British Security Service (MI5) was, by extraordinary coincidence, Hut. I suspect that The Hut in Ashtead, a mile from Cussen's home in Leatherhead, was a Secret Service meeting place under cover of Captain Sulis's riding stables and the Paddock Club.

On 28 April 1955, when Cussen was questioned at the magistrate's court, he stated he had known Blakely just over two years, maybe three. He lied. It is clear from Bob Wallis's statement that Cussen had known Blakely a lot longer. At Ruth's trial at the Old Bailey, when asked how long he'd known Blakely, he lied again saying: 'Approximately 3 years.' He lied to cover the secret world they'd been part of for over five years – a world that Ruth could have blown wide open if she had lived.

It's taken fifty years to find out the truth. Ruth was loyal to that underground bunch – she hanged for them. Fifty years they've been protected. Now I want everything out in the open for everyone to see that my sister was an innocent pawn in a dangerous game of espionage, planned by master craftsmen who wanted her disposed of. Ruth was the victim. What chance did she stand against them?

Epilogue

My life has revolved around trying to clear Ruth's name. It has not been easy. For years I have scribbled my thoughts, horrible thoughts, on anything I could get my hands on. Picking through episodes of dreadful confusion in Ruth's life that I hardly knew about but wanted to understand. All I've ever wanted is for people to remember Ruth with her name cleared. I want justice for her.

In June 2003 I heard from the Criminal Appeal Office at the Royal Courts of Justice. My Appeal against Ruth's conviction had been listed for hearing on 16 and 17 September 2003. I prayed that the truth would come out about the murder for which she hanged and that it wouldn't be another whitewash.

On 16 September everyone in Court 4 stood up as the three judges, Lord Justice Kay, Mr Justice Leveson and Mr Justice Silber entered. Mr Michael Mansfield, my barrister, faced the judges and raised points that he would be expanding before them. Most significantly he said there was a 'substantial error' at the trial in 1955: the judge, Justice Havers, had not allowed a defence of provocation to be put to the jury.

Mr Perry, the barrister acting for the Crown Prosecution Service, later set out to show that the murder verdict in 1955 was correct.

I listened to long legal sentences about provocation, for

example, the difference between 'sudden passion and lingering passion' and if the shooting was 'sudden and proportionate'. I felt helpless, listening to legal people arguing about Ruth being provoked into murdering Blakely. I said to myself: 'It was not true. Ruth did not shoot anyone. It was made to look that way though.' The same convincing Ruth Ellis story spun to the press and public in 1955 was being repeated. In my mind that was not fair and reasonable, not enough of the truth was coming out.

At about four o'clock on the second day, the Appeal finished abruptly. The judges reserved their judgment.

Twelve weeks later on 8 December 2003 in Court 9 at the Royal Courts of Justice, Lord Justice Kay announced that the Appeal had been dismissed.

I held back the tears, for the sake of my children, as I always have done.

Appendices I–IV

APPENDIX I: The Circumstances of Ruth's First Statement, HO291/235

At the Magistrates Court Hearing of 28th April 1955, Leslie Davies, Detective Chief Inspector of 'S' Division, Metropolitan Police, recalled:-

At about 11 p.m. on 10th April 1955 with Detective Superintendent Crawford, 'S' Division, I saw the dead body of the man I now know to be David Blakely at Hampstead Mortuary, and whose photograph is No.1 of Exhibit 3. At about 11.30 p.m. the same day with Detective Superintendent Crawford and Detective Inspector Gill I saw the accused detained at Hampstead Police Station. Superintendent Crawford said to her, 'I have seen the dead body of David Blakely at Hampstead Mortuary. I understand you know something about it.' He cautioned her and she replied, 'I am guilty. I am rather confused.' She paused and then said, 'It all started about two years ago when I met David Blakely at the Little Club, Knightsbridge.' Superintendent Crawford then stopped her and said, 'Would you like this to be written down?' She said, 'Yes.' Inspector Gill then wrote down what she had to say after she had again been cautioned and which caution she signed.

STATEMENT OF WITNESS

Metropolitan Police,

Hampstead Station,

"S" Division.

11th April, 1955.

Name:- RUTH ELLIS (Mrs)   B. 9.10.26.

Address:- 44, Egerton Gardens, Kensington, W.14.

Occupation:- Model.

Statement:-

I have been cautioned that I am not obliged to say anything
unless I wish to do so and that anything I do say will be taken
down in writing and may be given in evidence.

(Signed) Ruth Ellis.

I understand what has been said. I am guilty. I am rather
confused."

About two years ago I met David Blakely when I was manageress
of The Little Club, Knightsbridge; my flat was above that. I
had known him for about a fortnight when he started to live with
me and has done so continuously until last year when he went away
to Le Mans for about three weeks motor racing. He came back to
me and remained living with me until Good Friday morning.

He left me about ten o'clock a.m. and promised to be back
by eight p.m. to take me out. I waited until half past nine and
he had not 'phoned, although he always had done in the past.
I was rather worried at that stage as he had had trouble with
his racing car and had been drinking.

I rang some friends of his named Findlater at Hampstead
but they told me he was not there, although David had told me
he was visiting them. I was speaking to Mr. Findlater and I

311

STATEMENT OF WITNESS

Metropolitan Police, Hampstead Station, 'S' Division

11th April, 1955

Name: RUTH ELLIS (Mrs) B. 9.10.26

Address: 44, Egerton Gardens, Kensington W.14

Occupation: Model.

Statement:
I have been cautioned that I am not obliged to say anything unless I wish to do so and that anything I do say will be taken down in writing and may be given in evidence.

(Signed) Ruth Ellis.

I understand what has been said. I am guilty. I am rather confused.'

About two years ago I met David Blakely when I was manageress of The Little Club, Knightsbridge; my flat was above that. I had known him about a fortnight when he started to live with me and has done so continuously until last year when he went away to Le Mans for about three weeks motor racing. He came back to me and remained living with me until Good Friday morning.

He left me about ten o'clock a.m. and promised to be back by eight p.m. to take me out. I waited until half past nine and he had not 'phoned, although he always had done in the past. I was rather worried at that stage as he had had trouble with his racing car and had been drinking.

I rang some friends of his named Findlater at Hampstead but they told me he was not there, although David had told me

312

he was visiting them. I was speaking to Mr. Findlater and I asked if David was all right. He laughed and said 'Oh yes, he's all right.' I did not believe he was not there and I took a taxi to Hampstead where I saw David's car outside Findlater's flat at 28, Tanza Road. I then telephoned from nearby and when my voice was recognised they hung up on me.

I went to the flat and continually rang the door bell but they would not answer. I became very furious and went to David's car which was still standing there and pushed in three of the side windows. The noise I made must have aroused the Findlaters as the Police came along and spoke to me. Mr. Findlater came out of his flat and the Police also spoke to him.

David did not come home on Saturday and at nine o'clock this morning (Sunday) I 'phoned Findlaters again and Mr. Findlater answered. I said to him 'I hope you are having an enjoyable holiday and was about to say 'Because you have ruined mine' and he banged the receiver down.

I waited all day today (Sunday) for David to 'phone but he did not do so. About eight o'clock this evening (Sunday) I put my son Andria to bed. I then took a gun which I had had hidden and put it in my handbag. This gun was given to me about three years ago in a Club by a man whose name I do not remember. It was security for money but I accepted it as a curiosity. I did not know it was loaded when it was given to me but I knew next morning when I looked at it. When I put the gun in my bag I intended to find David and shoot him.

I took a taxi to Tanza Road and as I arrived, David's car drove away from Findlater's address. I dismissed the taxi and walked back down the road to the nearest pub where I saw David's car outside. I waited outside until he came out with a friend I know as Clive. David went to his car door to open it. I was a little way away from him. He turned and saw me and then turned away from me and I took the gun from my bag and I shot him. He turned round and ran a few steps round the car. I thought I had missed him so I fired again. He was still running and I fired the third shot. I don't remember firing any more but I must have done. I remember then he was lying on the footway and I was standing beside him. He was bleeding badly and it seemed ages before an ambulance came.

I remember a man came up and I said, 'Will you call the Police and an ambulance?' He said 'I am a Policeman.' I said 'Please take this gun and arrest me.'

This statement has been read over to me and it is true.

(Signed) Ruth Ellis.

Statement written down and read over by Peter Gill, Detective Inspector 'S' in the presence of Det. Supt. Crawford and Det. Ch. Inspector Davies.

APPENDIX II: Ruth's Final Statement, HO291/238

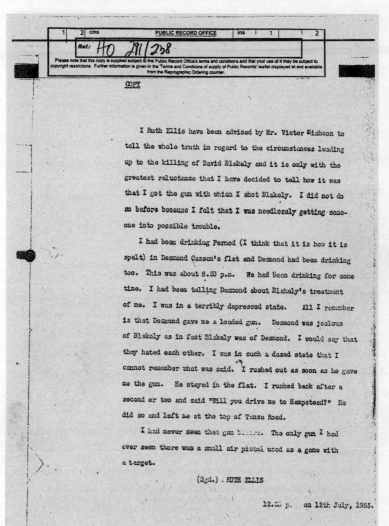

COPY

I Ruth Ellis have been advised by Mr. Victor Mishcon to tell the whole truth in regard to the circumstances leading up to the killing of David Blakely and it is only with the greatest reluctance that I have decided to tell how it was that I got the gun with which I shot Blakely. I did not do so before because I felt that I was needlessly getting someone into possible trouble.

I had been drinking Pernod (I think that it is how it is spelt) in Desmond Cussen's flat and Desmond had been drinking too. This was about 8.30 p.m. We had been drinking for some time. I had been telling Desmond about Blakely's treatment of me. I was in a terribly depressed state. All I remember is that Desmond gave me a loaded gun. Desmond was jealous of Blakely as in fact Blakely was of Desmond. I would say that they hated each other. I was in such a dazed state that I cannot remember what was said. I rushed out as soon as he gave me the gun. He stayed in the flat. I rushed back after a second or two and said "Will you drive me to Hampstead?" He did so and left me at the top of Tanza Road.

I had never seen that gun before. The only gun I had ever seen there was a small air pistol used as a game with a target.

(Sgd.) . RUTH ELLIS

12.30 p. on 12th July, 1955.

315

APPENDIX III: The Missing Tapes

Bindman & Partners
Solicitors

1 Euston Road, Kings Cross, London NW1 2SA
Tel 01-278 8131

Geoffrey Bindman   Wendy Mantle   Sarah Leigh
     Anthony Portner   Felicity Crowther
       Consultant: Leo H. Gillis

The Executors of Mr. John Bickford,
c/o 16-18 High Street,
Kingston-upon-Thames,
KT1 1EY

Your reference   Our reference 3049/GB/DC/CB   Date   15th September, 1977

Dear Sirs,

We act for Mrs. Jakubait, sister of Ruth Ellis for whom we
understand Mr. Bickford acted in connection with her trial
for murder in 1955.

We are informed that before her death Ruth Ellis expressly
stated that she wished all her belongings to be taken by her mother,
Mrs. E. Neilson who is also, of course, the mother of our
client. We understand that certain tape recordings were made
by Ruth Ellis before her arrest. Mrs. Neilson knew of the
existence of these tapes but not their whereabouts. She is
now regretably aged and infirm and confined to hospital.
However, it is come to the attention of Mrs. Jakubait that the
tapes were in the possession of Mr. Bickford before his death.

Our client has been considerably embarassed and upset be the
recent publication and broadcast of some of the tapes. We
are instructed to request therefore by what means the tapes
came into Mr. Bickford's possession and by what right he retained
them. We presume that they are now in your possession and request
that they be handed over to our client on behalf of her mother
as she is most anxious to attempt to forestall any further
publication which would result in distress to her and her family.

We regret writing in this manner so soon after Mr. Bickford's
death and have no wish to cause distress to his family. We were
proposing to write to Mr. Bickford himself and it is purely
coincidence that we write at this time.

Yours faithfully,

Bindman & Partners

APPENDIX IV: Cussen's Stay At The Atlantic

Number of | 15133
Company | /40

Form No. 49

THE COMPANIES ACT, 1948
(No Revenue Stamp Duty chargeable)

Declaration verifying Memorandum of Satisfaction of a Registered Mortgage or Charge
(Pursuant to Section 100)

Insert here
Name of the
Company

CUSSEN & CO.

REGISTERED
16 JUN 1964

Limited

WE   DESMOND EDWARD CUSSEN

of Flat 543 Atlantic Hotel, Queens Gardens, London, W.2.

a Director of   CUSSEN & CO,   Limited

and   Geoffrey Harry Searle

of   107, Hindes Road, Harrow, Middlesex   ,

the Secretary thereof, do solemnly and sincerely declare that the particulars contained in the Memorandum of Satisfaction endorsed hereon are true to the best of our knowledge, information and belief.

And we make this solemn Declaration conscientiously believing the same to be true and by virtue of the provisions of the Statutory Declarations Act, 1835.

Declared at Harrow
in the County of Middlesex

the 29th day of May
One thousand nine hundred and sixty
four

Before me,

A Commissioner for Oaths. (*)

(a) Or Notary Public or Justice of the Peace.

The Solicitors' Law Stationery Society, Limited
22 Chancery Lane, W.C.2; 3 Bucklersbury, E.C.4; 49 Bedford Row, W.C.1; 6 Victoria Street, S.W.1;
15 Hanover Street, W.1; 55-59 Newhall Street, Birmingham, 3; 31 Charles Street, Cardiff; 19 & 21 North
John Street, Liverpool, 2; 28-30 John Dalton Street, Manchester, 2; 157 Hope Street, Glasgow, C.2.
PRINTERS AND PUBLISHERS OF COMPANIES BOOKS AND FORMS
Companies 4B

[P.T.O.

Index